COMPANY OF KINSMEN

'This book, by a leading economic historian of South Asia, addresses a long-standing problem ... that of the dependent or independent role of social organization in the working of an economy ... [and] advances our understanding of an important economic region in both the past and the present.'

— Sumit Guha, *Journal of Interdisciplinary History*

'The book makes an invaluable contribution to Indian economic history, business history, and global history more generally. It is a welcome addition for scholars working in these fields.'

—Latika Chaudhary, *Journal of Economic History*

'[A] real tour de force ... a creditable attempt to present a connected and conceptualized narrative of the great transition in the Indian economy from the eighteenth to the twentieth century.'

—Claude Markovits, *Economic History Review*

COMPANY OF KINSMEN

Enterprise and Community in South Asian History
1700–1940

TIRTHANKAR ROY

OXFORD
UNIVERSITY PRESS

OXFORD
UNIVERSITY PRESS

Oxford University Press is a department of the University of Oxford.
It furthers the University's objective of excellence in research, scholarship,
and education by publishing worldwide. Oxford is a registered trademark of
Oxford University Press in the UK and in certain other countries.

Published in India by
Oxford University Press
2/11 Ground Floor, Ansari Road, Daryaganj, New Delhi 110 002, India

© Oxford University Press 2010

The moral rights of the author have been asserted.

First Edition published in 2010
Oxford India Paperbacks 2018

ISBN-13: 978-0-19-948680-9
ISBN-10: 0-19-948680-8

Typeset in Minion Pro 10.5/13.3
by Sai Graphic Design, New Delhi 110 055,
Printed in India by Repro Knowledgecast Limited, Thane

For
Sujata Sengupta
and
Dr Prasanta Kumar Sengupta

Contents

List of Figures — viii
Preface — x

INTRODUCTION — 1
Indian Society and the Economic History of India

1. CONTEXT — 29
   Economic history and 'culture'

2. STATES — 45
   A political theory of the community

3. MERCHANTS — 89
   Guild as corporation

4. ARTISANS — 130
   Guild for training

5. WORKERS — 153
   Collective bargaining

6. PEASANTS — 190
   Property and market

EPILOGUE — 220

Bibliography — 224
Index — 250

Figures

1   Surat from the sea, c. 1630. European view of Indian
    society was influenced by doing business in Surat shown
    here in a Dutch painting. © National Maritime Museum   8
2.1 'Hindu Village Council'. From Miss Droese, *Indian Gems
    for the Master's Crown*, London: The Religious Tract
    Society, 1892, p. 45. Another version of this engraving
    appears in a book by the Society published in 1857,
    which suggests that the illustration was made in the
    early nineteenth century.   72
2.2 A bewildered judge. Satirical look at 'our judge ... his
    judicial soul ... saturated with appeals, criminal cases,
    decrees, circular orders ...', G.F. Atkinson, *Curry and Rice
    (on 40 Plates). Ingredients of Social Life at 'Our' Station in
    India*, London: Day and Sons, c. 1900   79
3.1 Anticlockwise from top, Surat merchant, Parsi merchant
    of Bombay, and Marwari merchants of Calcutta, c. 1860.
    Source: Louis Rousselet, *India and its Native Princes*,
    London: Bickers and Sons, 1883   112
3.2 Bankers of Delhi. Source: *Lippincott's Magazine of Popular
    Literature and Science*, 17(99), 1876   114
4.1 Bengali silk weaver in Mushidabad region, c. 1900. Source:
    Nityagopal Mukherji, *A Monograph on Silk Industry in
    Bengal*, Calcutta: Government Press, 1903   141
5.1 The indigo factory, north Bihar, c. 1870. Source: James
    Inglis, *Sport and Work on the Nepaul Frontier*, London:
    Macmillan, 1878   161

5.2   Jobber watching over his tenters, c. 1920. Source: Arno
      Pearse, *The Cotton Industry of India*, Manchester:
      International Federation of Master Cotton Spinners and
      Manufacturers, 1930   181
6.1   Jat peasant, c. 1820. Source: Tashrih-al-Aqvam. © British
      Library   198
6.2   Peasants of the Doab, c. 1870. Source: Louis Rousselet,
      India and its Native Princes, London: Bickers and Sons,
      1883   200

Preface

The book shows how the idea of organizing people to serve economic ends took concrete shape in early modern and colonial India. It describes rules of cooperation, why people came together, how disputes were settled, and how cooperative communities became increasingly unstable in more modern times. The story moves along five dimensions—actor, agent, time, purpose, and region. The leading actors are—merchants/bankers, artisans, peasants, labourers, and not least, the states. The states respected the rules of cooperation that formed inside communities of merchants and others, and by being engaged with the society and economy, gave some firmness to the rules. In the time-span considered, these rules became unstable due to the action of new forces of change, namely, integration of India within a global-industrial economy, and a new rule of law albeit packaged in the old container of 'custom'. One consequence of these changes was that a kind of collective I call endogamous guild, which used marriage rules to secure cooperative ties, became weaker, and other forms of organization began being used more often.

All organizational forms were context-bound. Collective cooperation served different goals, they controlled property, supplied training, managed resources, and conducted negotiations inside and outside the collective. The endogamous guild was particularly relevant in the case of control of property, and less relevant in collective bargaining. Merchants and skilled artisans depended relatively more on endogamous guild. Other bases for cooperation, such as fraternity or village-based kinship, characterized peasants and labourers the more. The regional angle is important too for regions differed on the

composition of enterprise, and globalization and colonialism unfold-
ed in an uneven way across space.

It will be clear from this brief outline of the project that I aim
to write an economic history of institutional change in South Asia.
Assumptions about institutional change remain implicit in any
attempt to write an economic history of the region. The important
link between enterprise and community is more than implicit in
business history. These points supply a good reason to address the
link in a direct fashion. Moreover, a sense of history should inform
any understanding of enterprise and community in present-day South
Asia. For example, the book shows that, by being subject to diverse
pulls, institutional change in the region happened in a discordant
way. Community has been a field of serious discord in recent decades,
partly due to similar kind of pulls as in the past.

To avoid misplaced expectation, it is necessary to clarify the two
things that this book is not trying to be. First, this is not a comparativist
work. In particular, the book is not a contribution to the currently
ongoing discourse among global historians about the origins of
'divergence', which offers a variety of explanations on why the North
grew rich and the South stayed poor, or in some accounts, the South
declined from its past glory. My project is rooted in the historiography
of economic change in South Asia, and does not quite share in the
keenness with which global historians study the wealth and poverty of
nations. I do not wish, however, to suggest that global historians will
find nothing of interest in this book. Doing so would cause the book
to lose a valuable readership and a lucrative market, and amount to
doing injustice to Chapter 1, which revisits the archaic but resilient
notion that India stayed poor because of its collectivist past. There
is more than an indirect link between the two projects, divergence
on one hand and the institutional history of South Asia on the other,
and that link is formed of an idea present in economic sociology and
analytical economic history, that all collectives potentially carry gains
for its members and costs for society. I explore the trade-offs that
exclusive clubs such as these might involve in Chapter 1.

Second, the book is not a substitute for a descriptive history of any
of its elements. The narrative draws mainly upon existing historical
scholarship. It also draws on new source material, new in that not

all of it has been read so far with the purpose that this book aims to serve. Still, the project is an interpretive one. I wanted to paint a big picture based on material contained in social and political history, and not revise the detailed picture, which historians have done before at greater depth and with far more skill than evident in this work.

I am reassured nevertheless by the fact that some of the leading members of the craft have read the product and vetted the project, while also offering constructive criticisms. These conversations have alerted me to weaknesses of argument and presentation in earlier drafts. I have addressed them, if not always in a convincing fashion. I am indebted to Binay Bhushan Chaudhuri, Chris Fuller, Douglas Haynes, Patrick O'Brien, Om Prakash, Peter Robb, Tom Tomlinson, and two readers of the Oxford University Press (OUP), who read and commented on the whole text or parts of it. Some of the material has been published recently as articles in *Continuity and Change, International Review of Social History, Modern Asian Studies,* and *Journal of Global History.* I wish to thank the editors and referees of these journals, and specially Jan Luiten van Zanden, Tine de Moor, and Jan Lucassen, who read one or more of these articles and suggested changes.

A number of seminars and workshops provided occasions to write papers that reincarnated as chapters in this book, or indirectly influenced its contents. Discussions with participants, and reading or listening to other contributors, helped me rethink South Asia. I wish to acknowledge in particular 'Factor markets' and 'The return of the guilds' (both organized by Utrecht University and Global Economic History Network, 2005, 2007); 'Regimes for the development of useful and reliable industrial knowledge in the West and the East before the age of Institutionaised R and D' (Fondation Maison des sciences de l'homme Paris, 2007); 'Law and economic development: a historical perspective' (Utrecht University, 2007); 'S. R. Epstein memorial conference: technology and human capital formation in the East and West', and 'States and long-term economic growth' (both at the London School of Economics, 2008). The last-mentioned workshop was jointly organized by Debin Ma, Oliver Volckart, and myself. Conversations with these two colleagues, and with Jonathan Parry, contributed to my reading beyond India and beyond economic history.

All said, I should call this attempt to understand the long-term and changing relationship between state, market, and guilds in South Asia a work in progress.

London   TIRTHANKAR ROY

Introduction
Indian society and the economic history of India

Before modern forms of property and commercial law came into wide usage in the nineteenth century in India, organization of business was an extension of the organization of society. Allocation of scarce resources in this region, as in other commercial–industrial regions of the world, was performed by means of guild, caste, kinsmen, and family. Market exchange tended to be limited in factors of production, even when extensive trade existed in consumer goods. Groups organized the supply of labour, credit, and land. In agriculture, peasant lineages controlled ownership rights on land, or more commonly, the right to use land. In commerce, clusters of firms and families made available trade secret, cheap credit, insurance, safety and security, systems of law and justice, to their members, and restricted access to these services to those who were not members of these groups. In industry, groups consisting of artisan families in possession of valuable skills shared know-how, set technological standards, and sanctioned innovations. Adam Smith's famous dictum, 'the division of labour is limited by the extent of the market', worked less well in the world before the commercial revolution began. Division of labour was regulated by collectives.

That collectives like these framed and enforced the rules of doing business in the past is recognized in new institutional economic history.[1] The present work is an exploration of that idea with Indian evidence. In recent times, economic theory has been revised to accommodate the idea that the pursuit of individual rationality in the

[1] For discussion, see the next chapter.

competitive market is not necessarily conducive to economic growth. In the presence of costs of market transaction, economic growth would also require cooperative action. Members of cooperative bodies have symmetric access to information. The more the business world relies on personalized information, as it did in the past centuries, and the more the world is exposed to information asymmetries as a result, the more critical do cooperative bodies become for transacting parties.

And yet, organized groups were not just responses to specific economic needs as one might naively conclude from reading new institutional economic history. They were a business model no doubt. But they were nothing without the cultural–political blood that flowed in their veins. The groups we encounter in this region among economic actors in possession of valuable assets consisted of professionals who were also usually related amongst themselves by strong social ties. On most occasions, 'guilds' were made up of individuals related to each other by birth and marriage. Rules about professional relationship, therefore, overlapped with rules about social interaction. In some cases the social rules were present as norms that were so strong that groups became moral communities as well as corporate bodies.

I call this formation the endogamous guild, and propose in this book that this form of association was more commonly found in early modern India than elsewhere in the world, and that it became increasingly unstable in colonial India. It was not the case that all professional guilds in India in the eighteenth century could be characterized in this fashion. As elsewhere in the world, corporatism could draw on other ties, and social ties were flexible enough to adapt to changing economic realities. Nor was India unique in the world in respect of the presence of guilds that formed on the basis of kinship and marriage. Purely profession-based guilds were perhaps more common in the cities of late-medieval Europe. But cooperation among individuals who hailed from the same social pool was not rare in Europe either. Such cooperation could be found throughout the non-western world, especially in the societies of medieval East Asia. When workers recruited apprentices and entrepreneurs recruited partners from the extended family in early modern India or Qing China, such practices provided occasions to pass on jointly owned capital to the next generation. Sympathies of a filial nature created incentives to teach trade secrets. By extension, a similar sort of incentive to cooperate and stay together could work when collectives formed out of a cluster of interrelated families. So universal indeed were practices such as these, that keywords like 'family firm' and 'kinship ties' are hardly useful in doing comparative economic history.

That being said, not all professional combines that formed out of blood relations and marital ties were alike. Nor were they equally common throughout the world. In East Asia, for example, although kinship ties were present among guild members, notably in the form of regional collegiality in early Qing China, the dependence of professional relations upon kinship was neither significant nor systematic. Collegiality, corporatism, and brotherhood were on the whole more powerful bases for cooperation than blood and marriage.[2] In India, they were not. The systematic and strong association that we come across in India between marriage and profession, and the systematic use of marriage as a tool to serve the interests of a corporation, especially among merchants, bankers, and skilled

---

[2] Joseph Fewsmith, 'From Guild to Interest Group: The Transformation of Public and Private in Late Qing China', *Comparative Studies in Society and History*, 25(4), 1983, pp. 617–40; Christine Moll-Murata, 'Chinese Guilds from the Seventeenth to the Twentieth Centuries: An Overview', *International Review of Social History*, 53 (Supplement), 2008, pp. 213–47; Marie Louise Nigata, 'Brotherhoods and Stock Societies: Guilds in Pre-modern Japan', *International Review of Social History*, 53 (Supplement), 2008, pp. 121–42; Gary Hamilton, 'The Organizational Foundations of Western and Chinese Commerce: A Historical and Comparative Analysis', in G. Hamilton, ed., *Asian Business Networks*, Berlin: Walter de Gruyter, 1996, pp. 43–58. In premodern Western Europe, ordinarily 'trade was not conducted among individuals without any social affiliation'. However, these affiliations themselves tended to form on the basis of places of origin and language rather than considerations of purity of blood and the marriage rules that served to protect purity. A short account of the community in European history can be found in Avner Greif, 'Impersonal Exchange and the Origin of Markets: From the Community Responsibility System to Individual Legal Responsibility in Premodern Europe', in Masahiko Aoki and Yūjirō Hayami, eds, *Communities and Markets in Economic Development*, Oxford: Oxford University Press, 2001. In seventeenth century England, local communities 'were held together less by dense ties of kinship than by relationships of neighbourliness...', and ties of patronage and clientage'. Keith Wrightson, *English Society 1580–1680*, London: Routledge, 2006, pp. 69. Kinship did not play a large and systematic role in the recruitment of industrial apprentices and trade partners.

artisans, was only weakly and randomly present in medieval China, Tokugawa Japan, and premodern Western Europe.[3]

Despite their cultural roots, groups were powerless to perform their useful roles without direct or indirect political sanction. The other side of the collective, therefore, was a regime that recognized its rights and privileges. The economic power of endogamous guilds was sustained by juridical autonomy that such groups tended to receive from regional states on matters of property rights, terms of transaction, and contract enforcement. States occasionally did more. They offered particular groups protection from the competition of other groups. Collectives were either too powerful or too useful for their demands to be ignored by the rulers. Warrior chiefs, military tribes, and dominant peasant lineages organized tax collection and the clearing of forests, merchant firms financed bankrupt states during wars or imperial collapse, and bands of artisans were necessary to beautify the capital city.

These economic, social, cultural, and political traditions formed a compound. By 'economic' I mean participation in commodity markets; by 'social-cultural', the conventions and codes of honour that cemented the collectives and secured factor supplies; and by 'political' tradition, statecraft that upheld these norms and values. But the ingredients of the compound were variable between groups and over time. Many cooperative groups used marriage and kinship, but they still did not serve identical objectives. With merchants and bankers, who possessed valuable tangible and intangible assets, the main duty of the cooperative group was to maintain trust, secure conflict-free and fraud-free partnerships, and conduct a peaceful transfer of capital between generations. With skilled artisans, who possessed valuable knowledge, the main job of cooperative groups was to organize training

---

[3] The antiquity of a high degree of selectivity in marriage in South Asia is an established scientific fact. An earlier scholarship within South Asian ethnography, which went back to the colonial times, suggested that long-standing differences between population segments in South Asia could be attributed to endogamy. Recent genomic studies support that inference by showing that 'differences between groups in India are larger than in Europe, reflecting strong founder effects whose signatures have been maintained for thousands of years owing to endogamy.' David Reich, Kumarasamy Thangaraj, Nick Patterson, Alkes L. Price, Lalji Singh, 'Reconstructing Indian Population History', *Nature*, 461, 2009, pp. 489–95. The sample in this study included traditional business communities.

and apprenticeship, and restrict access to knowledge to insiders. With workers, who were individually vulnerable in any labour market, cooperative communities provided solidarity and means of collective bargaining.

The internal and external forces working on groups changed over time. In particular, enormous expansion of foreign trade and investment in the region created new and varied actors in the eighteenth and nineteenth centuries. Colonization altered, albeit within limits, laws of property and contract. The new environment narrowed the scope of informal–personal ways of doing business. The availability of formal laws of association brought out into the open the disputes and disputatious potentials lurking within business communities. Endogamous guilds were rarely cooperative and democratic clubs. Indeed, they often resembled the situation that game theorists call asymmetrical cooperation. Richer members and the elders could arm-twist the younger and weaker members into cooperation. Pent-up resentment against such practices found an outlet in the colonial court room.

Colonialism and globalization, in this way, thrust big changes upon collectives still rooted in older cultural–political traditions. It would be a mistake to exaggerate the revolutionary character of the transformation, however. New types of market risks facing the migrant workers or migrant merchants were often met by drawing upon the bonds of kin. 'Imagined communities' formed, making use of the idiom of caste. Further, new laws of property continued to be embedded in community practices; a result of implicit compromise between pre-colonial lineages and colonial rule. Modernity, thus, opened up conflicts between parts of tradition on the one hand and the imperatives of global market exchange on the other. The 'modernization' of economic institutions used local roots, and yet was a shackled and discordant one, being subject to contradictory forces and contradictory policies. The process continues to the present day; in a discordant way because of the persistence of these opposite pulls.

The present book describes the discordant evolution of a kind of corporatism that was possible only in colonial India. The book explores the experiences of major economic actors—merchants, artisans, peasants, and workers—in relation to the unfolding political and commercial environment. In each case, the narrative begins from the seventeenth century and ends between 1900 and 1940, depending on when the important processes of change under discussion seemed to run out of steam. The only exception to this format is a chapter on states, which considers statecraft in a longer time-frame.

The book targets two types of readers—those interested in the economic history of modern India, and those interested in business organization. Those readers interested in the economic history of India, and particularly in a work that could form a bridge between world history and Indian history, may find this book a useful first step. Historians of India suggest that the period between the inauguration of British rule in Bengal in 1757 and the end of the nineteenth century saw important changes in economic institutions. But they do not offer a coherent model of change.[4] The absence of a theory of institutional change anchored in a conception of the society has made it difficult for historians to handle long time-spans. The lines of continuity and change between the medieval and the modern, the pre-colonial and the postcolonial, remain obscure, and specializations are too tightly drawn around dates marking conquest and colonization. The book tries to weaken these borders.

To students of business, the book offers two points for reflection. First, the content of 'business organization' is social and time-bound. If the leading figure in the business history of the twenty-first century is the risk-taking entrepreneur, the leading figure in the business history of the eighteenth century was the risk-reducing community. The industrial corporation, joint-stock banks, universal property, and commercial law—staple ingredients in a modern notion of business organization—did not exist in India in the eighteenth century. Yet, India then was one of the more successful commercial-industrial societies of the world. The success owed to the cultural–political

---

[4] An influential text in economic history offers suggestive remarks on the possibility of an institutional history, B.R. Tomlinson, *The Economy of Modern India*, Cambridge: Cambridge University Press, 1993. Deepak Lal's work, *The Hindu Equilibrium: India c. 1500 B.C.–2000 A.D.*, Delhi: Oxford University Press, 2007, does institutional history of a kind, but few historians would find it easy to connect with its assumptions of 'cultural stability' and 'long-term stagnation'. A symposium published under a promising title, while presenting essays that are individually useful and relevant, does not quite fill the gap, Burton Stein and Sanjay Subrahmanyam, eds, *Institutions and Economic Change in South Asia*, New Delhi: Oxford University Press, 1996.

traditions that merchants and bankers drew upon to build cooperation. Second, merchants and bankers were not alone in possessing such resources. Similar cultural–political traditions helped also workers, peasants, and artisans. Business organization was not a preserve of the rich in the early modern world. Organizationally speaking, the distance between different professional categories was narrower than it became later when capitalists, peasants, and workers came under the purview of different laws.

This brief discussion leads us to identify three questions. How did enterprise and community interact in pre-colonial India? How did colonialism and globalization change the relationship? Does the case of India clarify the sources and patterns of economic change in the modern world? The rest of the introductory chapter addresses the first two questions. Chapter 1 takes up the third.

MARKET, STATE, AND SOCIETY: 1650–1750

What were the salient features of the relationship between market, state, and society in pre-colonial India? For the purpose of this book, the convenient point to begin from would be the sketches of social organization of industry and trade that we encounter in the writings of European travellers, clergymen, ambassadors, and merchants in the seventeenth and eighteenth century India. A consistent picture emerges in their descriptions of the economic actors with whom these people came in contact.

François Bernier observed that in the mid-seventeenth century northern India, 'no one marries but in his own trade or profession; and this custom is observed almost as rigidly by Mahometans as by the Gentiles, to whom it is expressly enjoined by their law'. Bernier rued the unhappy consequence that this 'law' had upon 'many ... beautiful girls', who were 'doomed to live singly'.[5] Thomas Bowrey, a merchant who lived in Bengal in the last quarter of the seventeenth century, observed in the same vein that the professions

are not admitted to marry one Occupation with another. A Merchant must marry a Merchant's Daughter, a Weaver a Weaver's Daughter, a Taylor with a Taylor's Daughter, A Gold Smith with a Gold Smith's Daughter, and soe the

[5] *Travels in the Mogul Empire A.D. 1656–1668*, London: Humphrey Milford, 1916, p. 259.

Figure 1: Surat from the sea, c. 1630. European view of Indian society was influenced by doing business in Surat shown here in a Dutch painting. © National Maritime Museum

rest. Every man must Consequently traine their Sons up to the Occupation he is of himselfe, and not assume any Other.[6]

Significant social interaction with other communities was forbidden to skilled and wealthy communities. Banias 'are Strictly forbidden to Eat or drinke Or dwell under the Same roofe with any Save their Owne Cast'.[7] And if anyone disregarded 'every particular of their laws', the person committing the infringement would 'lose religion' and be excluded from society 'until he has regained his Cast'.[8] Bowrey, incidentally, was an admirer of the Indian merchant, unlike his contemporary John Fryer, and praised the merchant for subtlety, capacity to solve complicated arithmetical problems with agility, and for charitable expenditure, in which respect, 'they doe much resemble the Jews, relievinge and Encouradgeinge all of their own Cast'.[9]

About the same time in a different part of India, J. Ovington described the social organization of economic groups in much the same way, if with greater clarity and detail:

Each single Trade is diversified by some particular Opinions; the Goldsmith, and Scrivan, the Joyner, Barber, and Merchant, & c. as they have different

[6] Thomas Bowrey, *A Geographical Account of Countries round the Bay of Bengal, 1669 to 1679*, Cambridge: Hakluyt Society, 1895 (reprinted New Delhi: Asian Educational Services), p. 31.

[7] Ibid., p. 9.

[8] Ibid., p. 11.

[9] Ibid., p. 28.

Employments, so are they of divers Sentiments, and distinguished in the Ceremonies of their Worship; and mix no more in their Sacred Sentiments of Religion, than in their Civil Arts. Therefore all their Arts are Hereditary, and their Employments condin'd to their own Families. The Son is engag'd in the Father's Trade, and to maintain the Profession of it in his Posterity, it is transmitted always to the succeeding Generations, which is obliged to preserve it in a lineal descent, uncommunicated to any Stranger. Upon this account, all Marriages are restricted to one Sect, and contracted only between persons of the same Perswasion and Profession.[10]

Pietro Della Valle wrote, again apropos seventeenth century Surat, 'every one attends and is employ'd in the proper Trade of his Family, without any mutation ever happening amongst them, or Alliance of one Race contracted with another'.[11] John Fryer, an East India Company servant who visited India in the 1670s, noted likewise, 'Tribes were distinguished by their Occupations, espousing therefore Vocations as well as Kindred; and thereby, ... they stood upon their Nobility in that Imployment, never marrying out of it'.[12] Alexander Hamilton, a Scottish sea captain, observed of a particular craft in the western coast of India, 'all Trades and Occupations being listed into Tribes, none can marry out of their own Tribe'.[13]

The Carmelite priest Paolino da San Bartolomeo wrote in the 1770s that in Travancore society, 'no one is allowed to marry from one cast into another'. The 'painters; ... dyers of cloth ... garland-makers; ... smiths ; ... coblers; also the weavers, taylors, carpenters, silver-smiths, clockmakers, and other artisans ... form separate classes, the members of which cannot eat with each other, and much less

[10] *A Voyage to Surat in the year 1689*, London: Humphrey Milford, 1929, p. 165.

[11] *The Travels of Pietro Della Valle in India*, London: Hakluyt Society, 1892, p. 78.

[12] *Travels in India in the Seventeenth Century—Thomas Roe and John Fryer*, New Delhi: Asian Educational Services, 1993, p. 177; see also on Fryer and his scientific contribution, Geoffrey Fryer, 'John Fryer, F.R.S. and His Scientific Observations, Made Chiefly in India and Persia between 1672 and 1682', *Notes and Records of the Royal Society of London*, 33(2), 1979, pp. 175–206.

[13] *A New Account of the East Indies being the Observations and Remarks of Capt. Alexander Hamilton*, vol. 1, London, 1739 (reprinted New Delhi: Asian Educational Services, 1995), p. 316.

intermarry'.[14] San Bartolomeo was particularly struck by the effect this exclusivity had on education. 'In India', he wrote, 'every child receives the same education that was given to his father'. There was no one curriculum or notion of learning, as a result. Schooling was a tool of trade; being illiterate signified occupational situation rather than poverty. 'Hence it happens that the Indians do not follow that general and superficial method of education by which children are treated as if they were all intended for the same condition, and for discharging the same duties ; but those of each cast are from their infancy formed for what they are to be during their whole lives'.[15] In San Bartolomeo's opinion, hereditary transmission of useful knowledge helped diffuse (sic) 'the knowledge of a great many things necessary for the public good'. The long apprenticeship 'enabled farther to improve [skills] and bring them nearer to perfection'.[16]

All earners, then, were divided into groups that functioned as guilds and practiced endogamy. It is difficult to offer a detailed account of the internal organization of these collectives based on European records. Two features do receive frequent mention in these records, however. These are, juridical autonomy, and the presence of panchayats and headmen in charge of making and enforcing laws within the community and at times conducting negotiations between groups.

Bernier, Bowrey, San Bartolomeo, Niccolao Manucci, Luke Scrafton, and many others used the word 'law' when discussing social conventions. The usage was not accidental. Surely, merchants and artisans elsewhere in the world, at times, connected marriage with professional interests. In India, the connection appeared to them as more than a casual one. It had the force of law.

A century before the earliest of these writings, Duarte Barbosa had observed that in the capital of the Vijayanagar Empire, traders of all faiths, Moors, Christians, and Gentiles, 'may live according to

---

[14] *A Voyage of the East Indies, containing an account of the Manners, Customs, & c. of the Natives With a Geographical Description of the Country. Collected from Observations made during a Residence of Thirteen Years, between 1776 and 1789,* p. 308.

[15] Ibid., pp. 257, 267.

[16] Ibid., p. 268.

any creed, or as he pleases'.[17] Bowrey mentioned that professions had 'their own laws'; and described professions as composed of kinsmen. Bernier, who was one of the more critical of the commentators on the Mughal political system, observed that the state did not legislate in India. 'There is no one before whom the injured peasant, artisan, or tradesman can pour out his just complaints; no great lords, parliaments, or judges of local courts, exist, as in France, ... and the Kadis, or judges, are not invested with sufficient power to redress the wrongs'.[18] Yet, India was not lawless. Manucci wrote that 'customs ... of these lands ... have the force of law', whereas formal justice and jurisprudence remained far too costly of access and too distant for ordinary people.[19] Robert Orme, who like Bernier formulated many of the ideas that became staple ingredients in an imperialist conception of India's past, merely repeated a point discussed by others when he observed that 'the different methods of inheritance amongst the Gentoos, are settled by their religion, according to the different casts by which they are distinguished'.[20] San Bartolomeo, who spent several years in Malabar in the 1770s and wrote a detailed and authentic account of the Malayali society of his time, dedicated a whole chapter of his book to the 'laws of the Indians'. The chapter consists of a series of moral maxims, which his Malayali friends regarded as laws, and of which the most stringent in his view was the rule 'never to leave one's tribe (cast)'. The maxims also contained rules the kings needed to respect, such as, 'not to be a tyrant or despot', to respect property, and to ensure that artisans and workers received due wages.[21]

How did community justice work? In mid-eighteenth century Madraspatnam, settlements of people were segregated by ethnic-linguistic groups, and therefore, by trades, as indeed in any other Indian city in this time. San Bartolomeo observed that

[17] *A Description of the Coasts of East Africa and Malabar: In the Beginning of the Sixteenth Century*, London: Hakluyt Society, 1866, p. 86.

[18] *Travels in the Mogul Empire*, p. 225.

[19] *Storia do Mogor*, vol. 3, London: John Murray, 1907, p. 310.

[20] Robert Orme, *Historical Fragments of the Mogul Empire, of the Morattoes, and of the English concerns in Indostan from the year MDCLIX*, London: F. Wingrave, 1805, p. 441.

[21] *Voyage to the East Indies*, pp. 284–304.

when a certain quarter is in this manner assigned to the Indians for their residence, one of their countrymen is always placed over them as a superintendant, who is obliged to preserve peace and good order among them, and to take care that they do not transgress the laws. At Cottate, Padmanaburam, Tiruvandapuram, Cayancollam, and other towns on the Malabar coast, the same establishment is made, that no strife or contention may arise among the various tribes, castes, and religious sects, on account of the difference of their manners and customs.[22]

A reference to juridical autonomy is now joined with a hint of how that autonomy translated into practice. A similar hint can be found in Bowrey's description of Bengal. In the view of some observers of northern India, the autonomy amounted to an exchange, whereby the Hindu merchants 'doe annually purchase theire freedome of theire heathenish laws, with no small summs of moneyes, and condescendinge Obedience to the Mogol and his Omrahs', in an obvious reference to the capitation tax that could be imposed upon non-Muslims in lands ruled by Islamic law, and was used intermittently in India, especially by Aurangzeb to fund his wars.[23] When Indian merchants lived abroad, in Central Asia or the Persian Gulf for example, they enjoyed extra-territoriality, as foreigners do today. In the context of the eighteenth century, such autonomy did not mean being subject to another nation's laws but freedom to frame their own laws, indeed to recreate their own social worlds, divided again into endogamous guilds. In settlements of Multani merchants on the Caspian coast, for example, Muslims were forbidden residence.[24] Chapter 3 discusses more examples of this kind.

The European reading of Indian society finds confirmation in medieval Bengali literature, where again we get glimpses of a highly commercialized and yet highly segmented urban society. It is believed that of the major ballads produced between the fifteenth and sixteenth centuries in Bengal, several (such as the *Manasamangal*) were sponsored by merchants and extolled the spiritual might of the merchant, whereas others dealt with the heroic exploits of the rustic

[22] Ibid., p. 8.

[23] Bowrey, *Geographical Account*, p. 39.

[24] George Foster, *A Journey from Bengal to England*, vol. II, London: A. Faulder, 1808, p. 186.

king. A long conversation between the great merchant Dhanapati in *Manasamangal* and his Brahmin informers about suitable brides for a son shows how deeply such alliances were influenced by pecuniary advantage as well as purity.[25] Purity is also a concern in the most famous episode of *Annadamangal*, the great work of the Bengali poet Bharatchandra Ray (1712–60). The episode describes a secret affair between Vidya, a young Bengali princess, and Sundar, a south Indian prince travelling incognito. After the deed was done, and Sundar was caught by the palace guards, the courtiers pressed him to reveal his caste. Cheeky and evasive answers to this elemental question nearly cost Sundar his life.[26]

In a sixteenth century version of the ballad *Chandimangal*, there is an extended description of the founding of a town by a king, which describes the occupations essential for a new settlement, beginning with three dozen sects of Brahmins distinguished by places of origin, and moving on to the merchants, scribes, doctors, artisans, and finally menials. These occupations are referred by their *jati* names that reappear in nineteenth century ethnological directories. A parallel list of Muslims starts with the military gentry and ends with butchers, weavers and sword polishers.[27] These ballads do not always convey a clear sense of a hierarchical society, but they do carry strong hint of segmentation and exclusivity of communities. Bharatchandra, who completed *Annadamangal* in 1752, described a

[25] Dinesh Chandra Sen, *Banga Sahitya Parichay*, vol. 1 of 2, Calcutta: Calcutta University, 1914. There being many versions of each one of these ballads, each version representing the same episode in a slightly different way, I refrain from citing page references. See, however, Bijanbihari Bhattacharya, ed., *Ketakadas Kshemananda: Manasamangal*, Calcutta: Sahitya Akademi, 1961 (reprinted 2005), pp. 24–5.

[26] Brajendranath Bandopadhyay and Sajanikanta Das, eds., *Bharatchandra Granthabali*, Calcutta: Bangiya Sahitya Parishat, 1997, pp. 328–32.

[27] Sen, *Banga Sahitya Parichay*. The episode is discussed in Tapan Raychaudhuri, *Bengal under Akbar and Jahangir*, Delhi: Munshiram Manoharlal, 1969, p. 7. In the version attributed to Mukundaram Chakrabarty, a late-sixteenth century poet, the picture of castes and professions is especially vivid. Communities, as distinct from trades, should inhabit designated spaces in a new town, the rule was mandatory in sixteenth century town planning. On a description of the episode in Mukundaram, see Sukumar Sen, *Bangala Sahityer Itihas* [A History of Bengali Literature], vol. 1 of 4, Calcutta: Eastern Publishers, 1959, pp. 526–7.

town named Barddhaman in terms of a spectrum of castes; only the list of occupational caste names is much longer than that available in the sixteenth century literature.[28] A foreigner, in this account, is asked to reveal both *jati* and occupation, along with the evidence thereof, at the city gate. A similar picture of a socially segmented world of work appears in a late eighteenth century description of Kashi (Benares), written by the Bengali zamindar-poet and a friend of the Company, Joynarayan Ghoshal.[29] The autobiography of Banarasidas Jain, a sixteenth century merchant in north India, shows the propensity of urban merchants to form cooperative combines with their own relations.[30] Banjaras, who transported bulk commodities of trade over long distances, were organized into groups that managed branches of a business monopolized by one community. Overall, marriage secured allegiance, and headmen represented authority of the group. This was the situation in medieval India until the end of their profession.[31]

What do these pictures add up to? It would be unwise to dismiss the European records and reflections as mere 'representations', without much value as evidence. Needless to say, the authors of these statements were neither infallible nor unbiased. Indeed, they were Eurocentric in the general sense that in their attempt to conceptualize India, the benchmark was necessarily Europe. For me, that fact increases, not diminishes, the value of their observations as evidence in comparative business history. Unlike James Mill, these authors had no political axe to grind. Unlike Max Weber, they did not project a sanskritist copy of Indian society.[32] Few attempted a formal theorization of caste, beyond

[28] Bandopadhyay and Das, eds, *Bharatchandra Granthabali*, p. 216.

[29] Dinesh Chandra Sen, *Banga Sahitya Parichay*, vol. 2 of 2, Calcutta: Calcutta University, 1914, pp. 1513-4.

[30] R.C. Sharma, *Ardhakathanak*, Bombay: Indico, 19.

[31] For a description and references, see Gautam Bhadra, 'Mogaljuge Bharatiya Banik' [The Merchant in Mughal India, in Bengali], *Ekshan*, 4(3-5), 1980, pp. 56–91. On Banjara society in the early nineteenth century, see Edward Balfour, 'Migratory Tribes of Natives in Central India', *Journal of the Asiatic Society of Bengal*, 13, 1844, pp. 1–15.

[32] On nineteenth century Orientalism, see Ronald Inden, 'Orientalist Construction of India', in Peter Cain and Mark Harrison, eds., *Imperialism: Critical Concepts in Historical Studies*, London: Routledge, 1998, pp. 94–136. What part of the travellers' description did the nineteenth century imperialist historians retain? James Mill believed that caste was one of the principles of 'aggregation' at work in Indian society. Combinations formed from the necessity to protect

the commonplace on *varnasrama* picked up from their Brahmin informants (chiefly, Bernier and the seasoned gossip Manucci took this road). A theory of origins of social differentiation in South Asia was a nineteenth century pre-occupation. Few even used the word caste in describing Indian society. Bernier expressly avoided using it. Whereas Bernier left a deep impression upon nineteenth century orientalists, the travellers and letter-writers themselves wrote, as far as one can see, independent accounts rather than derived ones, with the minor exception of Olof Toreen, whose valuable report on Surat saw the city partly through the eyes of Bernier, and Luke Scrafton, whose letters skilfully distilled a concept of Indian society from specific knowledge of places and peoples.[33]

These remarks, I consider, came from observing a precise and real difference in the business organization between Europe and India. The kind of professional guild that these writers had seen working in their own milieu in seventeenth and eighteenth century Europe, where ordinary people faced little barrier to enter any profession except for possessing the money to pay for one's training and certification, did not exist in India.[34] And yet, Indian goods and business practices embodied just as refined, in some cases more refined, skills than did counterparts in Europe. How did the Indians manage this? Their answer was that the Indians harnessed the needed social capital by different means. Guilds almost always formed by using personal ties, in India. Desire for honour within the community secured efficient and trustworthy conduct. Such collectives had two characteristics—agreed

---

communities from 'the financial oppression of the state or against unauthorized plunderers'. It was the weakness of private rights that saw the strengthening of collective rights. Beyond these plain statements, Mill did not show serious interest in the constitution of Indian society. See *The History of British India from 1805 to 1835*, vol. 1 of 3, edited by Horace Wilson, London: James Madden, 1858, pp. 303–5.

[33] *A Voyage to China and the East Indies by Peter Osbeck ... Together with A Voyage to Suratte by Olof Toreen Chaplain of the Gothic Lion East Indiaman ...*, vol. 2 of 2, London; Benjamin White, 1771; Luke Scrafton, *Reflections on the Government of Indostan. With a Short Sketch of the History of Bengal, From MDCCXXXVIIII to MDCCLVI; and an Account of the English Affairs to MDCCLVIII*, London: W. Strahan, 1770.

[34] At least one of these authors noted a resemblance between India and Ireland in respect of the popularity of endogamous guilds.

and shared rules about which parties the members would exchange scarce resources with; and, agreed and shared rules about whom they would marry or whom they would eat with. In the nineteenth century and earlier, most endogamous groups tended to share a calling in India, and those who shared a calling tended to be endogamous.

Later reference to collectives in India often use three keywords interchangeably—joint family, caste, and community. To these three, I have added a fourth, endogamous guild. It is necessary to clarify how these terms are related between themselves.

WHAT IS 'COMMUNITY'?

In colonial practice of Hindu law of property, the strongest and clearest concept was the joint family. The definition and compass of the joint family varied from one region to another. In the strictest definition, which came from Mitakshara, the joint family included the lineal male descendants of a real ancestor, who usually shared in the property held in common.[35] Broader definitions also included wives and daughters. In all cases, the legal members of a joint family had rights to a property; in that the property could not be sold or divided without the consent of every member. They were in this sense, 'coparceners'. In practice, the male head of a household acted as a legally recognized manager of a property, so that the rights of all other members were conditional on the real and formal authority of the elder.

If such was the family, in descriptions of peasant, merchant, and artisan collectives, we come across two broad and distinct notions of community, one tied to marriage and another not so tied. The word caste would come to mind in the former context. Caste as *jati* referred to a cluster of families that exchanged marriage partners between themselves, and did not recruit marriage partners from outside the group. Among Hindus, the endogamous unit could be defined to include all members sharing a caste name, or subsets of them. These subsidiary sets usually carried the sense of an extended family consisting of descendents of a mythical ancestor. In small-sized groups,

---

[35] Mitakshara and Dayabhaga were the two major smritis followed in British Indian courts as codes of Hindu law on property. The origin of Mitakshara is traced to Vijnaneswara, possibly a scholar in the Chalukya court of the Deccan, c. 1100, and that of Dayabhaga to a Nabadwip scholar Jimutavahana.

the joint family and caste tended to overlap. For example, heads of the powerful and wealthy merchant households in small towns were also often regarded as elders of the local merchant community. The boundary between the joint family and the endogamous unit, thus, was neither precise nor static.

There is another notion of community available in the social and economic history of early modern India, which had village or profession as its foundation. The seminal work of C.A. Bayly shows that in north Indian towns in the late eighteenth and early nineteenth century, 'cross-caste mercantile organization, both formal and informal, was critical to the organization of Indian business'.[36] Douglas Haynes makes a similar point with respect to merchant associations in Surat.[37] V.T. Gune wrote, with reference to the village community in Peshwa territories, that 'people not only of different castes but also religion sat together in a Majlis (assembly) convened to settle local problems'.[38] I show in Chapter 5 that communities secured by means of marriage were relatively weak among labouring peoples. Intermarriage was present, but it was one of a range of more fluid and contingent kind of associational rules. Among the factory worker, indentured labour, and migrant agricultural labourer in the nineteenth century, bonds developed along a number of axes—language, village, family, clan, or simply shared vulnerability to extortion. Migrant workers in the nineteenth century textile mills and tea plantations were predominantly male, and recruited by and supervised by individuals whom the employers considered to be 'castemen' carrying particular influence over the workers. Migrant agricultural workers in central Indian wheat fields moved in groups of families. The labourer collective, in short, was influenced rather more by context

[36] 'Epilogue to the Indian Edition', in Seema Alavi, ed., *The Eighteenth Century in India*, Delhi: Oxford University Press, 2002, p. 175; C.A. Bayly, *Rulers, Townsmen and Bazaars: North Indian Society in the Age of British Expansion*, Cambridge: Cambridge University Press, 1983. In a similar way, Mark Elvin criticizes Weber's Europe–China contrast, 'Why China Failed to Create an Endogenous Industrial Capitalism: A Critique of Max Weber's Explanation', *Theory and Society*, 13(3), 1984, pp. 379–91.

[37] 'From Tribute to Philanthropy: The Politics of Gift Giving in a Western Indian City', *The Journal of Asian Studies*, 46(2), 1987, pp. 339–60.

[38] *The Judicial System of the Marathas*, Poona: Sangam, 1953.

than tradition.

The coexistence of caste and cross-caste combines have induced historians to ask, did caste matter at all to economic history? The verdict remains open. While cross-caste combines could be found, studies on business communities in colonial India underscore the persistence and importance of *jati* in the formation of professional combines.[39] Reading that literature, one would think that the anthropological study of the mercantile group emphasizes caste just as persistently as social and economic historians discount its importance.

My own position on this issue can be summed up in two propositions. First, Bayly is right in emphasizing organizational diversity. I show in this book that in part, the diversity was historically contingent. Further, business organization differed between regions and between cosmopolitan port cities, small towns, and the countryside. We should recognize plurality. But we should also recognize that one can overdo the denial of caste. Eighteenth century Surat, Chapter 3 will show, yields examples of cross-caste combines and inter-caste rivalries, a type of conflict we would miss if we go too far in any one direction.

Secondly, 'does caste matter' is a spurious question. Caste and community on the one hand and cross-caste professional associations on the other, were both necessary, for they served different and complementary goals, and were not substitutes. What were these goals? Two functions of a collective were essential in the economic sphere, market negotiations, and management of property. Market negotiations necessarily involved a number of people not related between themselves by marriage or kinship. Disputes over terms of transaction, therefore, needed professional associations because insular community institutions such as the caste panchayat would be powerless to address disputes between communities. Confirming this prediction, the cosmopolitan business towns in India, such as Surat, saw well-developed professional associations emerge. On the other hand, professional associations had little role in decisions on the ownership, accumulation, succession, and management of property. These were matters that followed customs of the endogamous guild, defined and upheld by the elders of the community.

---

[39] See Chapter 3 for more discussion.

Different classes then depended on professional and community modes of coming together in different degrees. Merchants owned valuable property, and also struck deals all the time. They needed both kinds of collective. Skilled craftsmen and peasants were somewhat farther away from trade, but did have to decide, in common with the merchants, who should be the future owners of family business, whom to teach useful and complex skills, and who should manage land, pastures, livestock, or irrigation systems. The most visible community in these cases formed of kinship or marriage. The common expression of community in these occupations was lineage, family, and caste. Professional associations were not absent. Agriculture, especially in the dry zones, critically depended on services supplied by other groups on terms that needed negotiation. Wage labourers, who did not own valuable property, and did not have to address property related questions, did have to worry about market negotiation on wage. The collectives here were often based on a variety of recreated and contingent cultural bonds, not necessarily based on blood brotherhood or marriage ties, but also on village and linguistic commonalities.

The cross-caste organizations that Bayly, Haynes, and Gune discuss dealt commonly with what I call market relations, that is, issues of collective negotiation and bargaining. There is no question that groups of people, unrelated by marriage or kinship, did come together when facing similar problems, when negotiating with a shared counterpart, when dealing with the agents of the state, or defending against a common threat. An authority on the eighteenth century Surat finds 'no evidence at all that the Bohras and the Turks, the banias and the Parsis formed parts of a single organization. ... There was however a very real concern for the common good, and common action would often be undertaken in an emergency'.[40] I show how this broader principle worked during the Deccan riots of 1875 and the blue mutiny of 1860 in Chapter 6.

Groups did more than act in emergencies. They made rules for formation of partnerships and principal-agent relations, fostered cooperation and regulated competition among members, supplied

---

[40] Ashin Das Gupta 'The Merchants of Surat, c. 1700–1750', in E. Leach and S. N. Mukherjee, eds., *Elites in South Asia*, Cambridge: Cambridge University Press, 1970, p. 217.

instruction in useful skills, and framed property rights and successions laws especially where the capital and skills involved were valuable. Where any form of transaction in capital—land, capital, or skill—was concerned, cross-caste combines retreat from the scene. Was the average merchant family in the eighteenth century India likely to recruit partners or agents from families unrelated to itself by marriage? Were the urban silk weavers likely to recruit apprentices from families unrelated to them by marriage? Were peasant families likely to recruit coparceners from labouring families? In the overwhelming majority of cases, the answers to these questions would be firmly negative. On that point, the burden of evidence on specific groups confirms the observations of the European travellers and representations of economic society in Indian literary productions. In short, whereas cross-caste organizations could be found in shaping market relations, endogamous guilds were profoundly influential in shaping property rights and deciding individual access to scarce capital.

The two features that characterized the endogamous guild, sharing rules about marriage (or belonging in a *jati*), and sharing rules about professional choices, were present in most notions of caste. Are caste and endogamous guild, then, identical concepts? They are not, and the word caste should be avoided. It would be a mistake to try to understand guilds by means of an eccentric and supposedly immutable cultural propensity that was present only among Hindus in India. The Bohra Muslims, the Parsis, the three Jewish groups, and the Armenians would fit my description of the endogamous guild far better than the so-called Marwaris, or the people that the Europeans called Banians. The business model that combined occupation with marriage was more universal, and could be found across religious borders.

The word 'community' in this work refers to two kinds of collectives. One had endogamous guild and property relations in its core, other bases of cooperation and market relations on its fringes, and which at times overlapped with *jati* or its fragments, such as *gotra* and *kula*. This was the merchant-banker-skilled-artisan community. The other had cooperation and market relations at its core, and property relations and endogamy on its fringes. This was the tenant-peasant-labourer community. It is necessary also to distinguish the notion of community from that of the 'joint family', which was a nineteenth century British Indian legal concept that narrowed the definition of the family to members who had inheritance rights to common property. This juridical concept of the joint family symbolized a weakening of the endogamous guild in relation to dominant individuals and households within it. The process of weakening affected the capitalist groups more deeply than it did the workers and peasants.

Caste was not the foundation for endogamous guild, but the idiom of caste sometimes invested the guild with a moral force that had no parallel in the world history of the guild. 'The extreme emphasis on … the right family' in selecting marriage partners, especially of daughters, is a feature that continues down from the medieval society to the society today.[41] The classified matrimonial advertisements on any Sunday newspaper, that remain either deeply divided into caste and sect or emphatic about caste being 'no bar', will be sufficient evidence of this. Behaving like a *jati* provided means to seek exclusivity and erect barriers to entry among non-Hindu business groups. The case of the Parsis provides a revealing example. The adoption of the practices of a Hindu caste sheltered them from assimilation with the indigenous population.[42] Guilds elsewhere in the world did often use intermarriage to cement professional ties between families. But marriage among business families in India was far more than matters of convenience. It was an expression of allegiance of the individual to the wishes of the elders, it was tied with notions of purity, and it cemented a moral community that was parallel to, and served, principal-agent relationships within the firm. Marriage expressed being obedient, being pure, and being good, in addition to being profitable. Merchants, bankers, and skilled artisans often shared an ideology of cultural distinctness. Marriage was a device to protect distinctness (see also Chapter 2). Convenience played a subsidiary part in marriage alliances.

The moral dimension can be understood with reference to the three elements constituting the definition of caste. Sociologists identify three principal axes within caste—difference (and commonality), hierarchy, and pollution or what Célestin Bouglé had called 'repulsion'.[43] These

---

[41] Cited text from Raychaudhuri, *Bengal under Akbar and Jahangir*, p. 6.

[42] Jesse S. Palsetia, *The Parsis of India: Preservation of Identity in Bombay City*, Leiden: Brill, 2001, pp. 18-21.

[43] A good description of the analytical discussion on caste can be found in

ideas changed shape, but in some form, they were present in India for centuries. Manucci's account of seventeenth century southern India shows how powerful ideas of pollution and hierarchy were in relations between the outcaste and the others.[44] Contemporary Vaishnav poetry in Bengal carries numerous references to pollution. The *Manasamangal* contains a climacteric episode when the heroine Behula appears before her in-laws in the disguise of an untouchable, evoking attraction and disgust at the same time.[45] Devotional poetry of medieval India is replete with references to pollution. Still, the relevance of caste in the present case is a limited one, and confined to those manifestations of caste when the idea of difference/commonality and practices connected with maintaining distinctness/commonality could secure a guild.

If we must look for a theory of origin of this business institution, we should look at politics instead of religion. The word 'caste' obscures the political origin of guilds in India. We need to consider instead the aspect that the European observers called 'law'. More than religion, the power and distinctness of communities were sustained by the ideology of governance that proved remarkably resilient to shifts of regime until European colonization (Chapter 2). Communities received substantial juridical autonomy from regional states on matters of property and contract. Pre-colonial states in the Indian subcontinent were legislating states in a limited sense. Within the Indic notions of Kingship, Hindu as well as Islamic, the right to frame and administer civil law was to a large extent delivered over to communities. There were two notable features of this legal regime. First, both law and the institution of justice were to a considerable extent decentralized. For

---

Dipankar Gupta, ed., *Social Stratification*, New Delhi: Oxford University Press, 1991, pp. 23–7. Modern discourse on the social history of caste has concerned itself more with the origins of hierarchy and pollution, issues made central by the French anthropologist Louis Dumont, rather than with economic rationality and efficiency, which preoccupied the sociologist and economic historian Max Weber. On the former theme, the major debate in historiography relates to the influence of colonialism on restructuring hierarchy. See especially Susan Bayly, *Caste, Society and Politics in India from the Eighteenth Century to the Modern Age*, Cambridge: Cambridge University Press, 1999.

[44] *Storia do Mogor*, vol. 3.

[45] Bhattacharya, ed., *Ketakadas Kshemananda: Manasamangal*, pp. 106–7.

example, merchants and artisans settled disputes by the mediation of designated community heads and panchayats. And second, the jurisdiction belonged to communities rather than to professions. Merchants and artisans who did not share affinity did not share jurisdiction. In turn civil law, rules of succession for example, was driven by the goal of preserving allegiances toward family, kin, and lineage. Commercial law was not very different from codes of conduct among members of an extended family of merchants or artisans.

This form of business organization served contemporary markets and states efficiently. Indian society had always been a commercial one. Commodity trade was extensive in Mughal India, drawing momentum from the gigantic fiscal system, rich cities, safety and security in the core regions, prosperous military elite that lived in the cities and consumed large quantities of luxury goods, commercial and intellectual transactions with the Ottoman and Persian empires, and extensive maritime trade on the Indian Ocean littoral. Likewise, the Vijayanagar Empire saw urbanization, flourish of skilled crafts, temple building, and long distance trade conducted by powerful guilds. Markets and long-distance trade led individuals and communities to fashion commercial relationship between actors who represented diverse ethnicity.

These moves satisfied two larger patterns. First, the exchange of land, credit, and knowledge tended to be restricted within communities. In factor market transactions, relations of seniority and honour took the place of formal means of enforcement of contract. Second, much trade in final consumption goods avoided contracts and thus, the threat of fraud or breach of contract. Long-distance trade along the Indian coasts had always had segments dominated by spot market dealings and segments dominated by contractual dealings secured with advance payments. In the seventeenth century, the former segment included not only retail sales or sales in fairs and bazaars, but also the very large-scale trade conducted by Indian merchants in port towns like Surat. Some evidence of these spot market deals will be discussed in Chapter 3. By contrast, the European trade in Indian textiles had always been primarily organized along contracts, agency, advances, prior order, and predetermined terms. The forms of these contracts varied between regions. In any case, the words 'contractor' and 'agent' were more consistent with, possibly even originated in, Indo-European trade. Hindu and Muslim traditional law on contract in the main dealt with debts rather than sales (see also Chapter 2).

Whether within property relations or within market relations, groups became unstable as they became exposed to new kind of challenges from the eighteenth century. A major factor of change was Indo-European trade. The sheer scale of investment made in impersonal contractual deals grew to become unprecedentedly large. These deals, therefore, created a scope for breach of contract disputes that was also unprecedented in scale and complexity in this region. The European element in Indian commerce, therefore, intensified conflicts between communities and individuals. The need to ensure conflict-free deals emerged as a new problem, and a serious one. Informal ties of the community were simply not good enough bases to cope with breach of contract between communities.

MARKET, STATE, AND SOCIETY: 1750–1850

The eighteenth century introduced two new elements that affected the collective. First, the slow death of the imperial state and fragmentation of territorial power had ambiguous effects on collectives. Some peasant lineages became more powerful than before. Some banking families became less powerful than before. The second element concerns statecraft. The English East India Company state in the eighteenth century, which had inherited a business world dominated by communities and wished to maintain continuity in administrative ideology, instituted a new rule of law, uneasily straddling two worlds that had been very different one from another. In the style of the English legal system, the Company set up common law courts superseding community courts. And in deference to Indian political tradition, it filled the law books with maxims drawn from religious codes of the local population. The influence of the community in organizing production and exchange and in the framing of economic laws, therefore, persisted. And yet, the existence of common law courts had introduced a fundamental instability into that persistence.

Communities have never been perfectly stable institutions. Competition, conflict, migration, state formation, inflow of new knowledge from the outside, and a host of other factors could threaten an endogamous guild. Caste and community groups were often forced to learn new trades, and thus encroach on others' occupational preserves. Such moves would not have been easy to implement in a world where the state respected the juridical autonomy of communities. An individual could rarely survive as an economic actor outside the support group that supplied training, information, money, and bargaining assistance. Castes, therefore, broke up to give rise to new castes as long as political and ritual sanction from the elite was available. Rules could be broken, but there were stringent rules about breaking rules. This very principle became vulnerable in the eighteenth century when the new regimes instituted a mechanism for settling business disputes no longer dependent on the power of the collective. Disputes between and inside communities began to come into the public sphere, into the court-room, in a competing effort to establish common law precedence.

The desire to create a rule of law using Indian codes, as the East India Company had hoped to do, therefore, bogged the judiciary in a morass of case laws. Furthermore, because commercial law had no textual form, but had existed in the shape of community norms, the project of building commercial law using indigenous custom proved an impossible one. About 15 years after the mutiny (1857), legislative steps that marked a move away from tradition were no more uncommon.

MARKET, STATE, AND SOCIETY: 1850–1950

The move away from tradition, in fact, had begun earlier. With some exceptions, the nineteenth century saw relatively conflict-free commerce and industry. Political stability played a role in reducing conflicts. But the extension of universal laws that framed and stabilized contracts was important too. Joint-stock companies came into being. The stock market, modern banks, and insurance attracted household savings into new business ventures. Millions of workers left homes to work under indenture contract. Universities and technical schools opened up industrial knowledge to individuals who did not come from artisanal background. The markets for factors of production— capital, labour, and knowledge, and partially land—were opened out to people who did not necessarily hail from traditional families and groups. In both property relations and market relations, the groups of older times had become unstable.

A new world of enterprise was thus erected, and this world was founded on laws that allowed cross-community organizations to come into being and allowed them more space. Although communities based on honour were not always in step with this world of business and business law, collectives were necessary too. World markets carried new kind of risks. Formal law had limited reach after all, and the colonial courts were too slow, and because of its insistence on respecting the indigenous code, a haven of misinformation. A progressive disappearance of the collective was hardly to be expected in this scenario. The outcome, in fact, was more complex and more mixed.

The merchant-banker community experienced a creative destruction. Merchants, bankers, and industrialists forged unorthodox partnerships. Industrialization ushered in a public perception of entrepreneurship fixed upon individuals rather than communities. The elevation of Hindu and Muslim codes strengthened the joint family relatively more than it strengthened caste and religion. New associational principles, such as chambers of commerce, could in principle make professional relationships stronger than and less dependent on social ones, even though chambers of commerce in the nineteenth century maintained a strong bond with the ethnicity of their participants. In these ways, the endogamous guild suffered decay. At the same time, migrant trading groups, who did not form a homogeneous social unit before, fashioned a guild based on a recreated sense of community in the new business locations. A famous example of recreated capitalistic communities is the Marwaris of Calcutta.[46] Among skilled artisans the collective persisted, even though signs of adaptation were present in the cities.

More interesting changes can be seen with the labourers and the peasantry. A whole variety of new kinds of solidarity relations emerged in the labour markets. In some cases, the relationships fashioned by migrant industrial workers living in the city resembled the endogamous guild. Communities formed and tried to preserve jobs for themselves, while blocking access to these jobs to others.

---

[46] T.A. Timberg, *The Marwaris, from Traders to Industrialists*, New Delhi: Vikas Publishing House, 1978; Anne Hardgrove, *Community and Public Culture: The Marwaris in Calcutta, c. 1897–1997*, New York: Columbia University Press, 2004.

But usually the new collectives were hybrids. While using the shell of traditional and cultural bonds, at their core, they were responses to the particular problems faced at the work site, and the preferences of the employers.

Although the collective adapted, drawing equally on formal and informal resources, the adaptation carried social cost. In the market place, community could often become a cover for insider trading. Formal associations could be hijacked by ethnic combines. Among factory workers, strong collectives eased, for the employers, problems of managing and communicating with a culturally diverse work-force, but strong collectives also reduced the employers' control over the workers, and reduced technological flexibility. In interwar Bombay, the same little clubs at the work-site that had once served the managers well turned against them when 'rationalization' became imperative. Peasants in some regions had begun the time-span with a strong form of community, at times an endogamous guild, which enabled them to control land and complementary resources for cultivation. Formal property rights changed the pattern of control only partially, for the dominant groups in the village in most situations retained control in the formal regime, even though some of them took on a blow upon collective identity after being de-militarized. But commodity and credit transactions, on the one hand, and tenancy and credit legislations on the other, introduced competition and cleavages within the collective.

CHAPTER OUTLINE

The empirical core of the book consists of five chapters. Chapter 2 reads the origin of the business community in terms of a political contract between the king and the economic actor. The chapter suggests that both on the planes of theory and history, kingly power was regulated in India; regulated by legislative autonomy given to communities. Chapters 3–6 deal with the economic order alone.

Among merchant-bankers and among skilled urban artisans in pre-colonial India, technical knowledge and expertise, apprenticeship, knowledge of markets and clientele, and a sense of distinctness from the local society, tended to be shared and closely guarded. Chapter 3 shows how intra- and inter-group disputes in the wake of commercialization in the eighteenth century weakened endogamous guilds among merchants and bankers. And Chapter 4 shows how new commercial imperatives led to greater diversity in the nature of the artisan collective.

Between 1800 and 1940, millions of people left their homes and traditional jobs to work in new enterprises in India and beyond. Often, they offered their labour as members of a group led by a headman. Village, kinship, and family also influenced labour supply, usually via their influence on the constitution of the group. Chapter 5 ('Workers') explores the interplay between new work opportunities, managerial paradigms, and organized labour supply.

Agricultural growth in pre-colonial India was a group effort, and depended on partnership between military tribes and dominant peasant lineages. Administration after the 1790s strengthened private property rights, and took away the powers or the formerly armed elite. Commercialization, on the other hand, created cleavages within the community. How did these changes affect the community? Chapter 6 ('Peasants') explores this question.

Although mainly interested in South Asia, the present narrative uses global history as a reference. Economies, at any time, anywhere in the world, need collective regulation of land, labour, knowledge, and credit. Yet, the social organization of Indian business did not replicate patterns existing in Western Europe in the time studied here. Does that fact have implications for divergent experiences in the nineteenth century? Chapter 1 addresses this theme.

1 Context
Economic history and 'culture'

All societies used collectives in conducting market exchange in the eighteenth century. But all societies were not alike for that reason. They differed in the extent of market exposure. They differed in the nature of the collective, and therefore, in the consequences that these institutions might have on the costs of market exchange. Because they differed, they could develop along substantially different paths. Writing the social history of economic change in any one region, therefore, is a comparative project. That project attempts to answer the following question. Can cultural endowments explain divergent patterns of economic change? This chapter explores the question with reference to the Indian history.

CULTURE AND ECONOMIC HISTORY
What is culture? The Cambridge Online Dictionary defines 'culture' as the customs and beliefs shared between large numbers of people. Historians have long been familiar with the argument that customs and beliefs shared between large numbers of people influenced the genesis of modern economic growth and shaped world inequality.

Turn-of-the-nineteenth-century continental sociology saw progress in the Western world as a movement from community-orientation toward individualism, asking what virtuous qualities society had lost while emerging from the 'tyranny of tradition'. The same intellectual milieu had also seen the marginalist revolution in economics. Economics, especially the welfare theorems of Vilfredo Pareto, claimed that the pursuit of individual self-interest led to an allocation of social resources that could not be improved by state intervention. Classical political economy had established that the pursuit of individual self-interest would lead to economic growth. Together, these formal rules seemed to explain why economies grew and why that growth would be led by individuals acting unconstrained in the market. And yet, these formal rules of economics worked only for Western Europe in the previous 100 years. The initial and universal condition of humanity was not an assertion of individual rationality, but some sort of restraint on individual rationality. Why was growth born now and born here?

Max Weber's *The Protestant Ethic and the Spirit of Capitalism* (1905) answered the question with reference to work ethic. All religions of the world had notions of good work built into them. In Protestantism, that notion of good work took on a materialistic character. Good work meant not working for the community, or atoning for one's sins, but being diligent in one's calling. In countries where Protestantism was strong, individuals worked harder for personal gain. The pursuit of self-interest, in turn, produced collective gain. Protestant work ethic explained the time and place of the first modernization the world had seen. Weber further argued that in India and China, the dominant theologies shaped a work ethic that suppressed individuality.[1] For, in Hinduism, good work meant following caste customs. The key concept was *dharma*, or a divinely ordained calling. This work ethic was 'characterized by the dread of the magical evil of innovation'.[2] Caste, being an expression of a religion, militated against rationality and innovation by pre-ordaining choice of occupation, or by introducing 'vocational stability'.

Not all nineteenth century commentators on modernity placed individuality upon 'spirit', as Weber did. Henry Maine, one of those who did not, emphasized private *property rights*. Maine wrote—'private property, in the shape in which we know it, was chiefly formed by the gradual disentanglement of the separate rights of individuals from the blended rights of a community'.[3] This transition he called 'from status to contract'. In order to establish this thesis, Maine studied societies where individual rights were of recent origin. The Indian village offered

---

[1] Max Weber, *The Religion of India: The Sociology of Hinduism and Buddhism*. Translated and Edited by Hans H. Gerth and Don Martindale, Glencoe: Free Press, 1958.

[2] Weber, *Religion of India*, p. 122.

[3] Maine, *Village-Communities in the East and West*, New York: Henry Holt, 1876, Lectures III and V, p. 280.

models of joint proprietorship or collective ownership of assets, which, for him, were an important illustration of the prehistory of private property. These models showed that the administration of the Indian village encompassed legislative powers. Why did the legislative powers of the European manor become absorbed in the powers of the state whereas the Indian village community continued intact to the nineteenth century? The systematizing influence of Roman law in Europe provided one part of the answer. The other derived from the fact that the pre-colonial Indian state was not a legislating state.[4] It respected status and hierarchy more than contractual relations between individuals, or between the state and the people.

When the dust settled after the Second World War and decolonization, and economic development emerged as a new worldwide challenge in the 1950s, Weber made a comeback. The modernization theory retained the idea that modernization meant assertion of the individual rational actor, and that development therefore should mean not only a set of economic policies, but also the adoption of new customs and beliefs by large numbers of people.[5] Authors such as David Apter, David McClelland, Alex Inkeles, emphasized that becoming modern meant living in a society that valued the individual, valued innovation, and displayed personality traits more commonly found in the modern West. Walt Rostow, one of the architects of the theory in relation to economic history, emphasized the importance of 'scientific attitude'.[6]

Sociology and history in the 1960s disputed the specific claims about India that had informed Maine and Weber. Weber relied on texts produced by pundits, rather than on practice. Maine reified the village community, and underestimated the hierarchies and divisions ingrained within what might appear to outsiders as a council of equals. Attempts to discover a persistent core of orthodoxy in the Hindu religion, a definite connection between social organization and

[4] See Chapter 2 for more discussion on the point. See Maine, *Village-Communities*.

[5] For a useful and relevant early statement of the major issues, see S.N. Eisenstadt, 'Modernization and Conditions of Sustained Growth', *World Politics*, 16(4), 1964, pp. 576–94.

[6] W.W. Rostow 'The Stages of Economic Growth', *Economic History Review*, 12(1), 1959, pp. 1–16.

religious texts, a rigid historical link between caste and occupation, and a pre-rational Hindu work-ethic, have been shown to be futile quests. On all these points, the society of South Asia shows too many variations over time and between peoples to be reduced to a set of principles.[7] Based largely on readings of texts, Weber took the essential features of the caste system to be immutable, and moved back and forth between ancient and modern India as if caste formed a stable bridge across time. Historians more recently have rendered such methods untenable. Recent historiography of caste claims that the essential features of the idea were fundamentally restructured from time to time.[8] The religious route Weber took left him poorly equipped to deal with the Muslim situation, a weakness he covered up with tentative assertions about differences between Hindu and Muslim work-ethic, for example, 'the Hindu artisan is ... more industrious than the Indian artisan of the Islamic faith'.[9]

Modernization, then, raised more problems than it solved. The obituary of modernization as a tool in world history, however, was written not by sociologists, but by the impressive economic growth of the very regions that Weber had too hastily chosen as counter-examples to his theory of the rise of the West.

In the 1960s, economic anthropology discovered Karl Polanyi, who offered another argument on the link between culture and conduct.[10] Polanyi criticized economic formalism that behaved as if all economic actors were rational and individualistic irrespective of time and place. In fact, the pursuit of private gains by participating in market

[7] For a nuanced review of the critique of the Weber thesis, see Milton Singer, 'Religion and Social Change in India: The Max Weber Thesis Phase Three', *Economic Development and Cultural Change*, 14(4), 1966, pp. 497–505. The scholarship criticizing Weber is very large, and cannot be summarized in a footnote. Within this scholarship, Weber's position has often been caricatured by both 'vulgar' Weberians and their numerous critics, according to David Gellner 'Religion and the Transformation of Capitalism', in Richard H. Roberts, ed., *Religion and the Transformations of Capitalism: Comparative Approaches*, London: Routledge, 1995, pp. 21–46.

[8] On these themes, see especially Susan Bayly, *Caste, Society and Politics in India from the Eighteenth Century to the Modern Age*, Cambridge: Cambridge University Press, 1999

[9] Weber, *Religion of India*, p. 113.

[10] *The Great Transformation*, Boston: The Beacon Press, 1957.

exchange was a recent phenomenon. Nineteenth century Europe 'disembedded' the economy from social control. In the past, and in non-western societies, commodity exchange could reflect a variety of objectives, such as, the desire to ensure subsistence, acquire status, receive and give gifts, or build peace.[11] Like Weber, Polanyi considered that individuation was a modern western tendency; but unlike Weber, what remained outside these borders was not irrationality or other-worldliness, but other kinds of rationality. Polanyi's influence on the study of third world economic history can be seen particularly in the Marxist notion of communal or lineage mode of production and in Immanuel Wallerstein's use of modes of market exchange.[12]

If individual and collective rationality remain opposed in these formulations, institutional economic history of the 1980s emphasized their mutual compatibility.[13] Good collectives provided a bigger scope for assertion of individual rationality by reducing transaction cost. What do good collectives do which make them so indispensable? There are three benefits. They can deal with free rider problems in the supply of public goods. Public goods are goods that cannot be denied to members of a society; like the use of a road. For that very reason, individuals may be unwilling to pay for such a good. One solution is the state, which has the authority to tax. States also have the police power to see that rule-breakers are punished. But some 'impure' public goods can also be supplied by associations like the guild. Strong cohesive clubs, for example, could make internal agreement on how to

[11] Later appraisals of substantitivism underlined the need for combining both formalism and substantitivism in doing history, S. C. Humphreys 'History, Economics, and Anthropology: The Work of Karl Polanyi', *History and Theory*, 8(2), 1969, 165–212.

[12] For an original statement of the theory, see Claude Meillassoux 'From Reproduction to Production', *Economy and Society*, 1(1), 1972, 93–105. For a survey of related concepts, see Aidan Southall 'On Mode of Production Theory: The Foraging Mode of Production and the Kinship Mode of Production', *Dialectical Anthropology*, 12(2), 1987, 165–92.

[13] See Avner Greif, 'Impersonal Exchange and the Origin of Markets: From the Community Responsibility System to Individual Legal Responsibility in Premodern Europe', in Masahiko Aoki and Yūjirō Hayami, eds. *Communities and Markets in Economic Development*, Oxford: Oxford University Press, 2001. See also Douglass C. North, *Understanding the Process of Economic Change*, New York: Academic Press, 2005.

distribute the benefits and costs from common rules or common assets easier to effect. Second, collectives like guilds were strategic alliances, and helped bargaining, risk-sharing, and as market regulators.

The third significance of the group is highlighted in the literature on the transfer and diffusion of technological knowledge.[14] Guilds organized training of useful skills. That is, groups facilitated communication of good ideas. The process of diffusion of knowledge, before the era of cheap printed books and mass media, was influenced by the nature of collectives, for the simple reason that communication occurred more freely and swiftly within a collective than between members belonging in different collectives. And exchange of knowledge between peoples and societies was ordered by certain sanctioned routes. In the evolution of some modern laws and organization, we see a reflection of the pre-modern collective. The university, for example, is a surviving legacy of the medieval guild. The patent system is a legacy of a practice of paying fees to a guild for buying or using a piece of useful knowledge.

Economic history is not altogether clear about the conditions that make a group able to meet these goals or fail to meet these goals. What are the structural features of a group that make it more likely that it would be an effective group? Economic sociology offers two complementary propositions on this point.[15] 'Collective action that depends on overcoming free-rider problems is more likely in groups whose social network is dense and cohesive'. But if strong ties are good for coordination and forging agreements on change, weak ties are good for innovation, because 'more novel information flows to individuals through weak than through strong ties'. Individuals who have ties into multiple networks that are largely separated from one another, have access to diverse worlds of knowledge, and are particularly useful as information bridges between them.

This interesting hint of a trade-off connects with a larger problem. Preconditions that institutional economics considers are necessary

---

[14] Joel Mokyr, *Gifts of Athena: Historical Origins of the Knowledge Economy*, Princeton: Princeton University Press, 2002.

[15] Mark Granovetter, 'The Strength of Weak Ties: A Network Theory Revisited', *Sociological Theory*, 1, 1983, pp. 201–33; and 'Economic Action and Social Structure: The Problem of Embeddedness', *American Journal of Sociology*, 91(3), 1985, pp. 481–510.

for framing and enforcing a good set of rules can equally well lead to a bad set of rules. A strong state, for example, is necessary to protect property, but a strong state can equally well exploit the propertied (see also Chapter 2). A strong collective can build cooperation, but it can also restrain free exchange of information by erecting barriers to entry. Collectivization carries trade-offs. Culture matters to economic conduct by means of a balancing act—society needs collectives and yet must contain the costs of collectivization. Out of this problem emerge at least four distinct notions of necessary-yet-dysfunctional, good-yet-bad, collectivization.

Mancur Olson suggested that groups in modern western democratic societies were distributional coalitions that served their members, militated against change, and stifled individualism. Olson, interestingly, saw caste in India as a distributional coalition.[16] The economic theory of customary formations recognizes that some clubs persist even when they are opposed to the interests of individual members. George Akerlof explains such conformity with reference to 'a code of honor or a code of behavior in the relevant trading community'.[17] Proscriptive rules persist despite being to the disadvantage of some individuals because of the disutility from loss of reputation, or the 'stigma of the outcaste'. Collectives founded upon honour tend to perpetuate themselves because in an honour-based community individual's utility interacts with those of others.[18] Codes and honours need to be accounted for in turn, a task that Akerlof does not attempt. Modern usage of caste in applied development economics has gone further in explaining observance of the code in terms of reciprocity as opposed to penalties, and thus moved closer to the anthropologists' notion of

---

[16] *The Rise and Decline of Nations*, New Haven: Yale University Press, 1982.

[17] Akerlof and others treat caste as an abstract bundle of norms rather than as a real-life social or religious phenomenon. The two terms, community in this book, and caste as a bundle of norms, overlap. George A. Akerlof, 'The Economics of Caste and of the Rat Race and Other Woeful Tales', *The Quarterly Journal of Economics*, 90(4), 1976, pp. 599–617; and 'A Theory of Social Custom, of Which Unemployment May be One Consequence', *The Quarterly Journal of Economics*, 94(4), 1980, 749–75.

[18] George A. Akerlof, 'Social Distance and Social Decisions', *Econometrica*, 65(5), 1997, 1005–27.

community, especially the trading community.[19] Insofar as repeated play rather than moral beliefs is the foundation for the existence of a community, the subject of conformity has also attracted the attention of game theorists.[20]

Avner Greif's work on medieval merchant capitalism reveals a third kind of ambiguity associated with the constitution of groups.[21] An important distinction has emerged in the economic theory and economic history of groups through this research, between groups founded on rules of associational law, and groups founded on codes of honour. Both may pursue similar worldly aims. And yet they are different entities, for the spillover effects that they leave upon the formation of law can be quite different.[22]

Finally, in a recent article, I have explored the uncertain outcome of collectives upon exchange of knowledge.[23] My starting point is the assumption that significant innovation in processes of production usually requires partnership between diverse skills. An iron-master, a weaver, and a carpenter need to join their heads in order to design a radically new loom. The key to understanding industrial

[19] For a more comprehensive review, see Kripa Freitas, 'The Indian Caste System as a Means of Contract Enforcement', Northwestern University, unpublished, 2006.

[20] For a review of the game theoretic literature on reciprocity, see Rajiv Sethi and E. Somanathan, 'Understanding Reciprocity', *Journal of Economic Behavior and Organization*, 50(1), 2003, pp. 1–27.

[21] 'Cultural Beliefs and the Organization of Society: A Historical and Theoretical Reflection on Collectivist and Individualist Societies, *Journal of Political Economy*, 102(5), 1994, pp. 912–50.

[22] Paul Milgrom, et al describe the economy of medieval Europe as one 'without the benefit of state enforcement of contracts or an established body of commercial law', but nevertheless containing an efficient information-sharing system of private arbitration, or the law merchant. The very principle of association between unrelated individuals embodied in the guild principle was an impetus to develop legal rules of association, in which historians have found one root of the great modern innovation, the company. One could add that groups founded on written statutes were more likely than others to resolve conflict between goals. Paul R. Milgrom, Douglass C. North, and Barry R. Weingast 'The Role of Institutions in the Revival of Trade', *Economics and Politics*, 2(1), 1990, pp. 1–23; see also H.J. Berman, *Law and Revolution: The Formation of the Western Legal Tradition*, Cambridge Mass.: Harvard University Press, 1983.

[23] 'Knowledge and Divergence from the Perspective of Early Modern India', *Journal of Global History*, 3(4), 2008, pp. 361–87.

innovation, therefore, should be the ease or difficulty in the way of diverse professionals forming partnerships with each other in using and learning skills, or more conveniently expressed, the transaction cost of joint ventures. In a world dominated by guilds, the cost was market-based, that is, the payment of a fee. Knowledge was expensive but could be hired. In a world dominated by endogamous guilds, the ticket to entry into a collective was birth or marriage, and could not be purchased. Commodities could be purchased, but not knowledge. These barriers were not watertight, but they could be broken only with political resources rather than financial ones. The latter kind of collective dominated the Indian world, and the former was more common in Western Europe. These differences in barriers to entry into artisan communities provide one part of the explanation why industrial innovation from the eighteenth century focused on processes and tools in Western Europe, whereas innovation continued to focus on products, or more specifically design and craftsmanship, in India for somewhat longer. Exclusive communities were more adept at making new goods than new machines.

Do these concepts of cultural endowments explain the emergence of modern economic growth and patterns of world inequality?

THE GROWTH DEBATE

If the nineteenth century saw an institutional transition in India, the same time-span also saw the beginnings of modern world inequality. Between 1820 and 1950, nations in Western Europe and territories where European settlers had created new states saw a manifold rise in average incomes, whereas the old world regions of Asia, principally India and China, saw an increase of 10–20 per cent.[24] Averages are misleading. Many agents and activities in Asia taking part in the new world of commerce and industry succeeded as dramatically as their counterparts did elsewhere. Yet, more were constrained rather than enabled to better their conditions in this period of relatively rapid change. And they failed to gain from the new opportunities not because they shied away from market transactions, but despite taking part in them, and in some accounts because they did.

[24] F. Bourguignon and C. Morrisson, 'Inequality among World Citizens: 1820–1992', *American Economic Review*, 92(4), 2002, pp. 727–44.

Historical scholarship of comparative economic growth is perennially torn between two competing alternatives—one that explains the origins of international economic inequality mainly with reference to interactions between states, and another that explains economic growth and international inequality mainly with reference to characteristics of the local societies. The dependency and world systems schools are examples of the former approach.[25] Institutional economics applied to economic history is an example of the second, 'cultural', approach.

The interactionist approach implicitly assumes culture does not matter. What matters are modes of coercive control of labour, and how these were sustained by political means, including colonialism. Some authors also contend that colonization damaged or destroyed robust indigenous cultural traditions. These assumptions inform the major part of historical writings on colonialism produced within the South Asian academia. Irfan Habib, for example, suggests that the transition to colonialism led to a decline in commercial and industrial cultures resulting in de-urbanization and agrarianism.[26] A strand within nationalist historiography claims that Indian society before colonial rule was, in scientific, technological and educational attainments, equal to that of Europe if not better, and that colonialism destroyed scientific knowledge and systems of mass education.[27] A connected argument

---

[25] André Gunder Frank and contributors to the Latin American dependency school pioneered by Fernando Cardoso and Enzo Faletto made the early and influential statements of this theory. See Frank, *Capitalism and Underdevelopment in Latin America: Historical Studies of Chile and Brazil*, New York: Monthly Review Press, 1967. For an application of the approach to the developing world, see A.K. Bagchi, *The Political Economy of Underdevelopment*, Cambridge: Cambridge University Press, 1982. The dependency argument was incorporated in the world systems theory of Immanuel Wallerstein, *The Modern World System: Capitalist Agriculture and the Origins of the European World-Economy in the Sixteenth Century*, New York: Cambridge University Press, 1974. For subsequent scholarship on the interactions view of world development, see André Gunder Frank and Barry K. Gills, eds., *The World System: Five Hundred Years or Five Thousand?*, London and New York: Routledge, 1996. Frank's own conception of world development moved away from dependency toward inequality in resource and capital.

[26] 'Colonialisation of the Indian Economy, 1757-1900', *Social Scientist*, 3(8), 1975, pp. 23-53.

[27] For one example on education, see K.N. Panikkar, 'Cultural Trends in

is that the 'incorporation' of South Asia in a world capitalist system as a peripheral region, and the subsequent de-industrialization, led to obsolescence in knowledge of manufacturing.[28] These arguments together make colonialism the agent of an institutional regress.

The cultural approach to world history starts from an opposite assumption. Douglass North and his associates suggest that the modern West discovered secure property rights and contractual law in the seventeenth and eighteenth centuries.[29] If this was the origin of modern economic growth, one would need to explain the origin of world inequality by showing that the non-West had remained trapped in a business world that was unsafe and unpredictable. New institutional history takes it for granted that it was.

The belief that it was has much older antecedents going back to the nineteenth century. Karl Marx, informed by the writings of James Mill, believed that Asiatic society was founded on oppression. A vulnerability to conquest was the result of socially and constitutionally exclusive castes, tribes, and groups, which fragmented and weakened the society.[30] If the caste-fragmented society was the root of Asiatic despotism, the despot in turn acted as predator with respect to the merchants. The great imperial states of South, West, and East Asia pose an apparent contrast to the fragmented and competitive states that characterized Western Europe through much of its history.[31] J. Barrington Moore believed that this disparity had implications for

Precolonial India: an Overview', in S. Irfan Habib and Dhruv Raina, eds., *Social History of Science in Colonial India*, Delhi: Oxford University Press, 2007.

[28] For a perceptive review of this position, see David Washbrook, 'South Asia, the World System, and World Capitalism', *Journal of Asian Studies*, 49(3), 1990, pp. 479-508.

[29] North, *Structure and Change in Economic History*, New York: Norton, 1981, and Douglass C. North and Robert Paul Thomas, *The Rise of the Western World: A New Economic History*, New York: Cambridge University Press, 1973.

[30] A useful discussion can be found in Eric Stokes, 'The First Century of British Colonial Rule in India: Social Revolution or Social Stagnation?', *Past and Present*, 58, 1973, pp. 136-60. See also Daniel Thorner, 'Marx on India and the Asiatic Mode of Production', *Contributions to Indian Sociology*, 9, 1966, pp. 33–66.

[31] Karl Wittfogel, *Oriental Despotism*, New Haven: Yale University Press 1957. Roy Bin Wong explores the contrast in his comparative history of China, *China Transformed: Historical Change and the Limits of European Experience*, Ithaca, NY: Cornell University Press, 1997, Part 2.

security of property rights. 'In general, the attitude of the political authorities in India towards the merchants seems to have been closer to that of a spider towards a fly than that of the cowherd towards his cow that was widespread in Europe at the same time.'[32] William Moreland, the economic historian of medieval India drew a picture of the Mughal state as an extractive machine, leaving little space for a commercial culture to develop except in elite luxury goods or in moving grain. The Marxist anthropologist Eric Wolf saw the effect of the 'tributary' Mughal system upon merchants in much the same light.[33] In some recent works in world history, this difference has again been seen to imply a difference between a contained state and a predatory state.[34]

Supposing for the moment that this was the case, the misfortune of the non-West can be explained in broadly two fashions. First, the non-West started with bad collectives and remained stuck with these, an assumption that institutional economics often adopts by default. The analytical issue concerns 'path-dependence'.[35] Second, the non-West started with bad collectives, and the Western colonizers, the bearers of good tradition, proved unwilling to conduct institutional engineering. In one recent account, tropical disease environment or high settler mortality weakened the impulse to carry out radical policies in the tropics.[36]

It would perhaps be a mistake to pose these two approaches as

[32] J. Barrington Moore, *Social Origins of Dictatorship and Democracy*, Boston, 1967, p. 322.

[33] *Europe and the People without History*, Berkeley and Los Angeles: University of California Press, 1982, p. 86.

[34] For an argument on divergence that rests on rent-seeking, see Eric Jones, *Growth Recurring: Economic Change in World History*, New York: Oxford University Press, 1988.

[35] For a discussion of adverse path dependence as an analytical tool, Pranab Bardhan, 'Institutions Matter, but which ones?', *Economics of Transition*, 13 (3), 2005, pp. 499–532.

[36] Daron Acemoglu, Simon Johnson, and James A. Robinson, 'The Colonial Origins of Comparative Development: An Empirical Investigation', *American Economic Review*, 91(5), 2001, pp. 1369–401. The second view finds its most convincing application in interpretation of economic inequality in the New World. Kenneth L. Sokoloff and Stanley L. Engerman, 'Institutions, Factor Endowments, and Paths of Development in the New World', *Journal of Economic Perspectives*, 14(3), 2000, pp. 7–32.

exclusive alternatives. Each one of these would find relevant and useful applications in particular world historical contexts. Equally, a too hard-line application of either of these approaches would force us to rely on poorly testable propositions. For example the idea that India and Europe were institutionally similar on the eve of modern economic growth glosses over a difficult empirical question, and is contradicted by the testimony of European travellers in India on economic institutions discussed in the introductory chapter. The proposition that the only major difference between these world regions consisted in modes of labour control is speculative again. Similarly, the idea that Europe forged ahead of India owing to superior property rights entails assuming that the early modern business world in India was bereft of secure property rights, the early modern polity was despotic, and the available corporate entities were too weak and fragmented. To any serious student of medieval Indian history, points of entry such as these would seem bizarre at the very least.

INDIA IN CONTEXT

Chapter 2 shows that the notion of security of property rights was deeply rooted in the ideology of governance in this region. Political history of medieval India has substantially revised the idea of oriental despotism in order to accommodate evidence suggesting that merchants and bankers played a vital role in the business of governance in the early modern world. Indeed, without that political legacy, it would be difficult to explain the rise to political power of an association of European traders in the eighteenth century Bengal. European travellers did complain a lot about oppression of merchants by territorial states, but such instances should be read in the context of a particular contest between land-based power and naval might, which the maritime merchants controlled.

Were early modern institutions already dysfunctional? Colonial policy in India did stay away from radical institutional engineering. But we need to interpret that strategy with reference to *Indian society*, which the available theories from comparative institutional history do not do.[37] The commercial and industrial efflorescence in South

[37] The disease theory of inertia is unpersuasive. There is no evidence suggesting that officers of the East India Company governed India the way they did on

Asia in the eighteenth century calls into question any assumption about the intrinsic weakness of merchant and artisan collectives. The Europeanist construct that caste had made the Indian business world politically divided and weak, whereas professional guilds empowered capitalists in European cities, does not square with the experience of early modern commercial capitalism in the region.

In reality, there was little to differentiate Asia and Europe upon benefits that collectives carried for their members. The endogamous guild, seen in this way, was just as useful as any other kind of guild in the early modern world. For services that collectives performed then—training and apprenticeship, collective bargaining, and securing cooperation—India and Europe were possibly equivalent. In a world ruled by craft industries and informal law, there was little to differentiate an endogamous guild from a professional guild. Indeed in some respects, such as design development, the former model of long intra-family apprenticeship could perform better than the more open collective. The choice between guild and caste is a false choice not because caste was irrelevant in India, but because there is not sufficient ground to insist that the two models were qualitatively different.

We should here note that the early modern observer who compared India and Europe did not derive any conclusions about economic efficiency from observed cultural differences. In the 1710s, Danish missionaries in Malabar conducted a series of conversations with local experts on 'law and religion'. The missionaries were agitated about the cultural difference, for it was their business to be so. And yet, they evidently did not think that by becoming European in 'law', the Indian would become a better producer or merchant.[38] During one of these discourses an Indian merchant asked a Danish priest, are we not accomplished enough in 'manufactures, prepared by the Industry of the Inhabitants, and for its Goodness and Beauty, coveted by the Europeans'. What, then, 'should move you to change our laws?' The priest readily conceded, 'I grant ... that in relation to trade, and

---

account of a risk of infection. Another factor played a more direct, more obvious, and a larger role, the weight of indigenous tradition, in particular, the conscious desire to turn the existing groups into a tool of governance. See also Chapter 2.

[38] Anonymous, *Thirty Four Conferences between the Danish Missionaries and the Malabarian Bramans or Heathen Priests in the East Indies* (tr. From High Dutch by J. Thomas Philipps), London: St. Paul's Publishing, 1719, pp. 256–7.

the Things of this Life, you are a very understanding People, and no Ways inferior to any the wisest Nation'. The 'errors' of Indian ways related to the spiritual life, and spirituality alone. It had no material consequences in the eyes of the contemporary observer.

We now know better. And I believe that the one thing that does meaningfully connect culture with enterprise is the notion that all communities carry costs. Collectives involve trade-off. What kind of trade-off did the endogamous guild in India involve? On the nature of the trade-off, there will in all likelihood be differences between regions.

There were two types of costs of the endogamous guild. Modern industrialization builds upon inter-industry knowledge exchange, and wider range of contractual transactions. Professional associations, whose services are marketable, are better able to foster inter-professional learning than were the insular communities of India, wherein entry and exit were not traded and negotiated. Moving between occupational groups was not unknown in India, but such moves involved overcoming far stronger barriers than was the case in Western Europe. Further, the moral communities of India were neither well-suited to widespread contractual transaction, nor did they supply a sufficient basis for framing universal property and commercial law. Being embodied in codes of honour and conduct, informal law of merchant and artisan families were undocumented and opaque to an outsider, indeed even to insiders. The evolution of norms into universal commercial law faced barriers, and was ridden with conflicts.

The nineteenth century confronted economic agents in India with elevated risks of enterprise, a different technological paradigm, more impersonal and diverse market environment, and a new kind of state. Yet, the transition from one kind of collective to another proved too tortuous. It was slowed not by path-dependence, nor by the unwillingness of the state to do anything. Rather, it was slowed by a calculated and deliberate policy to do nothing; by a regulated inertia. Early colonialism in India saw itself as inheritors of a regional tradition of statecraft. Settlers did not see themselves as either settlers or carriers of a distinctly superior institutional heritage, though these feelings hardened in the nineteenth century. British colonial rule in India, at least the early nineteenth century version of it, was too traditional, indeed too Indian, a force of change. Colonial rule, in other words, slowed institutional change by means of a policy to preserve and use family, caste, and community to recreate an Indian kind of rule.

Despite the regulated inertia, the endogamous guild proved unable or poorly able to cope with the new world of commerce. Regulated inertia in politics and law had huge unintended consequences. Commercialization created rich merchants who did not believe in caste codes as strongly as did their forefathers. Battles for control over community associations and leadership in identity politics reflected these conflicts. Discords and differentiations fractured communities of merchants and bankers, particularly. These discords figure prominently in the narrative in the next chapters.

The journey begins with a theory of the origin of the endogamous guild.

2 States
A political theory of the community

Later chapters in the book will discuss forms of business organiz-ation in India. The present chapter discusses the nature of the relationship between the king and the economic order, and offers a theory of origin for the business community. All organized public conduct is shaped by ideology. If with private business the ideology is largely invisible and undocumented, with kingship, it is not. For that reason, among others, the point of entry into this subject of community formation is the written out tenets of kingship that we encounter in South Asia. None can claim that real governance was always conducted according to written rules. At the same time, rules of kingship dealt with the rights of those actors who could possibly trouble the king, were rules systematically broken. The individual king had limited power to alter the economic order, and had to take its existence and structure for granted. The texts should reflect the desire for a stable arrangement between the king and the wealthy. In the South Asian case, the texts did make explicit and quite stable assumptions about the economic order. This chapter extracts these central assumptions.

A short summary of the project is in order. The chapter proposes a political theory of guilds in the region. It shows that on the planes of ideology (and history) kingly power was regulated in India. Capitalists had substantial autonomy to frame their own civil law. But this freedom was enjoyed not by the individual capitalist, nor by an association of professionals, but usually by an association of families. Therefore, property and commercial law remained largely outside the boundaries of day-to-day statecraft; a fact of life changed, if fitfully, in the nineteenth century.

THE KING IN ECONOMIC HISTORY

Developing a theory of the state that could clarify the origin and form of economic institutions has engaged mainly the Europeanist. When transplanted to India, the Europeanist theories can produce odd results.

'It is the polity that defines and enforces the formal economic rules of the game', Douglass North reminds us.[1] Here, we encounter a fundamental problem in the theory of economic history. Polities that are strong enough to enforce the rules of the game are also strong enough to bend the rules in their favour. In *Structure and Change in Economic History*, North suggests a possible escape from this dilemma, the existence of potential competitors as in a contestable monopoly.[2] In another article, North and B.R. Weingast develop the idea that competition in the market for political power is likely to lead to credible commitments made by one dominant player to other players to work in mutual interest.[3]

When these ideas are generalized on a world scale, we get two propositions. First, political competition and credible commitments existed in early modern England, as North and Weingast claim in their paper. Second, political competition was weak in the great Empires of pre-modern Asia, the Indic, the Chinese, and the Ottoman. These regions saw little economic growth during and after Europe's take-off, presumably owing to poor enforcement of property rights. The second proposition fits neatly with a long, distinguished, and still vibrant scholarly tradition attributing the weakness of merchant capital and capitalism in pre-colonial India to Asiatic despotism. Key contributions to the despotism thesis owe to James Mill, Karl Marx, J. Barrington Moore, Karl Wittfogel, William Moreland, the Aligarh School, and more recently, Eric Wolf, and E. L. Jones. Some of their works were cited in the Introduction and Chapter 1. As historians later revealed huge evidence of economic dynamism in pre-colonial

---

[1] *Understanding the Process of Economic Change*, New York: Academic Press, 2005, p 57.

[2] *Structure and Change in Economic History*, New York: Norton Publishers, 1982.

[3] 'Constitutions and Commitment: The Evolution of Institutions Governing Public Choice in Seventeenth-Century England', *Journal of Economic History*, 49(4), 1989, pp. 803–32.

South Asia, the idea that the king in pre-colonial India was bad for business, has suffered irreparable wear.

Historians of pre-colonial India would find this formulation difficult to accept. There is first an analytical problem. States are defined in this theory in terms of their power to inflict damage upon society, or by the 'comparative advantage in violence'. The natural condition of states, owing to the comparative advantage they possess, is to become predators, unless contained. Mancur Olson's parable of the stationary bandit in his book *Power and Prosperity* expresses the same idea more directly, though in this case, the king contains oppression from calculated self-interest.[4] With this starting point, we reach the conclusion that competition is a good thing in state formation as in other walks of life. We can, however, just as well start from the other end, and define states in terms of their comparative advantage in *containing risks*, including risk of violence among constituents of society. In short, it is not clear why a predation theory of the state is a better tool for economic historians than a modern version of the social contract theory. What we have in essence is the assumption that armed elites are dangerous, unless contained by competitors or strategic alliances, which gives rise to rule-bound states. We can equally well start from the opposite assumption and suggest that states necessarily form out of consensual alliances and are by definition rule-bound systems; violence is a symptom of the breakdown of these alliances.

Empirically, historians of India have long taken for granted a contract theory of the state, as one would expect in a region where the theory of kingship occupies a gigantic corpus of texts developed over more than two thousand years. States subsist crucially on fiscal success. And such success built in this region, not on arms, but on alliances. As a disciplining device, far more effective than political competition, was the fear of famine when the populace was left without food and the king without money. Historians of India and China suggest that property rights were reasonably secure and protected in these regions in the seventeenth century or before, and the rights of the wealthy were respected. One of the reasons for this respect was that the need for cooperation, alliances, and mediation between rulers, tax-

---

[4] *Power and Prosperity*, New York: Basic Books, 2000.

collectors, and tax-payers was very great in pre-modern Asia, where taxes came mainly from peasant agriculture. Information costs were huge, terrains extremely varied and difficult, societies diverse, and the threat of rebellions and invasions always present. Tropical monsoon agriculture was notoriously famine-prone. In this environment, by definition, states' comparative advantage lay not on organizing coercion, but on meeting the constant risk of famines. These were impossible jobs without the cooperation of the elite.

All major pre-colonial states in India incorporated alliances, compromise, commitments, and a great deal of respect for property. The element of compromise can be explained on two levels—intellectual and economic. The subordination of the political to the intellectual leadership of the Brahmans runs through Hindu political traditions. The success of Hindu kings depended on cooperation of the Brahmans rather than on an efficient police system. The Brahmans supplied spiritual resources essential for legitimacy of states. Moreover, public accounts, statecraft, and fiscal rules were codified not by the ruling class of military tribes, but by Brahman scribes, who lived partly on the generosity of the merchants. Taxation rules, therefore, were packaged within dire warnings about the hell that awaited the king who overtaxed his subjects, including 'the wealthy'.[5]

The second reason why alliances were essential was a fiscal one. Offer of secure property rights to military chiefs, large landholders, original settlers, and resourceful adventurers interested in lands that were difficult to till or difficult to collect taxes from, has been a route to securing fiscal success of imperial states in medieval north and south India. Nearly all pre-colonial states in the South Asia region explicitly respected 'hereditary rights' to tax, to till, and to officiate, however defined. These rules were partially and indirectly continued by the British. Such moves carried risks, for the chiefs could become too powerful when they combined and tried to carve out their own empire. Making alliances, thus, could mean walking on a knife edge. This dynamics has been at play in the rise and fall of the north Indian empires; in the rise of the Chola empire in south India, and its demise

---

[5] P.V. Kane, *History of Dharmasastra (Ancient and Medieval Religious and Civil Law in India)*, Poona: Bhandarkar Oriental Research Institute, vol. 3, 1946, p. 191.

in the fourteenth century with the entrenchment and consolidation of peasant-dominated local assemblies.

This chapter first explores the Indic notion of kingship underlying alliances, and argues that the association between state and institutions cannot be understood in terms of predation (in the non-West) and containment of predation (the West). The institutional consequences of polities can be understood better in a framework of the implicit contract between the powerful and the wealthy, the identity of the wealthy, and the consequences of that contract on the conduct of business.

INDIC IDEOLOGY OF KINGSHIP

I begin with a consideration of that body of literature which created, to use Cynthia Talbot's phrase, 'an Indic discourse of Kingship'.[6] The textual sources that this discourse built upon goes back to the Vedic age, most texts that this section relies on were produced between 400 BCE and AD 600. But the practices that used elements of this discourse had a much longer life. The attempt here is not to discover 'structures' but to suggest assumptions about the private economic agents who carried on their work outside the palace, and upon whom the king depended for his own livelihood. These assumptions were framed usually with reference to shastric norms.

This discourse moves on the plane of theory and not history. But then, the one context in which theory had a big obvious influence on real life was kingship. In this sphere, history needed the sanction of theory, and thus the two maintained interdependence. As recently as the time of the Maratha and Rajput kings of the seventeenth and eighteenth century, the Indic discourse could be seen to play a more than symbolic role.[7] These texts established a strong norm, possibly unparalleled in age and complexity in the history of the world. That does not mean practice followed theory on every occasion. It does mean that practice needed to either reinterpret the norm or risk being considered amoral. The most authoritative commentary, by P.V.

---

[6] *Precolonial India in Practice: Society, Region, and Identity in Medieval Andhra*, New York: Oxford University Press, 2001, p. 7.

[7] See, for example, the symposium, 'Brahmans and the Legitimation of Hindu Kingship', Norbert Peabody; C. J. Fuller; Adrian C. Mayer, *Man*, New Series, 27(4), 1992, pp. 879–80.

Kane, moves between theory and history. That is, it frequently asks the question—what concrete situations might the apparent shifts in theory be reacting to? Nevertheless, as J.D.M. Derrett reminds us, 'a wholly consistent picture can hardly be expected from two millennia of texts'.[8] In this case, the texts were interspersed with 'rogue' texts that were written to contradict orthodoxy, and with administrative projects such as the *Arthasastra*, a cynically practical guide containing, among other helpful tips, instructions to the courtiers on how to murder an unpopular king. Exegetic theories of political practice, furthermore, run up against the difficulty of fitting Islam with Hindu, and north with south India. This section will follow modern scholarship on the Hindu theory of political science, and try to distill from it lessons concerning the relationship between statecraft and economic institutions.

We may begin by noting that the classical language of kingship has the sense of 'institutions' built in. *Rajaniti, rajadharma*, or *dharmasastra*—all have the two keywords, *niti* (moral conduct) and dharma (order) in them, suggesting the existence of a moral order to which the kings belonged. Surely individuals could break rules, but such actions would be seen as unjust.

According to shastric texts, the king's authority was regulated in two ways, and both reflected their dependence on Brahmans. First, the texts specify fairly clear rules of taxation, framed by the Brahmans. And second, the legitimization of kingly power depended on the cooperation of the priests, because nothing moved without Vedic rituals and only the Brahmans knew how to conduct these rituals.

As for formal rules, taxation was a contingent payment. The king's functions consisted, first and foremost, of maintenance of peace or protection, for which service, taxes were to be collected from all sources. Squeezing the rich could be at times consistent with the textual guidelines, that is, asking the merchants to pay up more money would not necessarily be seen as extortion in times of famine and war. Still, in the normal course, the kings would have to earn their keep. Tax was a wage the king received for supplying peace.[9] Accordingly, 'the first principle was that the king could not levy, according to the

---

[8] 'Rajadharma', *Journal of Asian Studies*, 35(4), 1976, pp. 597–609.

[9] Kane, *History of Dharmasastra*, vol. 3, p. 187.

smṛtis [literally tradition, in practice, usages, codes, and laws], taxes at his pleasure or sweet will. That the rates of taxes which the king was entitled to levy were fixed by the smṛtis and varied only according to the commodity and also according as the times were normal…'.[10] If this cardinal rule was disobeyed for long periods and especially if the traders 'were neglected, they may disappear from the country and dwell in forests'.[11]

The coincidence of kings and robbers is a frequent occurrence in Indian history, and nothing in the theory of politics suggests that such conjunction of roles would be necessarily a bad thing. But being a robber rarely meant being a predator. Indeed, generosity and extortion were often two sides of the same coin. Kingship had a close bond with gift. The king should be generous, while the king should also, to cite Jonathan Parry, 'fund his generosity … through force and valour'.[12] As Nicholas Dirks shows, histories of long-ruling communities carried a sense of transformation, rather a many-layered transformation, from disorder to order, from forest to field, from lawlessness to law, and from robbery to justice.[13] The notion of order included taxation rights, but not collection by force from one's own subjects. The restraint did not have to flow directly from what the religious texts ordained. The fear of famine, as Derrett recognizes, was enough to instill discipline over the king's actions and intentions.

The formal relationship between kings and Brahmans is the subject of a long and distinguished debate, which we need not go into. Briefly, the orthodox view posits a split between kingly and priestly duties, and places the former in a subordinate status with respect to the latter. Louis Dumont and the colonial historians of India, for example, represented

[10] Ibid., p. 185.

[11] Ibid., p. 199.

[12] 'The Gift, the Indian Gift and the "Indian Gift"', *Man*, 21(3), 1986, pp. 453–73.

[13] 'The Pasts of a *Palaiyakarar*: The Ethnohistory of a South Indian Little King', *Journal of Asian Studies*, 41(4), 1982, pp. 655–83; 'From Little King to Landlord: Property, Law and the Gift under the Madras Permanent Settlement', *Comparative Studies in Society and History*, 28(2), 1986, pp. 303–33. For a critique suggesting that the gifts observed by Dirks had a historically contingent character, see Jonathan Parry, 'Mauss, Dumont, and the Distinction between Status and Power', in Wendy James and N.J. Allen, eds., *Marcel Mauss: A Centenary Tribute*, New York and Oxford: Berghahn Books., 1998, pp. 151–74.

a view that saw the secular form of power to be encompassed within the sacred. This view now stands revised, and contributors do suggest that the king could at times establish his divinity. In one modern view, the superiority of the Brahman over the king was a colonial fiction and part of a political project that involved emasculation of the chiefs or 'little Kings' who ruled the south Indian countryside when British rule began to settle in.[14] The mainstream position, however, seems to be that royal power and Brahman power were two sides of kingship, and that these two actors were engaged in a symbiotic, dependent, and occasionally conflicting relationship, which only changed after the ascendancy of British colonialism in the region.[15]

Kingship could accommodate varieties of actors from varied classes. Supplies of military skills were remarkably broad-based in the region. Yet, in nearly all cases, the legitimization procedure by means of Brahmanic agency would be required. Along with maintenance of peace, a second important duty of the king was to see that the rituals were correctly performed—lest the rains failed. The pre-Aryan indigenous peoples believed that the success of the Aryan invaders owed to the assistance of the deities who could be bribed by such means; the correct forms of which only the ritual specialist knew. Derrett considers that the Brahmans' superiority flowed from this belief and from their command over the Vedas.

If ritual knowledge counted for so much, why was it not learnt more widely? The reason why the Brahman was badly needed was not the subordination of the secular to the sacred, or not only that, but also a carefully preserved communal monopoly of knowledge. A guild was at work. This guild relied on a cultural strategy. The Brahmans' claim to being a spiritual mentor rested on 'purity'. Purity involved a collective strategy towards disciplined acquisition of professional skills, or exclusive hereditary systems of apprenticeship and education, and strict marriage rules, which represented the visible, public, and interactive face of purity. In turn, such hereditary transmission implies that it was difficult, if not impossible, to stake claims to Brahmanhood

[14] Nicholas Dirks, 'Castes of Mind', *Representations*, 37, 1992, pp. 56–78.

[15] An interesting point is the meaning of the gift the king made to the Brahman; did it represent the king's inferior or superior status? See discussion in Gloria Raheja, 'India: Caste, Kingship, and Dominance Reconsidered', *Annual Review of Anthropology*, 17, 1988, pp. 497–522.

by anyone who was not already a member of a Brahman clan. In practice, a great deal of marriages and unions did occur outside caste. And yet, perhaps reflecting a constant anxiety that purity might be threatened, the texts unambiguously call upon the king to protect the clan, not only of Brahmans, but of all others.

Along with maintenance of peace and the performance of rituals, a third duty of the king was to protect castes. Indeed, the distinctive aspect of Indic kingship is that the king's duty included this patently cultural element. 'Manu ... requires the righteous king to consider carefully the dharmas of castes, countries, guilds and families (to find out whether they are opposed to the Vedas) and uphold those dharmas (that are not opposed) as binding (on those respective persons)'.[16] Dharma, in this case, does not mean religion for the Hindu king was an expressly tolerant figure (the shastric texts specified how religious heresy could be legitimized within statecraft). Dharma here meant the internal order of the castes themselves. A simple meaning of order would be professional economic codes. The king should enforce and respect 'the usages and conventions of occupational guilds, merchants ... they had followed from ancient times ...'.[17] But statements such as these refer to more than professional rules, and refer particularly to purity of blood.

One of the king's duties was to prevent the mixing of castes.[18] From the earliest times, union across castes was considered a heinous crime by nearly all shastras. When a sudra man had an affair with an upper caste woman, the punishments prescribed for such wickedness were more horrific than those for simple murders.[19] The progeny of cross-caste marriage or cohabitation were several degrees inferior in their claims to their fathers' property, and occasionally, left out of inheritance altogether. How enforceable these rules were is beyond the point. The point rather is that political theory considered regulation of marriage to be one of the king's duties. Caste, in short, was hardly autonomous from the state; it was central to the business of the

[16] Kane, *History of Dharmasastra*, vol. 3, p. 158.

[17] Ibid.

[18] P.V. Kane, *History of Dharmasastra (Ancient and Medieval Religious and Civil Law in India)*, vol. 5, part 1, Poona: Bhandarkar Oriental Research Institute, 1962, p. 1634.

[19] Kane, *History of Dharmasastra*, vol. 3, p. 401.

state; it was influenced and shaped by the state. The persistence of this tradition can be seen in medieval Deccan, where the state was enmeshed in inter-caste and intra-caste disputes.[20]

From an economic history point of view, how do we account for such a cultural policy? How might protecting caste help fiscal success? The simple answer is that castes represented endogamous guilds. The professions demanded, as professions do everywhere, royal protection from competition. In the Indic world, professions consisted of endogamous units. And therefore, protection meant rules prohibiting intermarriage of castes. The king's duty was to ensure that members of groups followed their traditional occupations, which would mean denying the right to follow the occupation to anyone not a member of the guild.[21] In turn, the guarantee of such economic protection necessarily tied a strategy to maintain the purity of blood. The king's cultural duties, fiscal policy, and business organization, in this way, became parts of a whole. I am suggesting that guild and purity joined early on, and the king, trying to protect guild, needed to protect purity.

The assertion that professions consisted of endogamous units needs to be qualified. That professions were in fact so constituted is undoubtedly a fact of business history in India before the arrival of Islam. The third century BCE Greek ambassador in the Mauryan court, Megasthenes, observed that in India, 'no one is allowed to marry out of his own caste or to exercise any calling or art except his own'.[22] But at the same time, the types of assemblies that get mentioned in the texts were not all formed of families. The *sreni*, for example, was an association of professionals unrelated by caste, and the *gana* an association of relations. The usual example of srenis came from artisans. It is noteworthy that artisans did not possess a great deal of valuable capital to restrict access to. On the other hand, shastric rules suggest that a tighter bond existed between caste and profession when professions involved considerable capital. It is also likely that the association between guild and intermarriage became closer over

[20] Hiroshi Fukazawa, *The Medieval Deccan: Peasants, Social Systems and States —Sixteenth to Eighteenth Centuries*, New Delhi: Oxford University Press, 1991.

[21] Kane, *History of Dharmasastra*, vol. 3, p. 158.

[22] P.V. Kane, *History of Dharmasastra (Ancient and Medieval Religious and Civil Law in India)*, vol. 2, part 1, Poona: Bhandarkar Oriental Research Institute, 1941, p. 50.

time. Kane, for example, offered a theory of how professions 'petrified' into castes through increasingly strict rules proscribing intermarriage between *jatis*, a process that he dated to the period between the second and the sixth century AD (the approximate period of the *Yagnabalkasmrti*).[23] The kings did not exactly make endogamous guilds, nor merely adapt to endogamous guilds. Kingship and guilds formed out of mutual interaction over centuries.

Whether within professional guilds or endogamous guilds, the presence of strong collective bodies is mentioned in all texts. 'Professional castes were ... well organized'.[24] Organization meant that these bodies 'had a measure of self-government'.[25] Self-government was a legal concept. Outside the royal and the highest court of justice, which usually had a monopoly over cases involving sedition, serious crimes, and those deserving corporal punishments, other tribunals consisted of village councils, guilds, and caste councils, or assembly of families. Collectives 'had authority to investigate disputes', and settle disputes 'by the evidence of the old men in the village or town or of guilds'.[26]

The one concrete rule where theory and history, ancient and modern India, can be joined with a relatively unbroken line is the law of inheritance of immovable property. A number of features of shastric law had the implication of creating a tight bond between caste and property. 'Customs of ... castes, villages and groups [regarding] rules of partition and inheritance should be enforced by the king'.[27] Partitioning of family estate was in actual fact possible, but extremely difficult. P.V. Kane states, 'in the earliest period of Indian Law, partition of property was an entirely unknown proceeding'. As Kane qualifies, partitioning was sanctioned in the major texts (especially the ones that were adopted by the British Indian law as benchmarks on the subject), even though there were restrictions signifying that 'such partitions were looked upon with disfavour' by the law-makers.[28] The important obstacle to a free market in private property was partitioning of coparcener interests. Coparcener meant kinsmen. As the discussion

[23] Kane, *History of Dharmasastra*, vol. 5, part 1, p. 1633.
[24] Ibid., vol. 2, Part 1, p. 66.
[25] Ibid., vol. 3, p. 97.
[26] Ibid., vol. 2, Part 1, pp. 66, 68.
[27] Ibid., vol. 3, p. 566.
[28] Ibid., p. 567.

further qualifies, 'whether kinsmen are joint or separate they are alike as regards immovable property'. Shastric authority, and as we shall see colonial law, agreed that 'no coparcener ... can dispose of his undivided interest by gift, sale or mortgage ... except with the consent of the other coparceners'.[29] Before Muslim conquest, in states ruled by Hindu law, land sales were reported but they became worthy of reporting precisely because they were very rare. And they were rare because sales required 'the assent of the villagers, the agnatic relations, the neighbours, the co-sharers and with the offering of gold and water', the permission of the local administrators, the help of the village headman in measuring the land, and the services of the record-keepers who decided the title.[30] Transaction costs were so large that the academic debate over whether or not alienable private property right could exist in land is indeed not much more than an academic debate. The undivided-interest-of-coparcener principle was applied just as earnestly by the civil court judges in India through much of the nineteenth century, and began to be overturned in a series of High Court cases only about a hundred years ago.[31]

The argument, in short, is that guilds in ancient India were usually (and increasingly) made up of endogamous professionals. This business model received the sanction of the states in the form of shastric respect for marriage rules and juridical autonomy of castes. Possibly a Brahmanic discourse of purity added more force to exclusive marriage rules. To use J.C. Heesterman's words, the secular order was organized around 'brotherhood', which was the 'institutional form' for defining property rights and distribution of these rights in Indian society until the advent of colonialism.[32] What applies to land rights should also apply to useful knowledge, which the merchants and artisans possessed.

The institutional order of the endogamous guild rested on two techniques—exclusive skill acquisition system and exclusive marriage rules. The word 'monopoly' that frequently appears in Derrett's treatment of *rajadharma* might fascinate the economic historian, and

[29] Ibid., p. 593.
[30] Ibid., p. 497.
[31] Ibid., pp. 593–4.
[32] *The Inner Conflict of Tradition: Essays in Indian Ritual, Kingship and Society*, Chicago: University of Chicago Press, 1985.

rightly. The king enjoyed a moral sanction to protect a monopoly of power. The Brahmans enjoyed monopolistic access to spiritual mediation. Generalizing this series, everybody else tried to erect a professional monopoly using purity (marriage) as strategy. There was a strong norm, and barring random deviations, any individual king should find it in his self-interest to take cognizance of that norm. As in any pre-modern commercial system, it could not have been easy for anyone to break norms. For, by the logic of this system, if a few major skills were monopolized by endogamous groups, others would have to fall in line, or face extortions from the more organized groups.

Supplies of essential services to the state and the urban elites were organized around families of merchants and craftsmen before Islamic rule began in northern India.[33] Illustrations of these organizations and these norms can be found in the history of the Vijayanagar Empire, the last great Hindu empire in the Deccan.

The imperial capital was dependent on merchants who came from beyond the borders. When formulating a rule of law about private business, the court took the equation of profession and caste for granted. In Vijayanagar, 'most ... craft producers were members of hereditary groups—castes, subcastes, and lineages—each with a unique history, social identity, traditional occupation, and social status ...'[34] In present-day historical scholarship on medieval south India, a picture is drawn in which merchant groups were integrated in the royal-cum-sacred authority.[35] One author draws on the works of other scholars and on textual and epigraphic sources to propose that merchant groups in medieval India (c. AD 500–AD 1200) influenced rulers and the courtly elite to incorporate mercantile conventions into particular scriptures and royal edicts.[36] The actual contexts when this was successfully done are not many, and suggest that powerful

[33] R. Champalakshmi, 'Urbanisation in South India: The Role of Ideology and Polity', *Social Scientist*, 15(8/9), 1987, pp. 67–117.

[34] Carla M. Sinopoli, *The Political Economy of Craft Production: Crafting Empire in South India, c. 1350–1650*, Cambridge: Cambridge University Press, 2003, p. 5.

[35] For a discussion, see Champakalakshmi, 'Urbanisation'.

[36] Donald R. Davis, 'Intermediate Realms of Law: Corporate Groups and Rulers in Medieval India', *Journal of the Economic and Social History of the Orient*, 48(1), 2005, pp. 92–117; Kenneth R. Hall, 'Peasant State and Society in Chola Times: A view from the Tiruvidaimarudur Urban Complex', *Indian Economic and*

urban merchant groups tried this course in the presence of specific sorts of threat, or to deal with serious cases of infringement of convention by one of the insiders. For my purpose, the point to note is that these privileges were usually specified in the idiom of caste, and contained stipulations about social intercourse and social distinctions between communities. For example, in several cases, royal business licenses granted by the Vijayanagar rulers took the form of privileges granted to castes. A famous dispute that occurred during the reign of Krishnadevaraya suggests that the courts became involved in trade disputes via caste disputes. License to trade was handed to castes. 'Certain subcastes like the Komatis claimed to be vaisyas ... [They] were styled vijatis [foreigners] by their rivals'.[37]

When we move from Hindu to Islamic statecraft in medieval India, it might at first appear as if we are moving into a different world. But in fact, we are moving along a line of substantial continuity on the plane of the relationship between the king and the wealthy.

DEBATE ON THE MUGHAL STATE

Historians of medieval India disagree on the nature of the pre-colonial states, the point of debate concerning the degree of centralization of power at the imperial core.[38] The conventional view, first stated by European travellers in Mughal India, was that the pre-colonial north Indian polity was a despotic and sovereign state. Merchants and producers in this system were a cog in the gigantic wheel of imperial taxation, and if not exactly oppressed, were not very vital either. The Aligarh school of historiography is the sophisticated modern representative of that idea.

But this view is being rethought. Instrumental in the rethinking have been interpretations of polities that ruled southern India. 'Ideologies of shared sovereignty and the recognition of domains of

---

Social History Review, 18(3-4), 1981, pp. 393–5; Meera Abraham, Two Medieval Merchant Guilds of South India, New Delhi: Manohar Publications, 1988.

[37] Kane, History of Dharmasastra, vol. 3, p. 252.

[38] See M. Athar Ali, 'The Mughal Polity—A Critique of Revisionist Approaches', Modern Asian Studies, 27(4), 1993, pp. 699–710. The rethinking on the Aligarh view of the Mughal state as a grand unitary system is discussed in 'introduction', Muzaffar Alam and Sanjay Subrahmanyam, eds., The Mughal State 1526–1750, New Delhi: Oxford University Press, 1998.

autonomy', using David Washbrook's words, have become mainstream constructs in the historiography of the early modern state. And these ideologies stand in sharp distinction with the European notion of the sovereign state, which colonialism introduced into the eighteenth century India.

Burton Stein used Aidan Southall's concept of a 'segmentary state' to argue that groups that formed along caste or religion played a bigger role than did the state behind the formation of social institutions in south India between the ninth and the twelfth centuries. The concept of a decentralized polity was later found to be a useful construct for medieval Deccan, Maratha states, and for northern India itself.[39] Earlier, Kathleen Gough had interpreted the Chola state in south India as a rule that allowed communities to retain substantial social and economic autonomy.[40] Another closely related notion is suzerainty, wherein tax-payers enjoy some domestic autonomy in exchange of a promise to pay taxes, as opposed to sovereignty. Suzerainty was applied in the context of the Ottoman imperial state, and found useful by Southall to describe the Chola and Rajput lineage states. The principle of leaving lineages alone was common between those examples of Africa and South Asia in which the term segmentary state was used. When we come to south India, the 'most distinctive' feature, in Southall's words, 'was the capacity of local leaders—*inspired, fired, and legitimized by Brahmanical exhortation, beliefs, and values*—to extract from the direct producers a nominally specific percentage of their product and transmit it, with subtractions on the way, to the central ruling class' (emphasis added).[41] The view of the pre-colonial polity constituted of weak states or vulnerable states supported by

[39] Burton Stein, 'State Formation and Economy Reconsidered: Part I', *Modern Asian Studies*, 19(3), 1985, pp. 387–413; Frank Perlin, 'State Formation Reconsidered: Part Two', *Modern Asian Studies*, 19(3), 1985, pp. 415–80; André Wink, *Land and Sovereignty in India. Agrarian Society and Politics under the Eighteenth Century Maratha Svarajya*, Cambridge: Cambridge University Press, 1986. For fuller citation, see Athar Ali, 'The Mughal Polity'. See also Southall, 'The Segmentary State in Africa and Asia', *Comparative Studies in Society and History*, 30(1), 1988, pp. 52–82.

[40] *Rural Society in Southeast India*, Cambridge: Cambridge University Press, 1981; 'Dravidian Kinship and Modes of Production', *Contributions to Indian Sociology*, 13(2), 1979, pp. 264–92.

[41] Southall, 'The Segmentary State'.

powerful local corporate groups, such as merchants, landlords, and territorial chieftains, appears also in a historiography of northern India after Mughal decline, according to which these groups are seen to consolidate their hold in commerce and politics during the eighteenth century.[42]

These ideas are not identical. The community exists in the nineteenth century notions of India as rooted in the village, changeless, and passive with respect to the state. On the other hand, the segmentary state idea contains a sense of contract and symbiosis between states and well-defined and dynamic corporate groups. It is a more dynamic relationship based on mutual dependence and constant negotiation. The king would not be able to function without the ritual sanction of the Brahmans, the services of the merchants in moving taxed grain, or the services of the artisans, shopkeepers, and entertainers in making the imperial city a paradise on earth. The consensual element makes the system far more dynamic than either Karl Marx or Henry Maine considered was the case in India (see Chapter 1). Groups could move up or become more diverse or do new things. But as long as groups remained useful to the state, their rights to create an insular community with their own civil laws would be respected by the state.

Common between all such notions of a decentralized state is the principle that the king does not legislate. The legislative process is fundamentally decentralized; laws being the prerogative of the merchant caste, artisan community, territorial chiefs, and 'little kings', to use a phrase popularized by Bernard Cohn. On this point about law, there is convergence between the Aligarh view on Mughal India, interpretations of medieval south India, the proponents of segmentary state, lineages, and suzerainty, and indeed, the classical writers on Indian society including Marx and Maine.

It is this element—constrained freedom to legislate—that made the Mughal state both Islamic and Hindu at the same time.

LAW AND JUSTICE IN MUGHAL INDIA

The standard text on Mughal judicial administration is a collection of lectures delivered by Jadunath Sarkar at the Patna University in

---

[42] C.A. Bayly, *Rulers, Townsmen and Bazaars: North Indian Society in the Age of British Expansion 1770–1870*, New Delhi: Oxford University Press, 1983.

1920. Sarkar's conception of the state is closer to that of the Aligarh view, whereas his description of the administration paints a deeply decentralized and segmented picture. Despite that anomaly, as far as I am aware, the general propositions on law and justice made in this book have not been revised substantially. This section, therefore, will follow Sarkar's conceptualization, supplementing it with other scholarly writings on the subject of law and justice when necessary.

Sarkar begins by recognizing that the Mughal emperor was jointly the ruler of the land and protector of the faith. The sovereign was protector of canon law for the Muslims, the basic structure of which had non-Indian and pre-Mughal origin. That very policy implied a huge disengagement from the laws of the non-Muslims. 'Towards [the] non-Muslim subjects [the sovereign] followed the policy of ... minimum of interference, he was content with discharging only the police duties and the collection of revenue'. In consequence, 'the vast mass of Indian customary law were respected so far as they did not run counter to the root principles of all Islamic governments'.[43]

The characterization of the judicial system as being rent into two parts had older roots and has not been revised in present-day discourse. European commentators on Indian law, from William Jones to James Mill, noted the presence of juridical autonomy of non-Muslims, and some of them saw it as the result of a bargain in which the latter populations were required to pay a tax in order to enjoy the fruits of the system. There is little disagreement among current authorities on medieval north India on the point that 'the Mughal state was not a legislating state'. In the words of one representative of the Aligarh school, 'No historian had ever laid claim that Mughal polity was in these aspects the equal of the European post-Reformation state'.[44] The theory and practice of statecraft underwent changes and refinements since the consolidation of Islamic empires in northern India. Yet, one component that changed slowly, if at all, was the principle of disengagement vis-à-vis the civil affairs of the non-believers, in effect withdrawing the protection of state law and state courts from the non-Muslim groups in the matter of settling property, personal, and contractual disputes.

[43] *Mughal Administration*, Patna: Patna University, 1920, pp. 3–4.
[44] Athar Ali, 'Mughal Polity', pp. 209–10.

This was a community system of law and justice, by which I mean a system which defines jurisdiction of state laws by community rather than territoriality or citizenship. Layers of customary law co-exist, each community or ethnic group using one of these systems of common law, and statutes exist for only some or even only one of these layers. In the Mughal institution of law, civil, and administrative law (and a great deal of criminal law as well) was framed according to canon if the disputants were Muslims; and administered according to community-bound customary law if the disputants were non-Muslims.[45] The state did not see itself as a law-maker for everyone, but rather as an agent in upholding the canons for the believers. Kingship demanded, foremost, seeing 'that the dignity of Islam and the Islamic Law is upheld in his dominions'.[46] The state's engagement with justice being thus mediated by religion, it implied a withdrawal of official justice from populations belonging in realms outside Islam, subject to an assertion of Islamic law in cases where disputes over personal law are taken to the courts.

Where did this dualistic regime come from? The origins of the system were explained by Sarkar in terms of borrowings from pan-Islamic tradition—'Our Turkish conquerors brought with themselves to their new home the type of administration which had long been known to extra-Indian Muslim countries as the model'. But the religious and pan-Islamic foundation of Mughal law cannot be a very satisfactory theory. It is slightly anomalous in the first place. Even though the principle of decentralization can be borrowed, given that local customs vary, the practice of decentralization is bound to shift the contents of the legal regime in each society. In other words, the very principle predicts a model that can never be precisely defined. That point apart, the borrowing theory does not explain why the state would not want to convert all to Islam on the point of the sword, and

[45] Ahmad distinguishes four kinds of law—the canon law or Muslim personal law; the common law or the Islamic law of crimes, tort, and nuisance; regulations; and local custom. The second kind of law applied to Muslims and non-Muslims alike, with some distinctions. With offences against codes of righteous conduct, such as adultery or drunkenness, Muslims could be punished more severely than Hindus. See Muhammad Basheer Ahmad, *The Administration of Justice in Medieval India*, Aligarh: The Aligarh Historical Research Institute, 1941.

[46] Al-Mawardi, jurist, cited in Muhammad Akbar, *The Administration of Justice by the Mughals*, Lahore: Muhammad Ashraf, 1948, p. 1.

subject all to the same law. Why, after 700 years of Islamic rule, did the region Islamicize to such a limited extent?

I believe we can answer this question by drawing attention to something that the borrowings theory tends to overlook—a fundamental compatibility between Indic theory of kingship and the so-called Islamic borrowings. Let me illustrate the point with a story set in the early sixteenth century. While out inspecting his terrain, the Mughal Emperor Jahangir encamped at a small village in submontane Punjab that had been the home of a community who had converted from Hinduism to Islam about a century ago, and yet maintained several social practices associated with their Hindu past, including burial alive of widows and female infanticide. What particularly disturbed the Emperor was not this, but that 'they ally themselves with Hindus, and both give and take girls. Taking them is good, but giving them, God forbid! I gave an order that hereafter they should not do such things'.[47] Just as the Hindu king had seen protecting the purity of the community to be one of his duties, so did the Muslim king. The corollary of the policy was a disengagement from encompassing legislation.

If the Hindu texts projected a decentralized regime as the ideal, as the previous section showed, so did the Indo-Islamic states. The former saw the legislative duties of the state not in terms of encompassing codes and a single judiciary that subjected all citizens to one code, but the upholding of customs and usages. And they specified the carriers of these customs and usages to be castes and professions. Both Hindu and Mughal law share these features—respecting the autonomy of the group, and the concrete expression of such autonomy in the form of withdrawal from legislation.

The decentralizing legacy was neither Hindu nor Islamic. It was an organic response of all regional empires to an administrative imperative that all of them needed to come to terms with in South Asia. The professions that supplied the crucial services for the Imperial state were divided into tribes, castes, groups, religions, ethnicity, and language. We need look no further than the army itself, wherein the artillery was in charge of the 'Turkish', the cannon foundry of the Indo-Portuguese or the 'Feringhi', and musketry of the 'Bundela', 'Buxari',

---

[47] Henry Beveridge, ed., *The Tuzuk-i-Jahangiri*, vol. 2 of 2, New Delhi: Low Price Publications, 2006, pp. 180–1.

and 'Karnataki' Hindus. In Akbar's army, 'some of the cavalry were Mongols, some Persians, others Turquimanni, Chakattæi, Osbequii, Arachosii, Balochii, Patnanei, Indians and Gedrosi [Gujarati]. There were Musalmans and also Hindus, in whom he put a great deal of confidence', not to mention the diverse other smaller regional chieftains whose services became available during big battles. Imposing a single religious code of law on all would be suicidal for such a state.[48]

Few, if any, regime ruling in this fundamentally diverse society ever tried a serious policy of cultural engineering. In theory, a formally religious state ruling a populace that follows different faiths, speaks many tongues, and follows different customs would face two choices about law. The first option is to convert everyone on the point of the sword and subject the population to a single rule of law. As opposed to this stick-based policy, there could be a carrots policy, wherein the ruler offers social, cultural, and juridical autonomy to skilled communities, against voluntary, committed, and therefore reliable supply of craft skills, commercial skills, and skills in battle. Historians of medieval India suggest that the stability and legitimacy of Indo-Islamic rule in northern India, and the small extent of Islamicization, owed to the pursuit of a pragmatic policy of building consent by granting autonomy to those families and groups that supplied the critical skills.[49] Social contract, rather than predation, supplied the ideological foundation of the relationship between the king and the skilled people. What has received perhaps less emphasis than it deserves is that this was far more an Indic rather than an Islamic ideology. And, as we shall see, the same rule was more or less intuitively adopted by the East India Company in the eighteenth century.

Who exactly represented the legislative unit in such a fragmented system? Henry Maine considered the unit to be the village community. The idea of an unchanging administrative core in the village simplifies both the political position and the process of historical change. And yet, later scholarship has not strayed very far from Maine. Cohn, a precursor to the 1980s revisionism on state formation, focused on the

48 The cited text from S. N. Banerjee and J. S. Hoyland, *The Commentary on Father Monserrat on his Journey to the Court of Akbar 1580-1582*, London: Humphrey Milford, 1922., p. 83.

49 For a discussion, see Catherine B. Asher and Cynthia Talbot, *India before Europe*, Cambridge: Cambridge University Press, 2006., especially pp. 48-9.

power of the local landed lineages with which both the pre-colonial and the early colonial states negotiated terms of taxation. These 'little kingdoms', in his view, were 'the basic jural unit of upper India in the eighteenth and nineteenth centuries'.[50] This idea is in line with the segmentary state one. But it tends to be too focused on landed magnates. Personal law or mercantile law cannot be easily fitted into a conception dominated by the village, land taxes, and land rights.

A more flexible conception is that the law-making units were useful professions. The *right to legislation* in the Mughal state was given over to communities that formed around purity and profession. Communities were by right and not just by common law convention the 'jural units' in charge of property, succession, and contract. The consequences of decentralization pursued over centuries could create huge path-dependency. It would induce communities to create and harden their rules of governance, to strengthen caste, kin, and lineage identity in opposition to other castes, kin, and lineages. In short, the policy to offer communities autonomy would fragment society along skill lines. But consider its effects on the laws themselves first.

Outside ecclesiastical matters, both Hindu and Muslim law were preoccupied with personal relationships. A large part of these laws dealt with the relationship between sexes and persons linked by blood or by marriage. The core of the Hanafi jurisprudence as documented in the Indian context was marriage and divorce, slavery until the mid-nineteenth century, gifts including *wakf* or religious endowments, inheritance (including wills), titles of ownership of property (a great part of which consisted of *shoofa*, the legal title of one partner in joint property in relation to other partners, established specifically with respect to lands, houses, and orchards), evidence and procedure, and to a small extent, debt recovery. Breach-of-contract and tort were weakly developed concepts, except in reference to marriage. The reason for foregrounding the personal as against synthetic relationships such as mercantile contract was that virtuous conduct rather than fairness or equality was the value that these legal systems sought to protect. These systems evolved by textual interpretation rather than as a response to client needs and constraints. This large and somewhat diverse body of laws could and did evolve. But historians seem to agree that the jurists and the judges by and large did not see it their duty to make and perfect laws. They were interpreters of laws to a degree, but in a manner that could be claimed to be consistent with scriptural guidelines.

The regime had three signal characteristics. First, in the sphere of canon law, the state did not make laws but upheld laws. In other words, justice was seen as an executive duty. The hierarchy of state courts, in turn, reflected the political order rather than the contents of law or the nature of the offence. Second, in civil matters falling outside canon law, communities both made laws and administered them. And third, this institution did not need written statutes, case laws, written court procedures, records, lawyers, and an independent community of jurists or what Weber called 'the aristocracy of legal literati'. These three features are now discussed in turn.

There was substantial convergence of the executive and the judicial. The emperor symbolized this convergence, if not perfectly. This convergence was an expression of the particular jurisprudence that made the king the supreme protector of the canon. That said, the jurisprudence also admitted that the king was not above the law, and thus a tension between the courts and the judiciary was indeed present. There were episodes, such as a case that Muhammad Bin Tughlaq had fought as plaintiff in the qazi's court and lost (only to re-arrest the defendant on a fabricated charge), which illustrate this tension.

The reach of the state courts was more or less confined to the major towns and administrative centres. Any place not of sufficient military importance had no resident qazis, and formed a 'no-man's land' in Sarkar's parlance. Equally, the existence of courts of justice in the towns was an inducement for the relatively wealthy Muslims to settle in the town. The fact that the towns were seats of judicial authority did not always make them more peaceful, however. In Bengal, there is evidence of periodic conflicts between the authority of the qazi and the prominent residents of towns.[51]

---

[51] There is evidence from medieval Bengali literature of the uneasy relationship that existed between the qazi's courts and orthodox Hindu merchants in the towns. One example appears in various versions of the fifteenth–sixteenth century ballad *Manasamangal*, which extols merchant's spiritual might. Dinesh Chandra Sen, *Banga Sahitya Parichay*, vol. 1 of 2, Calcutta: Calcutta University, 1914.

The administration of justice was arranged in a 'concentric organisation' of courts.[52] Courts were arranged in a hierarchy, but that hierarchy did not match a hierarchy of offence, nor did it correspond to a regulated appeals system. Rather it followed the rank of the officer presiding.

By this principle, the highest order of court was the imperial one. The emperor set aside one day of the week to hold a public court. Various means were followed to screen and select the cases that would come before the highest court. Despite the existence of an apparently random queuing system, it goes without saying that access to the emperor was not based on the merit of the case, but on money, power, and the predilections of those functionaries who acted as filters between the king and the petitioners. A description of the court (of the late seventeenth century) is in order:

The Emperor came direct ... to the diwan-i-Khas (or Hall of Private Audience) at about 8 a.m. and sat on the throne of justice till midday. This room was filled with the law-officers of the Crown, the judges of Canon Law (qazis), judges of Common Law (adils), muftis, theologians (ulema), jurists learned in precedents (fatawa), the superintendent of the law-court, (darogha-i-adalat), and the kotwal or prefect of the city police. None else among the courtiers was admitted unless his presence was specially necessary. The officers of justice presented the plaintiffs one by one and reported their grievances. His Majesty very gently ascertained the facts by inquiry, took the law from the ulema and pronounced judgment accordingly. Many persons had come from far-off provinces to get justice from the highest power in the land. Their plaints could not be investigated except locally; and so the Emperor wrote orders to the governors of those places urging them to find out the truth and either do them justice there or send the parties back to the capital with their reports.[53]

Notwithstanding what the Europeanist historian might think about the Mughal emperor, this was manifestly the least corrupt and most rule-bound of all courts in the realm. But its reach was severely limited.

Below the imperial court, the provincial governors and other officers of comparable rank held courts. Below the governors' courts

---

[52] B.S. Jain, *Administration of Justice in Seventeenth Century India*, New Delhi: Metropolitan Book, 1970, p. 82.

[53] Sarkar, *Mughal Administration*, pp. 8–9.

were the courts of religious law. These were presided over by the qazis, and were found in large district towns. While there were no formal limitations to the jurisdiction of each of these levels, it was generally taken for granted that cases of a routine nature would first be tried in courts of lower order. The imperial courts usually handled serious offences of a political nature. Punishments for rebellions, acts against the state, or misdemeanours with respect to superiors were delivered according to the wishes of the emperor or his agent, broadly constrained by certain established precedents and conventions.[54] Any client could approach any one of these levels, but the three levels cost very different amounts of money. A variety of intermediaries were needed for a successful processing of a petition. The qazis themselves, European records and Indian historians agree on this point, could be bribed easily. The numerous injunctions in administrative guidelines on the desired moral attributes of the qazi (that he should valorize poverty, for example) confirm the generally negative view of the character of the provincial judge.

Disengagement touched both law and the administration of justice. Cases in villages were supposedly settled by caste courts and village panchayats. For crimes committed in larger villages, a qazi was often appointed. And yet, even as the qazi conducted investigations, the communal court was authorized to proceed on its own and take appropriate actions. There is little information on the 'village assemblies' to which the task of framing and implementing civil laws among non-Muslims was entrusted. 'We have no information about the Hindu caste courts and arbitration boards which administered justice according to Common Law', nor do we know very much about Akbar's brief experiment with Brahmanic courts that were supposed to follow the *smrtis*.[55] Whether the lack of information was a reflection of an extreme degree of decentralization, or the rarity of disputes,

---

[54] Sarkar believed that some of the governors administered justice according to common law whereas the qazi was entrusted with the task of enforcing canon law, *Mughal Administration*, (fourth edition), Calcutta: M.C. Sircar 1952, p. 92. Other historians, however, disputed this view, and believed that the distinction between the middle tier and the lower one was not associated with the kind of laws enforced, Jain, *Administration of Justice*, pp. 79–81.

[55] Sarkar, *Mughal Administration*, p. 10.

remains open to speculation. Far too little is known about the precise mechanisms by which trade disputes were settled.[56]

European accounts of seventeenth century India frequently complained of extortion of merchants and merchant communities by Muslim rulers. A close reading would reveal that the complaints were coloured by the uneasy political relationship that the Companies themselves maintained with the territorial rulers. The more general situation can be expressed, to use the words of an early nineteenth century Company historian, as 'a tolerably clear knowledge of their interest, a respect for certain classes, and a veneration for established usages, ... in the mind of the most unjust princes of India'.[57] In the case of the European traders, as with the Indian traders, 'established usage' can be understood as juridical autonomy of the merchant community rather than any particular notion of extra-territoriality.

Commerce thrives in common law, which builds on a foundation of cases rather than codes. The Mughal judicial system, however, was neither based on cases, nor on procedures, but on religious codes. The individuals who ran this system did not and could not take precedence set by other individuals too seriously. There was apparently an explicit understanding that judgments not in conformity with scriptural direction or the ulema's opinion would be valid only in the specific case. In other words, while the legislative philosophy did allow the judges some room for manoeuvre and offered them some scope for referring to 'equity, justice, and good conscience' (to quote a familiar refrain in common law) in deciding individual cases, judgments had little chance of becoming common law. For the same reason, historians of Mughal law believe that documentation was deemed unnecessary

---

[56] Jain, *Administration of* Justice, p. 83. The administrative decentralization was not a complete one, for the governors and qazis did on occasions have to hear cases of a civil nature that involved non-Muslim disputants, and decide on the basis of precedence or common law. The actual common law cases thus heard in higher courts usually involved property disputes among the Hindu political elite. By and large, the state judiciary kept a conscious distance from customary law, especially Hindu law, and the farther away one went from the district towns, the more decisive became the barrier between state institutions and dispensation of justice.

[57] John Malcolm, *A Memoir of Central India*, vol. 2, London: Parbury Allan and Co., 1832., p. 98. Malwa, significantly, was among the most unstable zones in the eighteenth century.

and therefore weak in the court proceedings, and that '...[j]udgment is delivered only verbally and is not recorded in writing'.[58]

European travellers to India in the seventeenth century commented on the absence of written statutes. Indeed, the first major attempt at codification of law was undertaken not before the late seventeenth century by the last of the great Mughals, Aurangzeb or Alamgir, in the shape of *Futawa Alamgiri*. Yet, the European view was based on a fundamental misreading of the situation with regard to law. If the objective of the state instituted justice was to uphold Koranic law in its wider interpretations and applications, the Indian courts could simply rely on the extensive jurisprudence of the Arab world.[59] All that the courts needed was the service of jurists who could form a bridge between the Arab world of theory and Indian practice. Jurists of foreign origin therefore formed a valuable component of the Mughal courtly culture.

Consistent with the communal character of laws, professional lawyers and judges had a marginal presence in this system. Nothing like a mandarin system could possibly develop within a rule by scripture. Lawyers were absent from the rural courts and remained rare in the state courts. François Bernier observed that 'they have fewer lawyers, and fewer law-suits, and those few are more speedily decided'.[60] The counterparts of lawyers that we do hear about either represented clients who could not plead their own case for social reasons, such as wealthy women, or negotiated terms of transaction between parties. Thus, European traders seeking trading privileges often employed *vakil*s to argue their case with the state agents.[61] During Aurangzeb's

---

[58] Ahmad, *Administration of Justice*; Akbar, *Administration of Justice*, p. 13. 'No Indian Emperor or Qazi's decision was ever considered authoritative enough to lay down a legal principle', Sarkar, *Mughal Administration*, p. 10.

[59] Al-Haj Mahomed Ullah Ibn S. Jung, *A Dissertation on the Administration of Justice of Muslim Law preceded by an Introduction to the Muslim Conception of the State*, Allahabad: Allahabad Law Journal Press, 1926.

[60] *Travels in the Mogul Empire A.D. 1656–1668*, London: Humphrey Milford, 1916, p. 236.

[61] P.B. Calkins, 'A Note on Lawyers in Muslim India', *Law & Society Review*, 3(2/3), 1968-9, pp. 403–6. In the seventeenth and early eighteenth centuries, the English, Dutch, and the Portuguese companies routinely appointed as broker, *vakil*, or agent, the person known to be the head of the merchant community. The principle was extended to the artisans in the late eighteenth century. In the

reign, a systematic attempt was made to appoint *vakils* in local courts to carry through state business, and also to represent the poor. In this respect, the *vakils* did not form a qualitatively different class than the multi-tasked and insufficiently professionalized attorneys and solicitors in eighteenth century England, with the difference that in India, few except the most visible public organizations employed any *vakil* at all.[62]

LOCAL JUSTICE IN THE EIGHTEENTH CENTURY

In times immediately before British colonization began, systems of civil law and justice displayed the same broad features that we see in the foregoing description of the Mughal north India, namely, disengagement of state courts from commercial and local disputes, and the prevalence of caste, community, and village institutions in the settlement of commercial and local disputes. For the first time in historical chronology, a detailed picture of village and communal justice becomes available only at the turn of the eighteenth century.

V.T. Gune's account of the administration of the Deccan sultanate shows fundamental similarities between judicial institutions in western-southern India and those in Mughal northern India. Gune proposes that 'under the Sultans of the Deccan, the Muslim Law was the law of the state. According to Muslim codes, the public tribunals could not interfere with the personal law of the "Zimmis" i.e. "Hindus". The local Majlis was allowed to follow the Hindu Law in civil suits, while adjudicating the suits of the Hindus'.[63] The sultan was the head of a concentric circle of courts. Qazis presided over these, but the reach of these courts was limited to a few major towns. This being the

late seventeenth century, Rustum Manock, soon to emerge as the leading Parsi business family of the time, acted as a *vakil* for the Portuguese in western India, that is, negotiated on behalf of the Portuguese with the government in Surat. Jagannath Laldas in the 1740s was the *vakil* of the English company. The term *vakil* meant 'representative', a position that clearly commanded more respect and power than that of the agent. David L. White, 'From Crisis to Community Definition: The Dynamics of Eighteenth-Century Parsi Philanthropy', *Modern Asian Studies*, 25(2), 1991, pp. 303–20.

[62] David Sugarman, 'Simple Images and Complex Realities: English Lawyers and Their Relationship to Business and Politics, 1750–1950', *Law and History Review*, 11(2), 1993, pp. 257–301.

[63] *The Judicial System of the Marathas*, Poona: Sangam, 1953, p. 68.

THE HEADMAN OF A HINDOO VILLAGE HOLDING HIS COURT

Figure 2.1: 'Hindu Village Council'. From Miss Droese, *Indian Gems for the Master's Crown*, London: The Religious Tract Society, 1892, p. 45. Another version of this engraving appears in a book by the Society published in 1857, which suggests that the illustration was made in the early nineteenth century.

point of similarity, various forms of local assembly were more visible, at least left more record, than in the case of north India.

Under the Peshwas, the institution of the qazi suffered a decline but the local assembly retained its old status. The majlis was replaced by the panchayat, the former having somewhat more religious character, the latter composed of local notables. It is reasonable to assume that through this transition, the influence of the *gotasabha*, *gota* referring to caste or extended family, upon the functioning of the local assembly persisted. As the British law-makers later recognized, the *Mitakshara* and the *Mayukha* were the principal texts followed in matters of succession and inheritance, where no other guidance was available. But more than religion, caste or gotra precedence provided the foundation of law. 'The customs of the different castes were scrupulously observed by the members of those castes and it seems that the state was not allowed to interfere with their customary right of delivering justice'.[64] In the villages the local assemblies were far from representative bodies. Rather they reflected the power of the mirasdars, literally sharers, and effectively the dominant peasant lineages.[65] Property rights were framed in a manner so as to erect and preserve stringent barriers to entry into the community. For some examples, Gune cites several judgments from the seventeenth and eighteenth centuries suggesting exclusion of sons born of outcaste mothers from property, exclusion of sons of daughters from inheritance of father's property, the requirement of consent of all members of a lineage on decisions to adopt a child, and prohibition on adoption from another family. These judgments did not just reflect the concept but the practice of property law.

A historical study of the panchayats of the Peshwas in a slightly later period found the panchayat system in decay in the second decade of the nineteenth century, at least partly because the local officers who earlier summoned and managed the courts and appointed judges had lost their authority in the new regime.[66] British ascendance by itself does not explain why this was so. In fact, the early administration in Bombay Deccan tried to revive and retain the system, which is why English sources contain a great deal of material on this institution. It was the 'glaring defects and dangerous abuses' that the panchayats could give rise to that made the remnants of the system vulnerable from within.

One important cause of decay was the exclusion built into the system. The panchayat excluded outcastes and Muslims, and rarely tried cases involving these groups except in criminal cases and adultery involving individuals who belonged in these groups. 'The Mohammedans were not only entirely neglected, but treated (says Pottinger) "with a degree of contempt and indignity"'.[67] Administrative authorities who investigated the history and functioning of this institution were generally of the view that this institution became caught up in the divisive politics that afflicted the Maratha state itself. Finally, the cases heard by the panchayat were mainly concerned with

[64] Ibid., p. 69.
[65] Ibid., pp. 20, 55.
[66] H. George Franks, *Panchayats of the Peshwas*, undated, p. 5.
[67] Ibid., p. 35.

land and landed families, and covered subjects such as boundary disputes, debts, adoption, and property divisions. Being dependent on precedence, trial by panchayat could take enormously long time, on average two years and frequently up to ten years, or about a third of the average male life-span. Panchayats rarely tried cases of dispute that were commercial in nature and concerned merchants, artisans, and wage-earners. These were also necessarily cases that arose within the caste. In such cases, 'heads of all castes ... settled disputes not exclusively by their own sole authority but in conjunction with the most respectable members of the caste...'.[68]

Francis Buchanan's (later Buchanan Hamilton) journal of his tour of Mysore in 1807 makes numerous references to caste disputes and caste courts.[69] This poor dry land region had only recently come under the influence of British administration, that too an indirect one. Institutionally speaking, Mysore displayed persistence of the pre-colonial conditions at this time. Three themes steadily reappear in Buchanan's descriptions. Nearly all communities possessed councils, hereditary chiefs, headmen, religious gurus, or assembly of some sort. These institutions settled internal disputes, provided alms for the destitute, and decided matters of expulsion from and readmission into communion. Second, the most common kind of disputes concerned women, or so it seemed to Buchanan. Why women? Surely we need to remind ourselves of the discourse on purity discussed before. But these features can be understood also with reference to the ecology of the region. In arid lands without a strong political centre, community support was of critical importance during famines. And equally, famines, wars, and the constant pressure of hard work seemed to make family relationships unstable in some communities. Not surprisingly, then, the region saw dedication of women to temples develop its institutionalized and socially sanctioned form, temples being the most reliable providers of sustenance. On the other hand, perhaps because soil was a relatively less valuable resource, property disputes rarely find any mention in these reports.

[68] Ibid., p. 16.
[69] *A Journey from Madras, through the countries of Mysore, Canara, and Malabar, etc.*, vol. 2 of 3, London: E. Caddell for the East India Company, 1807, pp. 7, 24, 28, 29, 67, 119, 120–1, 144, 152, 241, 244, 270, 272, on Mysore; pp. 329, 415, 491, 494, 498, 529, on Malabar.

Third, agents of the government at times played a role in sanctioning the authority of the chiefs. A peasant community in southern Mysore, Buchanan reported, 'have no hereditary chiefs ... but government appoints a renter, who collects four or five old men of the tribe, and by their advice settles all disputes; and by fines, laid on with their consent, punishes all transgressions against the rules of cast. The renter must always be a Torea, and he agrees to pay annually a certain sum'.[70] But this involvement of a powerful third party, aside from its mercenary quality or perhaps due to this very quality, could be a source of weakening of communal authority. Among the Kaikkolar weavers, the chief is 'assisted by a council, and pretends also to have a jurisdiction in disputes; but in these an appeal is commonly made to the officers of government'.[71] In the dry districts of British Madras, officers routinely interfered in caste disputes, or arbitrated the composition of the councils, illustrating how this breach of jurisdiction was beginning to work.[72]

The best description of state-instituted law and justice is available from Bengal after British occupation, where law and justice still followed the stylized picture of the Mughal system drawn by jurists, with some local colour added. In the 1760s, the system of justice in existence in Bengal was described in detail in a series of parliamentary reports. The judiciary had two parts, one presided over by the *dewan* or the prime minister, and the other by the ruler, the *nawab nazim*.[73] The dewan was in charge of all property disputes, though 'seldom exercises this authority in person'. The chief court was the *adawlut dewanee*, which dealt mainly in landed property disputes. Below the Adawlut were the courts presided over by the qazi, who settled mainly claims of inheritance and succession, and additionally functioned as master of ceremonies in marriage, circumcision, and funerals. The qazi was assisted by the *mohtaseeb*, who dealt with drunkenness; more importantly, by the mufti, who heard evidence and wrote the fatwa or decision, the *maulvi*, authority on religious law, and *qanungo*, the land

[70] Ibid., p. 152, also p. 178.
[71] Ibid., p. 266.
[72] Ibid., pp. 294, 309.
[73] For a counterpart description of provincial legal administration in Mughal India, see Manucci, *Storia do Mogor*, vol. 3, pp. 420–1, and Sarkar, *Mughal Administration*, pp. 48–9.

registrar. On the other side, the nawab nazim held weekly courts called *adawlut al alea*, settling mainly capital offences. The business of this court relied on the evidence of the *phouzdar*, or chief of police, who additionally could settle criminal cases that were not capital offences; and investigated capital crimes. Below the phouzdar was the kotwal, the peace officer of the night.[74]

Important property disputes were heard by three independent qazis. In case of one dissent, the case was referred to a general assembly summoned by the nazim. In practice, however, the assembly was rarely called. The reach of this system was limited to the larger towns. The courts, the assemblies, the investigating and presiding officers were all located in the towns. 'It is only the rich or the vagabond part of people who can afford to travel so far for justice'. Artisans and merchants were conspicuously missing from the reported working of the system. For 'the industrious labourer...' were he to take a dispute to the court and 'wait the tedious process of the courts ... the consequences in many cases will be more ruinous and oppressive, than an arbitrary decision ... passed ... without any law or process whatever'.[75]

Furthermore, procedurally speaking, the scope for arbitration was restricted in the system. A letter written by the Council of Revenue, Murshidabad, to the President and Council in 1772, cited a note from the *naib dewan* of Mushidabad explaining when lawsuits became subject to arbitration. Two types of cases were exempt from arbitration. All disputes of 'inheritance, property, purchases, assignments' were decided 'according to 'the orders of the Almighty and his Prophet ... [and] cannot be proper subjects of arbitration'. The same letter voiced a conflict of opinion whether or not the Brahmin should be admitted as an advisor to the Magistrate in settling disputes among Hindus. There was a great deal of resistance to the idea from the minister, objections that Warren Hastings eventually overwrote. Criminal cases likewise were not subjected to arbitration, but settled by 'officers of justice', meaning the police. On the other hand, 'cases of debt, account, or other commercial concern' required arbitration. The statement mentions that orders were issued to record the arbitration

---

[74] British Parliamentary Papers, *Seventh Report from the Committee of Secrecy appointed to enquire into the State of the East India Company together with an Appendix referred to in the said Report*, 1773, p. 346.

[75] Ibid., p. 347.

proceedings, but the description does not detail the procedures or the laws relevant to these cases, the implication being that commercial disputes were altogether rare in these courts.[76]

If this was the situation with state justice, local justice in the eighteenth century seemed to have remained decentralized and controlled by powerful landed groups and castes as elsewhere. A detailed survey of Bihar conducted in the 1830s reported the presence of village chiefs near Gaya, who held 'his office by hereditary tenure, and does not league with the owners of the land to oppress the tenants, but in general supports their interests; and, being a wealthy man of some education, assists the poor and illiterate in settling their accompts'.[77] Even as late as 1842, a survey of rural Bengal found that 'elders appointed by the right of inheritance, and supported by the caste at large with the necessary ease and comfort ..., preside at the caste gatherings and assemblies'.[78] But in Bengal, these courts found no mention in episodes of turbulent business disputes, such as indigo. They were either confined to social issues, or had already become marginal.

This history shows the increasing contradictions that community law courts faced in a period of political and economic transition. Village courts and panchayats had exclusions built into them. The dependence on custom and precedence made the judicial process slow, ineffective, and restricted. The state-instituted regime of law had limited reach and excluded religious groups. The Company regime was thoroughly disillusioned with the old administration, including and especially, administration of justice and police. A big change in law was inevitable, not only because parts of the region were being ruled by British merchants, but also the internal contradictions of the old regime had become unsustainable. The change that did come in was packaged in an old bottle.

[76] Ibid., p. 329.

[77] Montgomery Martin, *The History, Antiquities, Topography, and Statistics of Eastern India ... collated from the Original Documents of the E.I. House*, vol. 1 of 3, London: W.H. Allen, 1838, p. 316.

[78] 'Report on the State of the Police in the Lower provinces for the first six months of 1842', *Calcutta Review*, 1, 1844, pp. 189–217.

THE COLONIAL TRANSITION

In 1757, a force commanded by an East India Company officer defeated the Nawab of Bengal, then virtually an independent state though technically a province of the Mughal empire, and installed a friendly regime. In 1765, after Mir Qasim, the ruler of Bengal who had turned hostile to the British had been defeated, the Company received the *dewanny* of Bengal from the titular emperor in Delhi. Dewanny meant charge of fiscal administration. Following a time-honoured tradition, civil and military administration continued to be vested in a different authority, in this case the local state, the *nizamat*, already desperately in debt to the Company and wholly dependent for its own security upon the Company's army. Thus began British colonial rule in India.

When the British took control of the administration of Bengal they were confronted with a system, rather systems, of law and justice segmented by community practices and in some cases community courts of law. This is the system described in the previous section. The relatively known and familiar cases tried in these institutions concerned landed property. Commercial codes, courts, and cases, by contrast, formed an unfamiliar territory. For the next quarter century, the diarchic administration continued, with increasing dissatisfaction on the part of the masters of the revenue system over the incompetence and incomplete reach of civil law. Gradually, colonial courts and law-books engulfed the much enfeebled legal institutions of the nizamat.

The colonial rule of law in Bengal, in its beginning, persisted with tradition and framed rules of succession and inheritance of property with reference to community custom, defining community mainly in religious terms. Although a window of English common law had been opened in the Mayor's and Supreme courts in territories under the direct administration of the Company, as the Company's territorial authority expanded, and its bread and butter changed from merchant profits to land taxes, it was indigenous common law that was expected to supply the guidelines for legislation, leading to a drive to define, codify, and preserve indigenous common law. Significant outputs of this drive were essayed by William Jones, Henry Colebrooke, Thomas Strange, and the father and son, Francis and W. H. Macnaghten. Some of these commentators, such as the last-named, were judges in the Company's *sudder dewanny adawlut*, the chief civil court of Calcutta

Figure 2.2: A bewildered judge. Satirical look at 'our judge ... his judicial soul ... saturated with appeals, criminal cases, decrees, circular orders ...', G.F. Atkinson, *Curry and Rice (on 40 Plates). Ingredients of Social Life at 'Our' Station in India*, London: Day and Sons, c. 1900

in the nineteenth century. These digests based on scriptural laws were expected to be used by the judges in modern courts.

At the same time, and having dispensed with a role for military chiefs in collecting taxes and enforcing property rights, the state needed to create its own enforcement system technically applicable to all. Under this pressure, after a brief experiment in persistence with tradition, the courts system was overhauled in the first half of the nineteenth century. A hierarchical system was established in place of a segmented one, and appeals and evidence procedures were formalized. The early nineteenth century saw significant advances in the direction of creating a uniform code of procedures. The first major statutes or 'regulations' of the Company removed some of the sharp edges of the old penal law. The regulations allowed a larger space for contracts, debt recovery, and provisions related to property, especially property of the expatriates.[79] The nature of admissible evidence was defined

---

[79] A noticeable point of difference, for example, was in respect of maritime laws. The innovations in this regard were confined not only to laws, but extended to new institutions such as the Small Causes Courts and Insolvent Courts, both designed to deal with cases of debt and commercial contracts.

and made applicable to all courts of law. The major field of innovation in the early nineteenth century Bengal, in this way, took place in the court room. The characters that peopled the court room—the jury, the lawyers, the record-keepers—were fundamentally new elements. If the laws remained unchanged in theory, the colonial court-room still created whole new professions, new agents, new roles, and as we shall see, new forms of abuse.

The desire to create a universal legal regime on the basis of Indian traditional-scriptural law, as the Company officers hoped to do, was an impossible project. Administration of community law with a judiciary that would try to codify and integrate diverse conventions into one harmonized whole, carried enormous information costs, one that gave rise to contradictions and transaction costs in the shape of a 'veritable jungle' of case laws.

The codification job was a never-ending one. The costs of translation and interpretation of tradition were very large, given that the old Sanskrit or Persian law books were often ambiguous, and did not necessarily represent usage. Whereas the Mughal system of justice was based on a dualistic distinction between believers and non-believers—a core state law that was coded and peripheral community laws that were left uncoded—the British system involved in principle giving equal weight to all authentic claims to custom, and therefore, writing down everything. But the communities did not just consist of Hindus and Muslims, also Sikhs, Christians, Portuguese, Parsis, Armenians, Buddhists, and countless others besides. The Muslims and Hindus themselves were not homogenous communities, and the divisions within them were reflected in a highly diverse and often contradictory jurisprudence. Adherence to custom required assuming Hindu custom applied to all Hindus. These requirements were either anomalous or impossible to meet. Through millennia, cross-caste and cross-religious alliances and occupational diversification had led to a huge proliferation of castes and communities. Each one of these groups, when under a literate leadership, was determined in the new regime to establish its own juridical protectorate with reference to one shastric text or other. The project diverted the attention of the early nineteenth century judges from efficiency or fairness, to minding consistency between texts, norms, and judgments.

The dependence of the system upon cultural intermediaries was a recipe for opportunism.[80] A nineteenth century case judgment distinguished three types of authority on Hindu law—the pandits, the texts, and the European scholars on Hindu texts. The pandits and textual authority were frequently unhelpful because of irreconcilable conflicts between texts, some of which were separated by hundreds of years, and the fact that each pandit was schooled in a particular scholastic tradition and was trained to disagree with other pandits. And yet it was not just the 'natives' or the lower court officials who participated in a game of misinformation. European judges were notorious for settling cases based on whim when faced with an impenetrable point of religious law, or for showing off their knowledge of oriental codes in long judgments full of Sanskrit quotations that added up to nothing.

If Hindu law sources were thus often found unreliable, a similar problem arose with Islamic law. *Futawa Alamgiri* was not the document the British used very much in the nineteenth century as a model in deciding on customary law applicable to Muslims. The text used in practice was the substantially recreated *al-Hedaya* of Charles Hamilton. There were two problems with the *Futawa*. It was simply too large, and had remained untranslated for this reason until the nineteenth century. Secondly, the *Futawa* was a compendium of Hanafi interpretation of laws. By the early nineteenth century, an extensive region of northern India, Awadh, had emerged a strong state with institutions of its own. The rulers of this state followed the Imamite or Shia interpretations. The two institutions were similar in broad structure, but differed on important points of detail. The colonial codes, therefore, needed to move on both planes. Baillie's annotated translation of the *Futawa Alamgiri*, for example, necessitated a voluminous supplement on the Imamea code.

---

[80] An early nineteenth century description of the court-room observed, 'Within these few years the natives have attained a sort of legal knowledge… This consists of a skill in the arts of collusion, intrigue, perjury, and subordination, which enables them to perplex and baffle the magistrates with infinite facility'. Walter Hamilton, *The East India Gazetteer; containing particular Descriptions of the Empires, Kingdoms, Principalities, Provinces, Cities, Towns, Districts, Fortresses, Harbours, Rivers, Lakes, &c. of Hindostan and the Adjacent Countries beyond the Ganges and the Eastern Archipelago*, London: John Murray, 1815.

A subtle shift of emphasis had taken place in the decision to elevate Hindu and Mulsim codes to the status of universally applicable law. Codes have a personal character. They refer to good conduct, in this case conduct in respect of keeping the family estate together and making it last forever. The centre of religious codes was not community or guild, but the family. British Indian law, with its preoccupation with property rights, defined property ownership with reference to the joint family, thus drawing a formal bridge between economic conduct and religious–personal law that did not exist before. As I show later (Chapter 3), the formal recognition of the joint family had the potential to introduce differentiation inside the community. The new laws helped business families to contain potential disputes amongst members, and at the same time, made some families stronger and more resourceful in human capital terms than others. But the move also created conflicts between the interests of the individuals and the interests of the so-called joint family.

A larger field of distortion arose from the fact that community customs were by definition aimed at preserving the rights of the collective over capital assets, whereas the new economy and western conceptions of rights frequently demanded assertion of the rights of the individual over that of the collective. The land market suffered owing to this entanglement of private and collective rights (Chapter 6). Other fields where the conflict played out in a particularly transparent way in the nineteenth century were the rights of Hindu widows over the property of their deceased husbands (a claim routinely challenged by the 'joint family' of the husband), and the rights of Hindu widows to adopt a son, again an escape route from the collective rights and vehemently challenged by the husbands' family.

The assertion of Hindu widows to joint family property became a particularly animated channel through which the legal fiction of the joint family was repeatedly challenged. A good mirror of this dynamics is the early nineteenth century adoption cases. Those women without the means to stake a legal claim to maintenance, and often even those formally assigned some maintenance, had to either reconcile to a dependent existence or rely on the authority of their sons to claim a good life for themselves. In a society where a large number of women married before puberty, being widowed without children was common enough. Under Hindu law, then in force in Bengal, a woman had no independent authority to adopt a son and needed to produce documentary evidence showing her husband's consent to adoption. The Sudder Dewany Adawlut in the early nineteenth century had to frequently decide cases where a young girl produced a document purportedly signed by her dying husband sanctioning adoption, which was challenged by her mother-in-law or a brother-in-law.

On more than one such occasion, the family buttressed its case with questions about the moral character of the beneficiary. In one case, a Brahman woman's claim was disputed by the brother of the husband on the ground that she was not a rightful heir to the property due to 'diverse acts of impurity'.[81] The final judgment did not deny that 'impurity' was a rightful ground, but held that 'since there is no proof that the appellant has been excommunicated by her tribe, for having been guilty of any impurity, which would, according to the Shastres, have rendered her an outcast', the charge was not proven in this particular case. The court, however, held the so-called 'permission' to adopt to be unacceptable, which was often the decision in adoption cases. In an almost identical case 30 years later, the issues were the nature of the documentary evidence and the legal majority of the husband rather than character of the appellant.[82]

When a widow adopted a son, did she have the right to gift her husband's estate to the son overlooking the claims of the husband's family? According to the Mitakshara school practised in Mithila, widows did not have such rights. On the other hand, merchant families used adoption frequently in order to ensure the existence of a male heir, and in regions where mercantile families were numerous, customary adoption laws were somewhat more flexible than elsewhere.[83] Which one of these regional conventions would be followed when a widow's right to adopt was challenged in court? The point was whether the case for adoption, almost always couched in religious terms by reference to the fact that a 'son' was necessary to perform rituals for ancestors, could be given precedence over the dangers of leaving succession of joint family property to 'the caprice

[81] Moost. Soondur Koonwaree Dibeeah vs Gudadhur Purshad Teewaree, 1842.

[82] Jumoona Dassya vs Bamasoondari Dassya, Privy Council, 1873.

[83] Juggomohun Roy vs Srimati Neemoo Dossee, Supreme Court, 1831.

of a woman'.[84] Although a landmark judgment in 1862 made Hindu testamentary powers equivalent to those in English common law, the continuation of the joint family principle made all individual decisions on wills, probates, and adoption benefiting the wife of a deceased up for the grabs by all those stated in the scriptures as admissible legal heirs.[85]

Complications of a similar order arose with widows from an inter-caste marriage. Such marriages were almost never valid in Hindu law strictly defined. And therefore, the progeny from such marriages were technically outcastes, illegitimate, and could not receive their fathers' property. In one such case, the lower court ruled for the son citing 'fairness', and the Bengali judge of the High Court overruled, on the point that 'the question of custom ... was wholly lost sight of'.[86] The judge did not dismiss the case but remanded it instead, and no clear indications exist how it was subsequently decided. The Dewanny Adawlut judges often tossed such cases around between themselves unable to decide on an agreed mean between caste and equity.

A third distortion produced by the new regime was that community and custom failed to provide guidance for commercial law. In pre-colonial India, commercial laws were decentralized, existed as moral codes rather than as guild statutes, and had been enforced by means of community courts and a decentralized system of justice. In colonial India, bureaucratic centralization led to the creation of a single hierarchical system of justice and a single procedural law. But where was there a commercial law book? How were the judges in the colonial court-room to find guidance in cases of a commercial and contractual nature?

COMMERCIAL LAW IN THE NINETEENTH CENTURY

The early nineteenth century treatises, chiefly *Digest* (1804) by H. T. Colebrooke, *Considerations* by Francis Macnaghten (1824), and *Hindu Law* by Thomas Strange, a justice of the Madras High Court (1830), recognized areas of compatibility and overlap between Indian texts on the subject of sale and debt contracts and European usage. Indian texts,

[84] Sri Raghunadha vs Brozo Kishoro, Privy Council, 1876.

[85] Soorjemoney's Case, judgment discussed by George Rankin, *Background to Indian Law*, Cambridge: Cambridge University Press, 1946.

[86] Narain Dhara vs Rakhal Gain, Calcutta High Court, 1876.

however, incorporated a great many subjects that the commentators considered 'irrelevant matter, some, not in general classed under this title'.[87] The important examples were the contract of marriage and the duties that it entailed, and the contractual obligations connected with certain kinds of gifts. On other common subjects, such as the necessity of intention and consent in order for a contract to be considered valid in a court, debt recovery, principal-agent relations of a commercial kind, and mortgage, the law was adequately detailed and flexible to be considered usable by the law courts.

And yet, these texts did not prove a very effective aid in the court-room. Only very broad maxims could be derived from Hindu texts, and these were 'dependent upon ethics alone; upon principles which are universally admitted, which are immutable in themselves, and which cannot but be eternal in their duration'.[88] This peculiar hybrid between the communal and the universal was not often invoked by the judges themselves, because they did not find ethical strictures too helpful in settling real-life disputes. Macnaghten noted that contractual disputes hardly ever appeared before courts of law, even though in commercial life, disputes were pervasive. Strange observed too that Hindu law had been used as a benchmark only in a minority of cases. 'In practice, the English law, as far as applicable, is adopted by the Courts'.[89] One of the reasons for this was a procedural clause that stipulated only 'equity, justice, and good conscience' to be employed when at least one of the disputants belonged to a different religion.

I suggest in Chapter 3 that intra-community disputes increasingly came before the courts to seek a common law settlement. While this was certainly the long-term trend, overall the business of the court-room did not see many commercial disputes. There were other ways of avoiding problems. As the nineteenth century moved on, the family, as distinct from the community, became the main organizing unit of large-scale industrial and commercial enterprise (Chapter 3). The loosening of community ties and strengthening of the family might

[87] Thomas Strange, *Hindu Law with reference to Such Portions of it as Concern the Administration of Justice in the King's Courts in India*, (fifth edition), Madras: Higginbothams, 1875, p. 262.

[88] Francis W. Macnaghten, *Considerations on Hindoo Law as it is current in Bengal*, Serampore: Mission Press, 1824, p. 404.

[89] Ibid., p. 306.

have diffused the kind of commercial disputes (between brokers or between members of the Parsi panchayat, for example) that spilled over into the courts in the eighteenth century port cities.

At the same time, as peasant exports grew in the new era of globalization, a new and politically sensitive field of contract failure was opening up in relationships between foreign capitalists and Indian producers. Some of the more serious examples occurred in tea plantations over the desertion of indentured workers (Chapter 5), in indigo production in Bengal over terms of sale, and in the Deccan over terms of credit. These disputes, involving a pledge to work for wages, a pledge to repay loans or forfeit land, or a pledge to sell crops, did not form any part of traditional law. Sanskrit texts and Hanafi codes did not have very much, if anything, to say on either sale of goods, or the land mortgage, or on wage-employment. And yet, as the controversial breach of contract clauses that covered the indentured worker in Assam or the persistent frictions in indigo showed, in an environment where commercial law had long been neglected, business disputes could take on ethnic and political colour. What were essentially commercial disputes could acquire a class character, and become an embarrassment for a regime still recovering from the shock of the mutiny. Chapter 6 studies the blue mutiny, one such business dispute that had an important effect upon legislation.

CONCLUSION

I advance three propositions in this chapter about how statecraft and the economic order were related in Indian history.

The first proposition concerns the norms of kingship. I show that the kings in pre-colonial India were expected to function within a moral order that included the notion of a social contract. The principle of the contract was to respect the juridical-economic-cultural autonomy of those collectives that supplied essential services for the state. All states are built upon alliances. There was no essential difference between Europe and India in this respect. The difference was that in the latter region the groups were not organizations like the Church or the guild, but clusters of families that followed hereditary occupations and were usually led by a designated headman or a council. Caste and community as business models were partially the outcome of a centuries old principle of statecraft. Further, in the

Indian case, the alliances were not utilitarian or strategic ones, but founded on an organic principle of politics. A strong drive to back particular constituents of society, in the way the mercantilist states in early modern Europe supported their overseas merchants with arms, would be foreign to this notion of statecraft.

Second, the institutional consequences of statecraft were far-reaching. It hardened monopoly of skills in the hands of lineages. In effect, the king could enjoy his monopoly of violence by offering an implicit guarantee to protect monopolies of families to their own hereditary skills. This he did by allowing them autonomy with respect to contract and property. In the economic sphere, especially formation of partnerships and contractual exchange, this practice led to two possible consequences. It gave panchayats legitimacy and gave social practices the force of laws, and it made formation of partnerships and contractual dealings across communities an unpopular, if unavoidable, strategy. This enforced separation of groups did not necessarily mean that hostility marked social interaction between them. But it did have the implication of driving communities into insularity, and turning them into units that internalized long-term relationships involving contract, training, cooperation, and joint working of assets. Legal autonomy was the foundation on which the landed, artisanal, or mercantile communities could function in this fashion in business.

Third, during the colonial period, a hybrid Anglo-Indian system was erected. By creating a single system of courts, and by streamlining the judicial process, the English created a judicial system in India that resembled the English common law system. Unlike code-based legal regimes, the Anglo-Indian system upheld and gave importance to the judicial process and case laws. On the other hand, in framing the actual contents of the laws, the Anglo-Indian system decided to uphold, codify, and formalize community codes. In that respect, colonial India departed from common law, resembled a civil law system, and stuck to the Indic heritage. This hybrid was monstrously inefficient.[90] Not

---

[90] To see why it was so, imagine a football match in which a single referee ruled over all players; and yet, each time a player committed a foul, the referee had to reread the rule-book and call in experts to decide whether or not according to the customs of the caste of the player, a foul had been committed. The game would never end.

only was the judicial process expensive in time and money, it created a moral hazard by encouraging disputants to invent traditions and judges to show off their knowledge of tradition to other judges.

As time went on, the system was falling out of step with a globalizing and commercializing economy in which individuals asserted their claims to wealth in opposition to the rights of the joint family and community more frequently and more intensely than ever before. In the late nineteenth century, the perceived need for legal reform was widely shared, and the ideological support for translation of Indian codes had much weakened. Transmission of European law, an assertion of legislative authority of the state, and case laws, therefore, became inevitable.

In the interest of discussing political practices, the chapter placed all economic actors in one basket. We now need to untangle the evidence on the communities themselves, beginning with the merchant, banker, and the industrialist in the nineteenth century.

3 Merchants
Guild as corporation

Descriptions of business organizations in pre-colonial and colonial India have sometimes used the word 'guild'. The word is a borrowing from the context of medieval Europe. The borrowing cannot be an easy one. Whereas in Western Europe the term usually connotes a professional association with a charter of rights protected by local and supra-local authorities, associations having such attributes were rare in pre-colonial India. The counterpart of the guild in India was a cluster of families related by ties of marriage and kinship, and possessing its own rules of law that came closer to a moral code than professional statutes. The moral code incorporated respect for elders, a preference for settling disputes by consensus, and philanthropy. These endogamous guilds performed some of the same functions as any professional guild would. Yet, they belonged in a different social world. The present chapter shows how commercialization from the eighteenth century strengthened as well as weakened that world.

PRE-COLONIAL INDIA

The Mughal economy created an enormous space for mercantile enterprise engaged in financing grain trade, production and trade of luxury manufactures located in the cities, and banking and financial services. Some authors and contemporary observers, however, hold that the enterprise of the merchant and banker was at best dependent on, and at worst repressed by, the imperial court and its segments. Repression is a strong word. The emperor Akbar centralized currency management to the extent that he had to disallow some banking businesses in the realm.

In the late seventeenth century, economic dynamism derived from new sources, namely, textile exports, inflow of New World gold and silver, and cash crop production. These forces of change did not have similar or equal impact upon all regions. For example, whereas there was a general tendency for interest rates to fall between 1620 and 1720, there was no visible tendency for capital markets to integrate and rates to converge between regions.[1] Bengal rates remained above those of Surat. And the average remained above those in contemporary Europe. Nevertheless, new businesses played an important role in regional politics. In the eighteenth century, the mutually dependent relationship that had developed between the successors to the Mughal empire and bankers exposed the latter to local conflicts and led them into taking sides in these conflicts. Increasingly, in the late eighteenth century these conflicts involved the European companies. Mercantile activity, thus, derived partly from new forms of trade and finance, but also from weakening of and fragmentation of state authority.

The major activities in which large-scale private capital was engaged in the eighteenth century were trades in cotton, grain, cloth, and opium, tax-farming, lending to the state, money-changing, and internal remittances. Tax farmers and big bankers thrived on fiscal weakness and collapse of the successor states, often induced by or worsened by predation of neighbours. Money-changers flourished because of monetary fragmentation of a territory that had been relatively more united a century before. And the remittance business grew because of the emergence of new zones of insecurity and expansion, which regions nevertheless were quite central in commodity trade (Malwa, for example). When the East India Company consolidated as a state in the early nineteenth century, some of the older forms of financial dealings that thrived on state failure came to an end.

What kind of firms supplied this expanded demand for capital? The merchant and banking firms were organized in communities. Near Delhi and Agra, the Punjab, Rajasthan, and Sind, the prominent trading communities were the Khatris, Lohanas, Bhatias, Khojas, and Parachas, the last said to have been converted Khatris. In Gujarat, Hindu and Muslim trading communities conducted inland trade and extensive maritime trade. In south India, two prominent trading communities were the Telugu-speaking Komatis and the Tamil-

---

[1] Shireen Moosvi, *People, Taxation, and Trade in Mughal India*, New Delhi: Oxford University Press, 2008, pp. 12–15.

speaking Chettis. Among the 'brokers' of European trading firms in the eighteenth century were relatively new groups, such as Bengali Hindus and Parsis, traditionally artisans, carpenters, weavers, and ship-builders. Indigenous banking was conducted mainly by Hindu Vaishyas, such as the Jains, Marwaris, Chettis, and the Khatri and the Arora community in Punjab. Exceptions to the community as business firm did exist. Merchants and bankers from Multan and Marwar conducted business in small and tightly-knit settlements along trade routes connecting the heart of the Mughal empire with the Russian empire. Communities could be found in Bokhara, Herat, Meshed, and Kandahar, in towns on the Caspian coast, and in Moscow, in the eighteenth century.

In historical scholarship on early modern business, we do hear about prominent individuals, but perhaps more systematically we hear about castes, groups, and families. Usually, the individual, the family, and the community were tied together in a highly inter-dependent relationship. The family was the unit of property ownership, succession, and worked like a firm. The community or cluster of families supplied complementary services, mainly dispute settlement, and the provision of public goods. And the heads of families formed the courts of settlement of disputes.

Several features of indigenous commerce of that time that surprised outsiders, such as a propensity to form partnerships within the extended household, and wide divergence in the terms of transaction according to caste, can be explained by a persistent tendency to forge relationships dependent on trust between members of the same community. The extended household rather than the individual was the unit of ownership of asset. The household decided property rights and rules of succession. To quote a pioneering business history, 'The unit of establishment was ordinarily everywhere the family [in the eighteenth century]. It was also usually the traditional Hindu joint family... No forms like that of a continuous joint stock venture appear to have emerged, though ad hoc or short-period partnerships ... were common.'[2] C.A. Bayly describes business organization in eighteenth

---

[2] D. R. Gadgil, *Origins of the Modern Indian Business Class*, New York: Institute of Pacific Relations, 1959, p. 34. For perceptive discussions on the role of family and community in the historiography of Indian business, see Dwijendra Tripathi, *The Oxford History of Indian Business*, New Delhi: Oxford University Press, 2004;

century northern India in terms of the extended household and groups of families.[3] Court proceedings in the colonial city of Bombay in the third quarter of the eighteenth century reflected '...the tendency among local merchants to rely on community connections and to form associations that could frame collective decisions'.[4]

There is a view in the historiography of Mughal India that formal guilds in the Western European model were unattainable because royal patronage to merchants had been weak and erratic. The state did not need the merchants as an ally.[5] Taxing the merchant was not a significant source of income for the state, and the relationship was left to a certain degree of arbitrariness, even extortionist practices. A story of urban atrophy can be erected on the basis of a weak kind of corporatism. Towns were either garrisons or points of land-tax administration rather than centres of commerce and industry. Implicitly, a contrast exists with late medieval Europe where the state's dependence on land taxes had fallen, the town had emerged a source of taxation, merchants and urban administration could both be better-off by collaborating, and the guild acquired its distinctive rights, even though these rights were later sold and resold to others, and eventually revoked. This stylized story of an institutional divergence is unconvincing. The assumption that merchants were dependent and marginal adjuncts to agrarian states stands much revised. Indeed, key financial instruments of early modern India, the extensive discounting and promissory notes businesses 'for example, were inseparable from land taxation and grain trade. Further, the stylized story of business organization places too much emphasis on the needs of the state. Alternatively,

---

and Dwijendra Tripathi, 'Occupational Mobility and Industrial Entrepreneurship in India: A Historical Analysis', *The Developing Economies*, 19(1), 1981, pp. 52–68.

[3] *Rulers, Townsmen and Bazaars: North Indian Society in the Age of British Expansion*, Cambridge: Cambridge University Press, 1983, p. 377.

[4] Lakshmi Subrahmanian, 'Merchants in Transit: Risk-sharing Strategies in the Indian Ocean', in H.P. Ray and E.A. Alpers, eds, *Cross Currents and Community Networks: The History of the Indian Ocean World*, New Delhi: Oxford University Press, 2007, p. 274.

[5] S.P. Blake, *Shahjahanabad: The Sovereign City in Mughal India, 1639-1739*, Cambridge: Cambridge University Press, 1991; M.N. Pearson 'Merchants and States', in J. Tracy, ed., *The Political Economy of Merchant Empires. State and World Trade 1350-1750*, Cambridge: Cambridge University Press, 1990.

business organization can be explained as an established institutional principle to which the states had to adapt. Guilds were unnecessary in the region for another mode of control over entrepreneurial resources was already available, namely the community.

How did communities govern themselves? All stable professional relationships demand a dispute-settlement system carrying legitimacy. In the case of Indian merchants we see the play of two intermeshed systems—the formal panchayat or personal court, and a moral code.

Historical scholarship on medieval south India (twelfth to fourteenth centuries) shows that trading communities like the Ayyavole and Nanadesi displayed a great deal of unity and organization.[6] The presence of a *samaya*, or conventions about code of conduct and regulatory rules, has been noted. Merchants distinguished by locality, kin group, and community followed their own codes of conduct, known in the scriptures as *achara* or practices, which differed according to particular groups. In the same vein, William Moreland speculated that trading communities in the seventeenth century functioned according to the rules of law, but these rules were framed and implemented by the communities themselves. '[L]ike other such systems, it was substantially fair to every one who knew "the rules of the game"'.[7] But Moreland had nothing more to say on the constitution of these laws and principles of justice.

Paolino da San Bartolomeo wrote that in the eighteenth century Malabar, settlement of criminal cases, especially appellate cases, often required the intervention of community courts. 'In doubtful cases, the superintendants and elders of the cast are consulted. In these assemblies the first object of the members is to enquire into the laws, customs and usages formerly established in the cast, or in the town or city where the trial takes place ; and according to these old precedents the point in question is determined'.[8] The Parsi panchayat was formed in Bombay soon after the island came under British possession. This

[6] 'These communities are often described as guilds although indisputable evidence of their organization into a well defined, structured and cohesive body is hard to find'. R. Champakalakshmi, 'Urbanisation in South India: The Role of Ideology and Polity', *Social Scientist*, 15(8/9), 1987, pp. 67–117.

[7] W.H. Moreland, *India at the Death of Akbar: An Economic Study*, London: Macmillan Publishers, 1920., p. 249.

[8] *A Voyage to the East Indies*, London: J. Davis, 1800, p. 311.

was meant to be a court of civil justice, whereas matters religious were still settled by the priests of Navsari on the Gujarat coast. The leading member of the leading Parsi business family established the panchayat to settle disputes, and to aid Parsi newcomers to the city. Frequent internal bickering invited the intervention of the Governor in the middle of the eighteenth century, and effectively turned the panchayat into an assembly shorn of its juridical powers.[9] Thereafter, the panchayat regained its authority only to lose it again on several occasions.

With the Khojas of Muscat, 'the community had an elected shaykh and council of elders which governed communal affairs'.[10] In Muscat, the Danish explorer Carsten Niebuhr observed in 1765, the Kucchhi Bhatias 'are permitted to live agreeably to their own laws'.[11] The propensity of the Kucchhi Bhatias of Muscat to establish agreements with family members settled in other ports was noted. They stepped out of this mould only when the need arose of a contract where another Bhatia firm was not already established.[12] Bayly discusses examples of caste panchayat from the eighteenth century north India. In some of the larger port towns and market towns of western India, commercial disputes were heard by a council of mahajans or principal firms, headed by the nagar seth.[13] But such supra-community courts and laws did not represent a universal system. Among Bohras and Armenians, for example, institutions of law were bound up with the centrality of the priestly elite. Bohras were a community of Muslim merchants from Gujarat, who formed 'a distinct colony' wherever they settled. A description of central India in the 1830s stated that the Bohras were 'united under the spiritual rule of their elected Moollahs, or priests, to whose orders, ... They render implicit obedience. The good understanding in which they live with each other strengthens

[9] Douglas M. Thornton, *Parsi, Jaina and Sikh or Some Minor Religious Sects in India*, London: The Religious Tract Society, 1898, p. 34.

[10] Calvin H. Allen, Jr., 'The Indian Merchant Community of Masqat', *Bulletin of the School of Oriental and African Studies, University of London*, 44(1), 1981, pp. 39–53.

[11] Ibid.

[12] Ibid.

[13] B. Cohn, 'From Indian Status to British Contract', *Journal of Economic History*, 21(4), 1961, pp. 613–28.

their association'.[14] Local rulers, as long as they had a say in the matter, referred cases back to the organization of the merchants rather than to their own courts of law, not usually to the satisfaction of the European disputants.[15]

What was the precise constitution of commercial laws practiced by any one of these communities? The question is hard to tackle by conventional methods because of the scarcity of documentary sources. One clue to the question, and the very scarcity of material seems to confirm the point, is that the community panchayat was not a court of law in the modern sense. It was a mechanism to arrive at a negotiated compromise, rather than a mechanism to establish and uphold the truth. Bernard Cohn's speculation about the principle of justice followed in the village panchayats in the Benares region might well be true of the merchant caste panchayat as well. These courts did not establish *the* truth as opposed to falsehood, or sift *the* right from wrong, but were means of finding a mutually acceptable settlement of disputes.[16] V. T. Gune, the historian of Maratha justice, states that 'while deciding suits more importance was given to bring out reconciliation between the parties in dispute than to the rules of procedure and law'.[17] Continuity of the transaction mechanism along with cohesion within the community was of paramount importance. The shared interests of the disputants rather than the point of the disputes were given more importance. Therefore, laws were not necessary. Too specific laws might even be a hindrance to negotiation and compromise. It would not be inappropriate to apply the same principle on to the panchayat of merchants.

However, this characterization of commercial law and justice leaves open the question, how did disputes *between* communities get settled? My tentative answer is that disputes between communities were rare in the first place. In Asian trade before European entry, commodities were of known quality and sold in known markets by traders who knew

[14] John Malcolm, *A Memoir of Central India*, vol. 2, London: Parbury Allan and Co., 1832, p. 110.

[15] For an instance from Patna, see Kumkum Chatterjee, 'Trade and Darbar Politics in the Bengal Subah, 1733–1757', *Modern Asian Studies*, 26(2), 1992, pp. 233–73.

[16] 'From Indian Status to British Contract'

[17] *The Judicial System of the Marathas*, Poona: Sangam, 1953, p. 128.

each other well. Information cost of these transactions was relatively low, and could sustain auctions and spot deals without carrying much risk. Quite a large segment within early modern transactions between merchants and merchants, therefore, consisted of spot transactions that simply avoided breach of contract. The segment was the dominant one in dealings between and amongst Asian merchants. Spot dealings did involve intermediaries and agents, but did not usually involve predetermined terms of trade. In such trade, the expected earning of the agent reflected the state of demand and quality of goods rather than the risk of non-fulfilment of contract. With the scope of disputes reduced in inter-community deals, dispute settlement mechanisms could well be internalized at little cost.

Furthermore, spot markets and auction form of deals were particularly compatible with a business world divided into informal collectives. Extensive contractual trade in the early modern world would require two fundamental preconditions—cheap credit and good faith. Credit in India was usually more expensive than credit in Western Europe, the only exception being credit transactions when debtors belonged in the same community as the creditors. And a trading world divided into communities was not conducive to building faith, again with the exception of intra-community dealings. In offering this speculation, I follow George Forster, who observed among his fellow boarders on a ship across the Caspian bound for Astrakhan, 'there is not a sufficient credit or good faith established in Persia, to enable merchants to consign their effects to factors. The foreign trader, therefore, is necessitated to become a supercargo...'.[18] Jakob van Leur famously suggested that early modern Asian maritime trade could be characterized as peddling. The speculation can be read in two ways, that the average scale was small, and that the form of transaction was on-spot or auction rather than contractual. Van Leur has been mainly read in the former sense and criticized. However, in the second sense, the word 'peddling' as a characterization of how business was ordinarily conducted in the Indian coastal towns before European entry, and within large segments controlled by Indian merchants even after European entry, may not be inapt. Consider these examples.

---

[18] *A Journey from Bengal to England*, vol. 2, London: A. fauder, 1808, p. 250.

Duarte Barbosa, who visited the western coast and the Vijayanagar capital around 1515, observed that in the port of Chaul, which along with Cambay was the major trading point before the rise of Surat, business was timed with the monsoon and the shipping season. Consequently, only in three or four months in a year, foreigners and 'merchants from all the neighbourhood' met here, the rest of the year Chaul being deserted. 'They make their bargains during this period, and despatch their goods, and after that return to their homes until the next season, so that this place is like a fair in those months'.[19]

The picture of mode of import trade in Surat drawn in the seventeenth century by Manucci and in the eighteenth century by the merchant John Henry Grose, is not substantially different, except that the seasons of trade were less pronounced than before.[20] Manucci wrote:

Whenever a loaded vessel arrives, the Hindu traders go aboard, and ask if the captain wishes to sell the whole cargo of the ship. If so, they pay for it in money, or furnish goods for the return cargo, whichever is preferred. This is all done without delays, and merchants can thus acquire whatever merchandise they are in search of, and for which they have left home.[21]

And Grose elaborated the procedure further, a hundred years later:

On a ship's importing there, nothing more was to be done, than for the commander ... to bring his musters or samples on shore, together with his invoice; and the considerable merchants resorting to him, would immediately strike a bargain for the whole cargoe, if the assortment suited them, with no other trouble than settling the per centage upon the items of the invoice. ... the amount: paid down upon the nail, either in ready money:, or by barter, according as the vender and purchaser agreed, with as much good faith, at least, as is ever observed among the European merchants of the most established character of probity.[22]

Spot transactions could be very large and very diverse. The extensive capital of the Surat traders enabled them to take risks of some of the assortment being not up to the mark. Equally, the prospect of repeated transactions with rich clients made the captain of the ship interested

---

[19] *A Description of the Coasts of East Africa and Malabar: In the Beginning of the Sixteenth Century*, London: Hakluyt Society, 1866, p. 70.

[20] *A Voyage to the East Indies*, London, 1772, pp. 105–6.

[21] *Storia do Mogor*, vol. 1, London: John Murray, pp. 61–2.

[22] Grose, *Voyage*, p. 105.

in fair deals. Some of them would be forced to stay months in the port waiting for the reverse wind, and would be at the mercy of the officers were there cases of fraud.

Faith in fair bargain in spot transactions was universal. Of the 'banya' in India, '...those of them who are properly merchants, in the extensive sense of that word, are in general the faired, openest dealers in the world, and those of Surat were especially famous for the simplicity and frankness of their transactions'.[23] Grose also wrote of a quality among the bania that he called 'commercial courage', and which points to a constructed skill in negotiations on the spot—

... their invincible phlegm and coolness in the course of their transactions. Whether you offer them shamefully less than their goods are worth, or fly into passions at their under-rating yours, there is no such thing as provoking them into the least show of passion or indecency. They calmly suffer you to evaporate your resentment without interrupting you, and waiting patiently till your fit of drunkenness is off, for they look on it in no other light, they return cooly to the same point, as if nothing had stirred them from it.[24]

There is, in this fashion, a great deal of description on bargaining, and surprisingly little on contracts as such. It is not that such modes of trade did not exist, but there is strong ground to believe that the scope of contractual transactions increased enormously after European investments began to grow, and that it had been rather limited in earlier times and amongst Asian actors.

Along with opaque community laws and the rarity of disputes, there was a yet third feature that explains the quiet manner in which communities might be able to settle internal disputes. There was an ideology of righteousness that governed the conduct of the merchant with respect to members of the same merchant community. Consistent with Moreland's speculation that commercial law was present as 'conventional morality' rather than as statutes, later scholarship shows that the family firm was more than a firm. It was a firm 'embedded' in moral relations. It was 'a constellation of relationships through which honour was acquired'.[25] Patronage and charity, marriage alliances, and principal-agent relations were separated by invisible boundaries. Charity was the public form in which this moral code was expressed.

[23] Ibid., p. 105
[24] Ibid., p. 106.
[25] Bayly, *Rulers, Townsmen and Bazaars*, p. 377.

Leading merchant families supplied subsistence, cheap credit, and jobs to poorer relations. A great deal of organized charity was done by the temples, which were established by the leading merchants.

Within a family firm of Benares in the mid-nineteenth century, for example, 'when the immediate needs of the members' frugal eating and clothing habits and few servants had been satisfied, by far the most important category of social expenditure was connected with religion.'[26] A study of Parsi giving argues that 'one of the primary effects of gifting was to aid the community in defining and limiting the social boundaries of the community.'[27] This study also shows that as Bombay became the principal centre of the community, philanthropy took a more institutionalized character, more regular rather than crisis-induced as it was before, but also more insular than before.[28] In south India, merchant gifts were particularly associated with gifts to the temple. David Rudner suggests that the castes of itinerant traders engaged in trade by worshipping the deities of their customers, and making gifts to these temples that marked the trading zone.[29]

More interestingly, the valorization of social expenditure was usually, if not always, accompanied with a frugal personal lifestyle of the rich relations.[30] Historians are yet to offer an integrated view of merchant consumption that can account for frugality. Often, frugality was framed in the language of asceticism, as James Laidlaw has observed, though in reality austerity and economics were hardly separate spheres.[31] A simple economic theory of frugality would be that merchants needed to save more than other classes, not only because

[26] C.A. Bayly, 'Patrons and Politics in Northern India', *Modern Asian Studies*, 7(3), 1973, pp. 349–88.

[27] David L. White, 'From Crisis to Community Definition: The Dynamics of Eighteenth-Century Parsi Philanthropy', *Modern Asian Studies*, 25(2), 1991, pp. 303–20.

[28] A detailed factual account of Parsi charity can be found in the collection, *Famous Parsis: Biographies and critical sketches of patriots, philanthropists, politicians, scholars and captains of industry*, Madras: G.A. Natesan, 1930.

[29] 'Religious Gifting and Inland Commerce in Seventeenth-Century South India', *Journal of Asian Studies*, 46(2), 1987, pp. 361–79.

[30] Among exceptions to this pattern were the merchant houses located close to the Mughal court.

[31] *Riches and Renunciation: Religion, Economy and Society among the Jains*, Oxford: Clarendon Press, 1995.

they needed the money for investment, but also, they needed money to tide over bad times. In a tropical monsoon environment, business risks derived largely from the season, and seasonal fluctuations were acute. If the rich peasant stocked up grain, the merchant stocked up money. But this view does not explain charity very well; charity being an act of spending rather than saving. Perhaps display of wealth was eschewed from fear of the rent-seeking political elites. The fear-of-the-king factor would depend on how the merchant–state relationship is conceptualized, and we have seen in Chapter 2 that the notion that the state was normally extortionate in India, is exaggerated.

We can arrive at a more plausible theory of frugality by integrating consumption and community. History tells us that rich individuals within merchant families could at times exercise a degree of freedom about personal consumption denied to poorer members of a family. Subject to that qualification, we can speculate on the presence of a compatible relation between the goals of the individual and the goals of the community. Within the merchant community, enterprise could be an individual resource but consumption was a public act. The individual entrepreneur did not see oneself as a unit of consumption. The individual was a custodian of the wealth that belonged to the community. The minimalist lifestyle expressed the idea that the rich were heads of households rather than wealthy capitalists. Reflecting the same idea, the spending by the rich went to create public goods for the community, such as charity for caste members, or building a temple where entry for outcastes was restricted. But it was not acceptable to spend money on a silk garment for that would amount to a dissipation of the common wealth.

Along several fronts, both within and without, the community became unstable from the eighteenth century. The earliest instances of friction arose in relationships between the Indian and European merchants. In the nineteenth century, problems arose within the community, and the very institutions of governance of internal dissentions began to weaken.

CONFLICT IN INDO-EUROPEAN TRADE

I have already mentioned (Introduction and Chapter 1) that the fundamental reason why Indo-European trade had high disputatious potentials was that it relied almost wholly upon contracts, agency, and predetermined terms, and involved sums of money quite unprecedented in scale. Breach of contract on the part of the agent-headman-broker became a serious new worry, one that could not be addressed by available legal means that had been integrated within the community. And, I argue below, directly or indirectly, as courts of law were started outside the community, internal disputes also began coming into the public, threatening the very existence of the community.

There is much evidence of frictions in the context of Indo-European trade. Urban contracts over insurance and trade were subject to 'conditions of endemic conflict' in the eighteenth century port city.[32] Conflicts were endemic also in opium, textiles, and indigo trades, in the last case exploding in a small-scale 'mutiny' in the mid-nineteenth century. A contemporary observer, Robert Orme, noted that the entanglement of property with personal law had made public settlement of property disputes relatively rare in India, whereas personal law failed to settle commercial disputes. 'The free exercise of commerce [is] found to produce still more frequent occasions of dispute.'[33]

An earlier scholarship read the relationship between the European and the Indian merchant as a hierarchical one. In this view, the Indians were 'comprador capitalists', who had rather little say about terms of transaction, and who lost even the freedom they had when the Company became a raj.[34] Clearly, disputes in Indo-European trade cannot be completely understood in the framework of 'comprador' capitalism, where the fundamental axis of commercial relationship was a principal-agent one. One party set and dictated terms, the other had to take it or leave it. The comprador thesis has been questioned. Rajat Ray, for example, writes, 'not many among the promoters of the great twentieth century Asian corporate undertakings were "compradors" in the political propagandist's sense of the term, implying abject

[32] Subramanian, 'Merchants in Transit', p. 275.

[33] Robert Orme, *Historical Fragments of the Mogul Empire, of the Morattoes, and of the English concerns in Indostan from the year MDCLIX*, London: F. Wingrave, 1805, p. 442.

[34] For an example of the application of this idea, and a useful discussion of the literature, see Bonaventure Swai, 'East India Company and Moplah Merchants of Tellicherry: 1694–1800', *Social Scientist*, 8(1), 1979, pp. 58–70.

dependence.'[35] This approach, instead of making the Indian element secondary to the European, rightly observes that the two tended to be specialized in distinct but connected operations, maritime trade and country trade for example, requiring different and complementary kinds of information and skill. And yet, while they both gained from partnership, the contractual relation between them was unstable. Why was it unstable?

My hypothesis is that inter-ethnic contracts were inherently unstable. For, terms of contract in a community-bound world made sense and were relatively easily enforceable only between members of a community. The late eighteenth century and the early nineteenth witnessed great expansion of contractual transactions across sectarian borders, in new commodities and new markets that participants had not much prior knowledge about. To ensure that goods sell, merchants needed to control quantity, quality, and dimension exactly. They needed to depend on prior contract. Consequently, there was reduction in the sphere of spot market transactions. Commercial law, being tied to opaque community practices, fell behind this trend. More broadly, an institutional cleavage opened up between Asian trade and European trade.

Let me begin with a story. In the autumn of 1800, the aforementioned George Forster started on an ill-advised journey from Bengal to England by the land route across Afghanistan, Persia, Caspian, and Muscovy. He carried his savings in the form of a *hundi*, which was a promise to pay a sum of money ordinarily respected by Indian merchants along the overland route. By the time Forster had crossed the Hindu Kush, rain and snow had erased the writing on this piece of paper, and he found it impossible to cash the hundi and raise money anywhere. His travelling companion, and only friend in a hostile landscape, was an Armenian merchant with whom Forster maintained a relationship of dependence and distrust. The Armenian had the paper cashed in the bazaar, at a discount that devastated Forster and soured their relationship beyond repair.

The story carries a simple lesson. The hundi was a contracted promise to pay. But a European traveller outside community was less

[35] Rajat Kanta Ray, 'Asian Capital in the Age of European Domination: The Rise of the Bazaar, 1800–1914', *Modern Asian Studies*, 29(3), 1995, pp. 449–554.

able to enforce that contract than was an Armenian. For, the contract made more sense in a social world of which the Armenian was a part and the Briton was not. The story reveals to us another problem with the community model. Communities are clusters of people who command mutual 'trust' and 'reputation', but they are much more than that. They are also a predatory device. Forster was ripped off not because he had a bad reputation, but because he was a loner and an outsider. In the business world ruled by communities, loners and others are doomed to disaster. Communities stifle enterprise. For this reason, Indian business was never completely trusted by Europeans, and Europeans were rarely full members of the Indian inner circle.

I do not wish to suggest that European and Indian business institutions were discrete worlds. In the commercial world of the late eighteenth and early nineteenth century, the Company state as well as European businesses depended on Indian commercial instruments. There was a rough kind of comparative advantage in this dependence—*overland* remittances/trade in the South Asian landmass or in trans-Asia typically involved Indian instruments; *overseas* remittances involved instruments operated by the European agency houses and Company employees. Intra-Asian and coastal traded tended to be dominated by Asian merchants, and exports bound for Europe by Europeans.[36] But the balance between these two spheres was changing. The dependence of European trade on Indian business institutions was steadily in decline in the nineteenth century. Forster's experience reveals one reason why this was inevitable. Not all traders were members of the inner circle where instruments found easy acceptance. But that was not all.

One universal problem in early modern trade was the distrust of the interpreter-agent. Although neither the company administration nor private commerce could function without the indigenous agent, the distrust of the intermediary, the 'dupes of the intriguing servants' was as deep-rooted as was the dependence.[37] 'Since the English became rulers of extensive dominions and trade in Hindostan...', a Company

---

[36] In this sphere, Asian merchants remained entrenched. Sushil Chaudhury discusses overland trade, its scale, and complexity, in *From Prosperity to Decline: Eighteenth Century Bengal*, New Delhi: Manohar Publications, 1995.

[37] Eugene R. Irschick, 'Order and Disorder in Colonial South India', *Modern Asian Studies*, 23(3), 1989, pp. 459–92.

officer remarked, 'a new field was opened to a subtle class of people, who, until that time, held but a middle rank in the country, Banyans and Circars'. The degree of dependence of the European partners on these agents was so great, and their powers of negotiation and contracting with artisans and peasants so unrestrained by either their status as agents or any custom, that the former were veritably at the mercy of the agents, whereas the latter 'act in the two-fold capacity of seller and purchaser, reaping the advantages of commission and fraud from both'. The author held that these abuses arose from the extension of the contract principle to Indo-European trade, whereas spot transactions, '...instant payment without the chargeable and fraudulent mediation of brokers', would have averted these transaction costs.[38]

A second and broader field of conflict arose in inland trade over dealings between European and Indian merchants. One historian writes, 'preoccupation with various problems concerning contracts with the local merchants dominates the ... correspondence' of the French Company in the late seventeenth and early eighteenth century.[39] The trade history of Bengal in the eighteenth century is replete with instances of disputes between the Company servants conducting private trade and Indian peasants and merchants. The problems had been long-standing. But a veritable flood of complaints began when private traders moved, in the years after Plassey, into the interior to conduct opium and other trades in implicit violation of the licenses issued by territorial authorities. The merchant in command of a private army issued orders (*perwannas*) declaring terms of contract, and local agents (*gomashtas*) went to the peasants to force them to comply and collect protection money in the bargain. In response to numerous complaints, the last major trade treaty signed between the ruler and the Company stipulated that all commodity transactions by the Company should be done on spot market basis, or to use the

[38] William Thompson, *Travels in Europe, Asia, and Africa; describing characters, customs, manners, laws, and productions of nature and art containing various remarks on the political and commercial interests of Great Britain and delineating in particular a new system for the government and improvement of the British settlements in the East Indies: Begun in the year 1777 and finished in 1781*, vol. 2, London: J. Murray, 1782, pp. 97–8.

[39] Indrani Ray, 'The French Company and the Merchants of Bengal (1680–1730)', *Indian Economic and Social History Review*, 8(1), 1971, pp. 41–55.

contemporary phrase 'ready money', rather than on contract, and made disputes subject to the jurisdiction of local courts of justice. The treaty was seen by the English as a surrender of their rights. Matters did not improve by the aggressive tactics of the European merchants who ventured in inland trade, by 'the insolent attitude assumed towards the latter by the native magistrates in some outlying places', intense factionalism within the Company, rivalries among the Company servants seeking to stake a claim to the scramble for the interior, and the 'villainous practices' of the Calcutta agents engaged by the European private traders to procure goods there.[40]

A yet third field of disputes occurred between Indians and Indians. The particular quarrels that we know more about were of a new kind, occurred frequently, and left unintended political consequences. These disputes between Indians and Indians were of a kind that customary practices could not solve. How do we understand this failure?

COMMUNITY DE-STABILIZED

The obverse of the community principle was that professional identity among merchants tended to be weak. Class solidarity and class consciousness being weak, the business world was 'atomized'. This feature, ordinarily of little consequence, proved to be a hazard with the consolidation of European capital in Indian Ocean trade. Competition for English trade created scope for disputes between communities that the insular moral codes or panchayats were powerless to resolve. Merchant communities operated with small numbers, and the moral code and kinship networks that the members shared did not have much force or effect beyond their place of origin.[41] The moral code, therefore, was threatened all round. Individual entrepreneurship and private consumption became more assertive. The elders found their authority to rule being challenged more often. And above all, the very availability of courts and formal encoded commercial law on the margins encouraged disputants to bypass the community procedures.

[40] N.L. Hallward, *William Bolts. A Dutch Adventurer under John Company*, Cambridge: Cambridge University Press, 1920, pp. 10, 16.

[41] On this point, see P. Sudhir and P. Swarnalatha, 'Textile Traders and Territorial Imperatives: Masulipatnam, 1750–1850', *Indian Economic and Social History Review*, 29(2), 1992, pp. 145–69.

The Surat shroffs, who monopolized the bill discount business of eighteenth century western India, effectively consisted of a handful of firms. Yet, this market in credit instruments was not necessarily oligopolistic. In the view of one historian, they 'never acted as a unified group, no shroff organization ever came forth to impose a unified rate of discount, no single shroff or group of shroffs working in concert ever wielded sufficient power in order to force the Company to accept rates of discount less advantageous than those freely prevailing on the market'.[42] This was so because divisions along religion or caste prevailed over professional interests. This generalization may be too strong, for the potential to forge collaboration and agreement among shroffs in the regulation of discount rates was, in fact, often in evidence. But it would not be wrong to say that the professional interest and identity and communal identity were not always perfectly aligned. Indeed, it was this potential for a division that made it possible for the English to meddle in territorial politics rather easily in the eighteenth century world. In Surat again, that 'the shroffs could be played against each other was well known to the English'. In the eighteenth century Bengal, where merchants and financiers supporting a fiscally weak state played king-makers in alliance with the Company, the situation was not very different. While the overt or covert alliance between the individual European merchants and the European chartered companies helped the former, the weak professional identity of the Indian merchants made them only loose collections of communities and powerful individuals without strong potential for collective action.[43]

In part, the problem reflected the fact that Company trade was a stage in which commercial roles, and by implication codes, customs, and laws, were being recast. As the Indian Ocean trade expanded in scale, increasingly transactions occurred outside the realm of the traditional castes. On the south-eastern coast, for example, 'merchant

---

[42] Michelguglielmo Torri, 'Trapped inside the Colonial Order: The Hindu Bankers of Surat and Their Business World during the Second Half of the Eighteenth Century', *Modern Asian Studies*, 25(2), 1991, pp. 367–401.

[43] For a later period, Markovits writes: 'Indian merchants abroad tended to think of themselves as Chettiars, Memons, Khojas or Sindworkies rather than "Indian". This segmentation prevented the emergence of powerful Indian business lobbies'. Claude Markovits, 'Indian Merchant Networks Outside India in the Nineteenth and Twentieth Centuries: A Preliminary Survey', *Modern Asian Studies*, 33(4), 1999, pp. 883–911.

families and caste groups appeared and disappeared'.[44] A great deal of negotiating agency passed from the panchayat to the 'headman', a figure that had been around from before European trade, but who now straddled two worlds as a contractor in early modern commodity market transactions between Europeans and Indians.

Agency of this kind was many-layered, and included merchants, bankers, and master craftsmen. At one end were the Parsi or Gujarati brokers of Surat, and their counterparts, the Telugu 'chief' merchants in Dutch Pulicat or English Madras in the seventeenth and early eighteenth century, who were usually prominent representatives of already entrenched local commercial groups.[45] They worked as contractors of the chartered companies and therefore enjoyed positions of considerable economic and political power within the port city. Somewhat more amorphous were the *dubashes* of Madras, who worked as agents of both European businesses and households, had no particular background in commerce or manufacturing; they performed general rather than specialized commercial functions.[46] In Bengal, Om Prakash observes, intermediary merchants who entered contracts to supply textiles, 'were an extremely heterogenous group', including ship-owners such as Khem Chand Shah at one end and many marginal operators dependent on the custom of the Dutch company at another end.[47] Among the merchants who formed partnerships with European private merchants, were neo-rich citizens of Calcutta in the late eighteenth century. They did not emerge from traditional merchant communities. The Bengali partners of European agency houses in Calcutta in the early nineteenth century were drawn from both commercial castes and literate upper castes. The latter type did not represent a traditional commercial culture.[48] They joined in

[44] Sudhir and Swarnalatha, 'Textile Traders and Territorial Imperatives', p. 128

[45] Joseph A. Brennig, 'Chief Merchants and the European Enclaves of Seventeenth Century Coromandel', *Modern Asian Studies*, 11(3), 1977, pp. 321–40; Michelguglielmo Torri, 'Mughal Nobles, Indian Merchants and the Beginning of British Conquest in Western India: The Case of Surat 1756–1759', *Modern Asian Studies*, 32(2), 1998, pp. 257–315.

[46] Susan Neild-Basu, 'The Dubashes of Madras', *Modern Asian Studies*, 18(1), 1984, pp. 1–31.

[47] *European Commercial Enterprise in Pre-Colonial India*, Cambridge: Cambridge University Press, 1998, p. 168.

[48] Away from the zone of Indo-European trade, an important example of non-

commerce simply because the chance to do so presented itself. Indo-European trade, in short, had cracked the community wide open.

Community, far from resolving conflicts, at times became a weapon. In the seventeenth and eighteenth century Madras, competition for English trade worsened the already festering conflict between the Right-hand and the Left-hand castes.[49] In Surat, the competition among brokers took on the character of a long-standing quarrel between Parsi and Hindu merchant houses. Brokers who belonged in different communities used information supplied to the Company as a strategic device in competition between themselves.[50] In the early eighteenth century, the three sons of Rustum Manock, the leading Parsi house of Surat, had a dispute with the Bombay Council of the East India Company who accused them of overcharging on a previous transaction. The strained relation continued until, upon an appeal from one of them who travelled to London for the purpose, the Court of Directors set up a special tribunal that settled in favour of the brothers. The leading bania house of Surat in the 1730s and the broker of the Company, Jagannath Laldas was not so lucky. When a debt dispute arose between him and the Company, Laldas had to flee Surat and take refuge in the territory of the Peshwas. In part the dispute was engineered by his Parsi rivals the Rustumjis, who held the brokership briefly when the tables turned and Jagannath came back. Members of some merchant families on the south-eastern coast addressed competition by mutually agreeing to divide the market. Thus, one member contracted only with the English, another only with the French. In effect, the family resolved one problem to open up another.

---

traditional business was the Brahmans in western India, where protection and patronage of Brahman-dominated courts saw several *Chitpavan* families quickly rise to economic power and wealth. See V.D. Divekar, 'The Emergence of an Indigenous Business Class in Maharashtra in the Eighteenth Century', *Modern Asian Studies*, 16(3), 1982, pp. 427–43.

[49] Joseph J. Brennig, 'Chief Merchants and the European Enclaves of Seventeenth Century Coromandel', *Modern Asian Studies*, 11(3), 1977, pp. 321–40. For sources on this dispute, see J. Talboys Wheeler, *Madras in the Olden Time: Being a History of the Presidency from the First Foundation of Fort St. George. Compiled from Official Records*, vol. 2 (1702–1727), Madras: Higginbotham, 1861.

[50] Michelguglielmo Torri, 'Mughal Nobles, Indian Merchants and the Beginning of British Conquest in Western India: The Case of Surat 1756–1759', *Modern Asian Studies*, 32(2), 1998, pp. 257–315.

These strategies amounted to fragmenting the family into 'separate entrepreneurial units', the business family was 'breaking up'.[51]

How were these quarrels addressed? In the middle of the eighteenth century, urban merchant litigants dominated the proceedings of the new Mayors' courts established in the port cities under English jurisdiction. Histories of family firms in Bombay show how readily the merchants of the city resorted to Company courts for dispute resolution.[52] There was an association between diversity of business and preference for arbitration by the court rather than the panchayat. The largest of the Hindu and Parsi firms went to courts frequently. There was considerable cost to such moves. The courts exposed account books, which in these cases were inseparable from household accounts, to public scrutiny. Despite these costs, it would appear that city merchants had been waiting for an independent judiciary, especially one that gave the individual entrepreneur the option to bypass the trusteeship of the elders. There were two reasons for this preference. Some Indian litigants preferred the protection of private rights delivered by the English law. But another reason was that panchayat authority, real and symbolic, was in decline.

The rule of the panchayat was beginning to be challenged from the inside. Research on the Parsi panchayat in the nineteenth century confirms the centrality of this institution in regulating matters of property and succession, but also shows how the legitimacy of the institution came under threat from a variety of sources.[53] The dominance of the panchayat by a few leading families was resented in the late nineteenth century, especially when the number of neo-

---

[51] Sudhir and Swarnalatha, 'Textile Traders and Territorial Imperatives', p. 150

[52] Sheila Smith, 'Fortune and Failure: The Survival of Family Firms in Eighteenth Century India', in Geoffrey Jones and Mary B. Rose, eds, *Family Capitalism*, London: Routledge, 1993, pp. 44–65; and Subrahmanian, 'Merchants in Transit'. See also K. Mukund, *The View from Below: Indigenous Society, Temples and the Early Colonial State in Tamilnadu 1700–1835*, Hyderabad: Orient Longman, 2005; M.C. Setalvad, *The Common Law in India*, London: Steven and Sons, 1960, p. 17.

[53] Christine Dobbin, 'The Parsi Panchayat in Bombay City in the Nineteenth Century', *Modern Asian Studies*, 4(2), 1970, pp. 149–64. See also on the establishment of the panchayat, David L. White, 'Parsis in the Commercial World of Western India, 1700-1750', *Indian Economic and Social History Review*, 24(2), 1987, pp. 183–203.

rich contenders was on the increase.[54] 'Again it regained its power, and again it declined, chiefly owing to the injustice of having "one law for the rich and another for the poor"'.[55] Interestingly, one of the battles raging inside the Parsi panchayat in the nineteenth century concerned preventing 'members of the community diverting from strict Zoroastrian principles in the matter of matrimonial arrangement'.[56] The panchayat rules in this regard had been observed more in breach than in compliance, and some of the rich and younger members opposed the conversion of these codes into statutes.

The final point about instability is that the relationship between the individual members within communities and the community itself contained potential for change from within. The economic theory of caste discussed in Chapter 1 misses these chinks in the armour of custom. These potentials found new outlets in the nineteenth century, not only in the colonial court-room, but also by using a variety of other institutional means. Honour-based groups have a fundamental weakness in their structure. They are like contestable monopolies; in that they constantly encourage individuals to seek extra-communal ways of supporting enterprise. The new era of trade made such initiatives more successful.

THE RETREAT OF THE COMMUNITY,
THE RISE OF THE FAMILY

We should not assume that the relationship between the family, the individual, the firm on the one hand, and the community on the other

---

[54] A study on merchant charity in colonial Surat suggests that charity took on a political character under colonialism. Potentially such shifts would also weaken certain means of achieving cohesion. D. Haynes, 'From Tribute to Philanthropy: The Politics of Gift Giving in a Western Indian City', *Journal of Asian Studies*, 46(2), 1987, pp. 339–60. For a recent survey of the literature on community philanthropy in changing political order, see Jesse S. Palsetia, 'Merchant Charity and Public Identity Formation in Colonial India: The Case of Jamsetjee Jejeebhoy', *Journal of Asian and African Studies*, 40(3), 2005, pp. 197–217.

[55] Douglas M. Thornton, *Parsi, Jaina, and Sikh, or, Some Minor Religious Sects in India: The Maitland Prize Essay for 1897*, London: The Religious Tract Society, 1898., p. 37.

[56] Natesan, *Famous Parsis*, p. 86.

had ever been fixed. In fact, it was fluid and changeable, especially in the cities; so much so that one could even say that among the successful communities, there was a strong tendency for individual names to grow larger than communal identities. When a merchant firm or family became a large business enterprise and a name in its own right, it needed to break out of the boundaries of the immediate relations and recruit managers from talented and trusted agents from outside the family, in rare cases, outside the endogamous guild. Potential business rivals became more worthy partners in a risky enterprise than a novice from the family. Such moves became more possible in a big cosmopolitan port city of the nineteenth century. Furthermore, in Bombay and Calcutta, prominent individuals could earn reputation by participating in a variety of non-community institutions, for example, city administration, the legislature, or European business enterprises (some Parsi firms, for example, were the most reliable shareholders of the Great Indian Peninsular Railway through a difficult period); and by making benefaction in public institutions such as schools, colleges, hospitals, old-age homes, urban schemes, water-works, and libraries.

It would appear that the chances of such mobility varied between communities and forms of enterprise. In trading firms, for example, an assistant was often permitted to trade on own account and establish an individual name quickly. Banking firms rarely allowed such privileges to their junior partners and assistants. In the former case, individual mobility was more likely, and the identity of the firm was more dependent on individual initiative. One of the great Parsi entrepreneurs of the early nineteenth century, Jamsetjee Jejeebhoy, started career as an assistant in Parsi firms selling opium in China, while also trading on his own. When one of his former employers lost heavily, Jejeebhoy appointed him as a subordinate in the venture. When a merchant relation died, Jejeebhoy's own reputation was sufficiently established for him to take over the firm. Jejeebhoy also formed association with a prominent Gujarati Hindu and a Muslim merchant. Indeed, the history of Parsi business in Bombay perhaps illustrates in clear contours the earliest and most notable cases of fashioning inter-ethnic partnerships. The long-term success of some of the Parsi enterprises owes to this propensity that began quite early in the nineteenth century.

Figure 3.1: Anticlockwise from top, Surat merchant, Parsi merchant of Bombay, and Marwari merchants of Calcutta, c. 1860.
Source: Louis Rousselet, *India and its Native Princes*, London: Bickers and Sons, 1883

Within banking firms, the individual identity was rather more contingent. In this sphere of business, client relations were long-term and extended beyond one generation. Stability, and not innovation, was the key to their survival. The joint family, rather than individuals within it, therefore, became the point of reputation. And yet, the family itself did not have a fixed identity. For example, the great nineteenth century bankers of Mathura, Maniram-Lakhmichand, changed communal identity from being Gujarati Brahmin to Jain to being Hindu again, adapting to changing forms of religious charity, marriage alliances, and business partnerships.[57] Religious charity in this case served to announce each one of these moves.

It is necessary to remember that the individual was not necessarily a stable principle either in the new world, when community backing had been withdrawn, marginalized, or left behind. In Jamshetjee Jejeebhoy's case, the Parsi–Hindu–Muslim partnership, unorthodox for the early nineteenth century, faltered when it was suspected that one of the partners had traded too much on own account. A more famous case of business failure occurred in the second quarter of the nineteenth century in Calcutta, when a spate of bankruptcy nearly ended the Euro-Bengali joint ventures oriented to the indigo trade. While some of the prominent Bengali entrepreneurs did hail from traditional business families, this was one world of business where family ties had been used to the least extent. Unlike the Parsis on the western coast in the same time, few agents, partners, assistants in Euro-Bengali firms had gone through apprenticeships in businesses owned by relations; few had personal connections in businesses owned by other Bengalis; and while there was great one-upmanship amongst the Bengali neo-rich in matters of conspicuous consumption, there are almost no instances of institutionalizing mutual support, dispute settlement, and community sentiments. There never was a more atomized and more opportunistic world of business in the early nineteenth century India, and it is hardly surprising that it failed to weather the market risks in indigo export.

Bombay in the same time saw successful Euro-Parsi ventures; the Parsi partner being almost always already entrenched in a family

---

[57] F.S. Growse, *Mathura: A District Memoir* (third edition), Allahabad: Government Press, 1883, pp. 14–17.

Figure 3.2: Bankers of Delhi. Source: *Lippincott's Magazine of Popular Literature and Science*, 17(99), 1876

business of one's own. Dinshaw Manockjee Petit, for example, was an assistant and later partner to a European, whose firm had already long relied on Petit's father for brokerage services. The cotton famine in 1860s, which fed and then destroyed such enterprises in Bombay, forms a useful contrast with the parallel episode in 1840s Calcutta. In the former case, the end of a huge speculative bubble that destroyed a vastly larger sum of money than was lost in Calcutta did not end either Indian enterprise or the Euro-Indian ones, because of the presence of individuals (like Dinshaw Petit) who could deliver millions of rupees to refloat former partners and associates. Likewise, the contacts and reputation built by his father enabled another Parsi entrepreneur, Jamsetji Tata, to weather the storm and rebuild his lost fortune.

With such examples behind them, it is not surprising that the merchants and bankers of the late nineteenth century continued to use communal ties even as the scope for unorthodox choice of partners increased with new laws of company formation and with the onset of factory-based industrialization.

COLONIAL INDIA: HYBRID COLLECTIVES
From the second half of the nineteenth century, the commercial world began to change almost unrecognizably through the working

of three large new forces—commodity export, industrialization, and new laws. Lending money to the peasant expanded greatly, especially in new agrarian zones that exported grain and cotton to Europe. Industrialization required massive amounts of capital, which could not possibly come from the pockets of one's own friends and relations, forced upon communities the need to build unorthodox partnerships, and induced them to control formal financial institutions such as the stock market and banks. In the 1870s, legislation that addressed company formation, contracts, and negotiable instruments, placed formal sector enterprise on a more secure footing. Limited liability fostered joint-stock companies and banks that financed foreign trade and manufacturing. These latter raised capital in the London money market.

How did the old endogamous guild fare in this turmoil? It would be a truism to say that the community did not quickly disappear, but adapted to these three fields of change. So successfully indeed that the notion of a community formed of intermarrying families has remained the basic analytical tool for sociologists and anthropologists looking at business groups in the modern times.[58] Research on particular mercantile traditions not only reiterates the centrality of the 'family', but feels compelled to delve into family formation, family customs, hierarchies, and family laws, in explaining economic successes and failures.[59] Helen Lamb wrote, 'people emerge from

[58] D.W. Rudner, *Caste and Capitalism in Colonial India: The Nattukottai Chettiars*, Berkeley and Los Angeles: University of Callfornia Press, 1994; Shoji Ito 'A Note on the "Business Combine" in India', *The Developing Economies*, 4, 1966, pp. 367–80; Helen Lamb, 'The Emergence of an Indian Business Class', mimeo, 1953; Helen Lamb, 'The Indian Business Communities and the Evolution of an Industrialist Class', *Pacific Affairs*, 28, 1955, pp. 101–16; A.F. Brimmer, 'The Setting of Entrepreneurship in India', *Quarterly Journal of Economics*, 69, 1955, pp. 553–76; Markovits, 'Indian Merchant Networks Outside India'; Tirthankar Roy, 'Capitalism and Community: A Case-study of the Madurai Sourashtras', *Indian Economic and Social History Review*, 34(4), 1997, pp. 437–63; T.A. Timberg, 'Three Types of the Marwari Firm' in R.K. Ray, ed., *Entrepreneurship and Industry in India 1800–1947*, New Delhi: Oxford University Press., 1994, pp. 127–56.

[59] On the complex link between family and marriage customs, the family firm, and the trading community, see Brimmer, 'The Setting of Entrepreneurship'; Lamb, '*The Indian Business Communities*'; M.D. Morris, 'Modern Business Organisation and Labour Administration: Specific Adaptations to Indian Conditions of Risk and Uncertainty, 1850-1947', *Economic and Political Weekly*, 14(40), 1979, pp.

traditional business activities into modern business as members of a group.'[60] And Andrew Brimmer explained why this was so—'... there existed between the family-firm and the trading community of which it was a member an informal relationship symbolized by a strong sense of responsibility for the well-being of one's community fellows and an overt preferences for dealing with them.'[61] One historian calls the smooth convergence of family goals and business strategies 'personal capitalism.'[62] Field-studies of business organizations in the small market towns of twentieth century northern India point at '...the essentially familial organization of business ventures, and the trader's fear of larger commercial organizations because of distrust of nonfamily members'.[63] Collectively, these studies show the principal ways that kinship could secure cooperation and compliance in the new world of business. Community reduced risks and fostered trust.[64] The promise of a good marriage was the incentive and expulsion from the affinal group was the threat that ensured trustworthy behaviour among individuals dealing in goods or services. Community enabled sharing of quasi-public goods, such as credit, business contact with mobile groups, responsibility for individual liability, and apprenticeship. Masters of artisan trades or principals of merchant firms recruited students from the family or recruited promising students into the family by marrying them to daughters. Community also meant exposure to entrepreneurial culture.[65]

1680–7; H. Papanek, 'Pakistan's New Industrialists and Businessmen: Focus on the Memons', in Milton Singer, ed., *Entrepreneurship and Modernization of Occupational Cultures in South Asia*, Durham: Duke University Press, 1973, pp. 61–106.

[60] Lamb predicted that the same 'people' would tend to shed that 'communalism' in the course of associating with other groups via modern industry and banking, Lamb, 'The Emergence', p. 1.

[61] Brimmer, 'The Setting of Entrepreneurship', p. 557.

[62] Sheila Smith, 'Fortune and Failure: The Survival of Family Firms in Eighteenth Century India'.

[63] Richard G. Fox, 'Family, Caste, and Commerce in a North Indian Market Town', *Economic Development and Cultural Change*, 15(3), 1967, pp. 297–314.

[64] See Timberg, 'Three Types of the Marwari Firm'; Mattison Mines, *Muslim Merchants*, New Delhi: Shri Ram Centre for Industrial Relations and Human Resources, 1972; V. Krishnan, *Indigenous Banking in South India*, Bombay: Bombay State Cooperative Union, 1959, for discussions of these functions in a variety of contexts.

[65] Ashis Nandy, 'Entrepreneurial Cultures and Entrepreneurial Men', *Economic*

For the economic historian, however, the picture of an undifferentiated dominant community might seem too simplistic. What we see can best be described as the unfolding of diverse trajectories. Common to these various experiences was a tendency to straddle both the formal and the informal sector, take advantage of both social ties and relations of regard and respect, on the one hand, as well as laws that protected formal contracts, and a public sphere that gave chambers of commerce a powerful voice, on the other. There was stronger desire to build personal fortune, preserve it for one's own descendants, be more assertive in consumption, and yet give a little back to the community as charity. But the differences between groups were significant. A few key examples will illustrate these differences.

In one case of rural banking, we see the informal-communal element dominate. Natukottai Chettiars of Tamil Nadu were initially rural lenders, and found their options limited by strong land laws that worked against smooth transfer of assets. In the early twentieth century, they moved outside India. Lower Burma became part of the British Empire in 1852. At that time the economic potentials of the Irrawaddy delta were largely unutilized. A modified *ryotwari* system enabled land-holdings to be mortgaged. Between 1852 and 1900, cultivated acreage expanded, and rice exports grew from less than two hundred thousand to more than two million tons. Although in the early stages of the expansion local finance played a major role, after the 1880s, capital came from migrant financiers. Between 1880 and 1930, Chettiar firms with their headquarters located in a cluster of towns in south India, met an increasing part of credit demand of Burmese peasants.[66] This ascendancy has been explained in terms of

---

and Political Weekly, 8(47), 1973, pp. M98–M106; A.K. Bagchi, 'European and Indian Entrepreneurship in India 1900-30' in Ray, ed., *Entrepreneurship and Industry*; Omkar Goswami, 'Then Came the Marwaris: Some Aspects of the Changes in the Pattern of Industrial Control in Eastern India', *Indian Economic and Social History Review*, 22(3), 1985, pp. 225–49.

[66] Michael Adas, 'Immigrant Asians and the Economic Impact of European Imperialism: The Role of the South Indian Chettiars in British Burma', *Journal of Asian Studies*, 33, (1974), pp. 385–401; Raman Mahadevan, 'Immigrant Entrepreneurs in Colonial Burma—An Exploratory Study of the Role of Nattukottai Chettiars of Tamil Nadu 1880-1930', *Indian Economic and Social History Review*, 15(3), 1978, pp. 329–58. This article explores in detail the problems that agrarian finance in Burma faced after the end of the rice export boom.

the Chettiars' superior business organization, in particular, to long apprenticeship, training in business ethics and techniques (such as a special accounting system), group solidarity, inter-firm lending, and informal sanctions to minimize default within the group. Furthermore, by the very definition of a 'community', the Indian merchant communities combined business partnerships with marriage alliances. Chettiars too were an endogamous group. Consequently, along with shared financial stakes, they also shared much common emotional resource.[67]

In Calcutta and Bombay, the nineteenth century split the institutional picture into two halves. The informal world engaged in commodity trade, produced and traded in handicrafts, used boats and carts for transportation, and mainly used indigenous bankers for remittance and capital. A formal world owned mills-mines-plantations, was more global in commercial links, had easier access to ports and railways, joint-stock banks, and the formal capital market. These new businesses emerged first in the port cities, where indigo, opium, cotton, and rice export trades needed financiers, insurance agents, shipping firms, and money-changers. Leading industrial entrepreneurs moved between these spheres. They employed community ties to secure business in both spheres. The Marwari jute mill owners of Calcutta, for example, began as raw jute traders, and moved with equal facility in both trade and manufacture thanks to tacit cooperation amongst a group of leading Marwari families of Calcutta.[68] The vast network of trade that they depended upon had many participants, but loyalty and information within this network usually followed the ethnicity of the mill-owner. Indigenous banking firms also remained dependent on the family and community, while also transacting with the modern banks.

Who were the Marwaris? Throughout the eighteenth and the nineteenth century, a loosely constituted group of commercial people

---

[67] See Rudner, *Caste and Capitalism.*

[68] The history of prominent Marwari houses such as Birla, Badridas Goenka, Bansidhar Jalan, H.P. Poddar, Ramkrishna Dalmia, Babulal Rajgarhia and others suggest that their main interests around 1900 were in jute baling, mining, zamindari, and import agency. Some of them became industrial from the interwar period.

had steadily dispersed from their original home in south-western Rajasthan and resettled themselves in new business towns as money-lenders and revenue-farmers. From that base they began to enter trade. The prominent families of the city who shared such an origin had migrated to Calcutta during the last quarter of the nineteenth century. They neither were nor became one homogeneous endogamous guild. Professional and class divisions always kept them socially divided. The very term Marwari reflected the local Bengalis' perception of a people who seemed to them vaguely alike. And yet, as this diverse group urbanized and prospered, the attempt to consolidate a distinctive Marwari identity, if not one society, grew stronger too. A shared language, after all, was a great leveller. And deliberately or otherwise, linguistic and business identity was used as a guild resource to conduct insider trading in banks, trades, stock markets, and industries.

In both cities, the continued reliance on social ties explains one feature of Indian industrialization, the dominance of conglomerates, or business empires controlled by families almost all of whom had originated in old-style commerce and banking. Concentration and family empires is a familiar feature to historians of pre-war Japanese industrialization, and can be explained by a simple rule. Capital, which is available from diffused sources, chases reputation, which is scarcer. In the initial stages of industrialization, reputation could not be gauged by actual performance of an enterprise. Hence, reputation attached to proxies, such as clan or family, leading to concentration. In the nineteenth century India, reputation rested upon community for the reason that capital for industry came from members of the same community. Parsis were the biggest backers of pioneering Parsi firms in the 1830s or 1840s. One family business would be funded by a handful of other family businesses because the latter trusted the judgment of the former.

In both Calcutta and Bombay, while enterprise remained firmly in the hands of families and clusters of families, financing of enterprise began to reach out to other groups, and to the public at large. About the time of the cotton price boom in Bombay (early 1860s), the club of entrepreneurs-cum-financiers was still small and still dominated by members of mercantile communities, but ethnically more diverse. A Parsi business in this time could expect to be funded by a motley group of capitalists, including Gujarati, Bohra, Marwari, and European ones. The situation changed again with the development of a capital market, when public money began to finance industrialization. The ability to use public money was greatly facilitated by new laws of limited liability. Until 1850, partnership was the general form of ownership-cum-management. Limited liability was formally recognized in the first Companies Act of 1850, and its coverage became comprehensive in the 1860s.

Public financing and limited liability introduced a new dynamic in company formation. The brand name was still concentrated. But public capital did not necessarily chase a club. It chased individual family names. In 1950, the householder with money to spare for the stock market did not look for the Parsi origin of an enterprise, but would go for the name of Godrej or Tata. The family took precedence over community in the minds of the investor, which further weakened the cohesion within the industrializing groups. The elevation of religious codes into law slightly tilted the balance in favour of the joint family and against either the individual or the community, in respect of security of property rights.

Communities and families in this way could shape a hybrid world of their own composed of the informality of the bazaar and formality of modern business and modern law. The choice worked successfully sometimes, and failed sometimes. The costs of such hybrid collectives can be illustrated with two examples—the managing agency contract of the nineteenth century, and the bazaar's unhappy forays into joint-stock banking in the early twentieth century.

COSTS OF COLLECTIVES: MANAGING AGENCY AND PRIVATE BANKING

Should companies be managed by professional managers or community members? In the nineteenth century, there were not many trained managers available, so companies needed to be managed by members of the community. But, then, few members of a community of merchants and bankers understood, or had the time to learn, the intricacies of an industrial venture. They were perhaps willing to subscribe the share capital if one of their trusted brethren came up with a new idea, but they were not willing to take part in gathering the labour, training them, arranging to import the machines and foremen, and a host of other tasks involved with setting up a cotton spinning factory in Bombay. The solution was a simple one. Draw up a management contract that delivers management (for a fee) to one of the co-owners who first had the new idea. The contract drew a line between the community and the manager, and offered the manager an extra incentive to manage the firm while also earning a part of the income from return on equity. The limited liability format drew a line between the entrepreneur and the financiers.

In a scenario where there was so much asymmetry of information between the manager and the owners, merely the existence of a contract would not necessarily save the enterprise from being a victim of adverse or careless dealing by the manager. What did save it from abuses was the fact that socially speaking the owners formed the same club. The manager was a manager by virtue of the contract, but the manager was also a merchant, a banker, and a Parsi or Gujarati bania well-known to other members of the guild. The system could work because the owners had informal means to keep a close watch upon the affairs of that company. They could do so because both the manager-entrepreneur and the financiers formed a club. Their common origin ensured that capital would come forth into the new venture, while the contract created a legal space where financiers would not unnecessarily interfere with the management of the firm.

With such an origin, managing agency contract evolved into something different in the nineteenth century. When limited liability became popular, small investors bought shares of a new company. Reputation for enterprise increasingly fixed on families rather than communities. The substantial body of owners now had no personal or direct control over the managing agent, nor could they be well-informed about what might go on inside the company. The club was dissolved. The managing agent now began to change its identity.

From a member of the guild, the managing agent became a firm in its own right. As a firm, it symbolized reputation for good management, so that a new venture created by it could attract public subscription. As a private family firm whose shares were closely held and not traded, it became a holding company with more secure right to manage the industries with which it had an agency contract. The managing agent was now the nerve centre of the business empire controlled by a family.[69] It continued to save on two types of scarce resources—capital and managerial talent. Indian firms faced perennial difficulty meeting their fixed and working capital requirements out of paid-up share capital, and had to rely heavily on loans and public deposits. A large part of these loans the owners or the managing agent firms themselves supplied, but substantial percentages came from banks and the public. Loans require a guarantor, and deposits require the borrower to be a trusted and reputed name. The managing agents served these functions. Given limited information about the capacity of individual managers of individual companies, reputation concentrated in firms that represented the goodwill of a family.

Formally, therefore, the managing agency shed its social mooring and became a legal corporation. That very fact exposed the weakness of the contract system. The contract could be manipulated to enrich the agents. The agents could speculate in the trade, say, of raw jute to the detriment of the company manufacturing jute goods. The anonymous owners of a firm now had no credible means with which to punish a poor manager, because they no longer belonged in the same club. The absence of a credible informal or formal punishment system enabled mismanagement and fraud. When such a thing happened and a company went bankrupt, shareholders could rarely recover their money or change the laws. For good well-managed family businesses, on the other hand, the system became redundant in the mid-twentieth century, as the holding company performed the controlling functions of a managing agent, and the Board of Directors assisted by professional managers, now more easily available than before, performed the management function. The reputation functions were still critical in the small stock market and few banks, but it had shifted from managing agency firms to their thinly veiled real patrons, families, and conglomerates.

In the nineteenth century, the world of indigenous banking had continued on much the same footing as before. It thrived from financing export-import trade, remittances, and investment in

---

[69] I have been influenced by Dwijendra Tripathi's original interpretation of the managing agency system in western India, see *The Oxford History of Indian Business*, New Delhi: Oxford University Press, 2004.

government securities and private equity. But as the need for capital expanded with industrialization, community financial resources fell short, and public money became necessary. The stock market was still a fledgling institution. Formal banking consisted of government-sponsored Presidency banks, whose main clients were businesses connected with European enterprise and that small segment of Indian enterprise which the Europeans understood or could easily communicate with. The biggest bazaar bankers commanded liquidity with them, but the Presidency banks were not easily persuaded to lend money to small or medium-scale Indian business. Increasingly in the nineteenth century, business communities began to establish banks.

The bazaar's foray into modern banking was not a very happy one, however. The history of the Indian joint stock banks until the start of the Reserve Bank of India is a history punctuated by booms, crashes, and panics. The first boom occurred in Calcutta in the early nineteenth century. The 1830s and the 1840s crashes finished off the pioneers, including the famous Union Bank of India floated by the most successful Bengali entrepreneur of the time, Dwarkanath Tagore. The second boom occurred in Bombay in the 1860s, encouraged by cotton speculation and the formal recognition of limited liability. Again, the banks then started went later into liquidation. A third boom occurred with the spread of the spirit of *swadeshi* (or nationalistic self-reliance) from 1906. The centre of this movement was Calcutta, but Indian banks elsewhere also profited from the nationalistic wave. In 1913–14, a few major bankruptcies led to a widespread crash of these banks. These banks tended to fail partly because of a neglect of basic principles, such as adequate capitalization, partly from the absence of a lender-of-last-resort, but mainly from an excess of insider lending and fraud. Many firms used public deposit to lend to community enterprises, which entailed moral hazard problems. When a community member lent money to another member on personal security, the former could use ex-communication as a threat to enforce contract. When the manager of a bank used public money to lend to dubious ventures, monitoring was lax, and therefore, chances of bad loans relatively high.

These two cases—managing agency and banking—share a lesson. In a world rent in two halves, managing agents and Indian private banks stood in between the formality of law and the informality of the community. The hybrid character of their world perhaps presented entrepreneurs with more flexibility than possible in either a purely community-bound or a purely law-bound business world. But such a world also weakened both formal and informal checks upon predatory and irresponsible behaviour. Managing agents, on occasions, betrayed their principals by engaging in private trade. Community-bound banks were encouraged into insider trading. Endogenous collectivization carried social costs.

Social costs were also large when ethnic combines came in conflict and competition, as the final case study would show.

'BUSINESS CULTURE': EUROPEAN AND INDIAN BUSINESS IN COLONIAL INDIA

In regions of India, and principally in Calcutta city, European firms dominated the factory industry until the interwar period. By and large, these firms were engaged in making goods (tea, jute) that relied on exports, on financing themselves from London money market, and did not compete with British exports to the rest of the world. It was advantageous for them to belong in the trading world that centred itself in London.[70] Calcutta was also the home of the Marwaris. Around 1920, a number of Marwari families had established themselves as suppliers of raw materials to the European firms, as insiders in the stock market, and as owners of banks. Using these advantages some of these firms started jute manufacturing, and on a smaller scale, sugar, paper, cement, construction, and share-broking.

Business historians find the co-existence of foreign and Indian capital a phenomenon of great interest, and have seen their relationship and contrasting business styles, long-term success and failure, in terms of 'culture' and community. India was not exceptional in receiving foreign investment in the late nineteenth century. Many colonies did, in mines, plantations, and railways principally. However, India

---

[70] The large British managing agents in Calcutta were—Andrew Yule (jute, tea, coal, paper, engineering), Bird and F.W. Heilgers (jute, coal, engineering, limestone), McLeod-Begg-Dunlop (jute, tea, railways), Jardine-Skinner and George Henderson (jute, tea, engineering), Octavius Steel (tea, electricity), Shaw Wallace (tea, coal), Gillanders-Arbuthnot (jute, tea, coal), Macneill-Barry (jute, coal, electricity), Martin-Burn (coal, wagon, dockyard, cement), Balmer-Lawrie (coal, paper, engineering), and Kilburn (tea, coal, engineering). Smaller groups included Kettlewell-Bullen, McKinnon-Mckenzie, Thomas Duff (all three in jute), Williamson-Magor and Duncan Brothers (both mainly in tea).

was exceptional in the extent of factory-based industrialization; and India was exceptional in having a strong body of *indigenous* capitalists alongside the foreigners. Both groups controlled segments of long-distance trade and industry. The co-existence was not a static one, and after the Great Depression, the dominance of foreign capital was quickly on the decline and Indian capital was in ascendance. If culture matters at all, it cannot matter in a Weberian sense of relative weakness of Asian business in comparison with the Western European. The equation was neither one-sided, nor static, nor in a dynamic sense, Weberian. How does culture count, then?

There are three specific cultural questions historians ask about the phenomenon of co-existence and its end. Why did Indian and European capital operate in different segments? Why did European capital dominate Calcutta so long? Why did they lose that position after 1929?

Morris D. Morris proposes what we might call the two-fields thesis.[71] The Europeans and Indians specialized in distinct operations, driven by their comparative advantage. Indeed, ethnicity and factor markets were interrelated. Each group could access a distinct kind of capital market, product market, and raw material market better than the other in the initial stages of development of factory industry. Europeans raised money from London; their shares were purchased by other Europeans. These shareholders included former expatriate workers in India. Indians raised money from family and community resources. Europeans sold goods in export markets, through a transportation and communication network centred in London. Indians sold goods in India and China. Europeans relied on indigenous agents for procurement of raw material. Indian industrialists had been raw material traders themselves, in cotton as well as jute. 'Culture' in this case, would point at spheres of specialist knowledge.

A. K. Bagchi addresses the second problem of dominance. 'Culture' in this case explicitly refers to guild-like exclusive clubs. Bagchi suggests that colonial Calcutta created a platform for socialized communication to develop between three powerful groups—the political elite (Calcutta was India's capital), the British managing agents, and the government-

---

[71] 'South Asian Entrepreneurship and the Rashomon Effect, 1800–1947', *Explorations in Economic History*, 16(4), 1979, pp. 341–61.

backed Bank of Bengal. The European economic interests formed an informal cartel. Unlike colonial Bombay, in Calcutta, wealth and ethnicity were both defining features of the informal guild that was the outcome of these communication networks.[72] There were two fields no doubt, and the fields were separated not only by comparative advantage in information, but also by exclusive and ethnic clubs.

B.R. Tomlinson's work on corporate capital in the last days of the raj points at a broad-based shift in comparative advantages in the post-Depression years.[73] Collapse of the world market during the Depression, rise of nationalism, development of formal and informal institutions within India, and the growth of a home market under tariff protection from the late-1920s, led to a change in nearly all the parameters that had once secured the two fields of advantage and kept them separate. According to the two-fields thesis, Europeans and Indians had their own instruments of success. For the Europeans, these were access to the London markets in goods, money, and machines, proximity to local political elites, and cooperation amongst Europeans. For the Indians, the means had been control over domestic commodity markets, the domestic stock market, community resources, and participation in nationalist politics. From the 1920s, the economic and political environment ensured that the sphere of business, where the latter set of instruments had an advantage would enlarge, and the sphere within which the former set could score shrink.

Inevitably, as their relative sizes changed, the two spheres ceased to remain discrete and came in direct conflict. The conflict again had something to do with 'culture', although it eventually destroyed the old divide between cultures. Businesses throughout the world tried to cope with depressed demand by means of voluntary supply restrictions. Such moves worked in principle when the members of a cartel have identical interests, all incumbent and potential firms are members of the cartel, the number of members is small enough for there being credible

[72] *The Evolution of the State Bank of India, Volume 2: The Era of the Presidency Banks, 1876–1920*, London and New Delhi: Sage Publications, 1997. Especially the 'Introduction', pp. 1–69; and Amiya Kumar Bagchi, 'European and Indian Entrepreneurship in India 1900–30' in R.K. Ray, ed., *Entrepreneurship and Industry in India 1800–1947*, Delhi: Oxford University Press, pp. 157–96.

[73] 'Colonial Firms and the Decline of Colonialism in Eastern India 1914–47', *Modern Asian Studies*, 15(3), 1981, pp. 455–86.

enforcement systems, and when expulsion from the cartel might hurt anyone who does not play by the rules. Such moves tend to fail when the club is too large, too diverse, and excludes some participants. Confirming the famous prediction of Mancur Olson that large and diverse coalitions entail free riding risks, agreements could simply break down.[74] Cartels that form out of ethnic ties carry an additional risk. By definition, they exclude or fail to secure the cooperation of other ethnic clubs. One ethnic cartel, then, has every interest to prey upon the restrictionist moves of another ethnic cartel. This is what happened in Calcutta in the 1930s. The major European firms in jute and tea tried to shore up their prices by imposing supply restrictions using club ties. All that such moves did was invite the small Indian planters, commodity traders, and mill-owners, to expand and start factories. The Europeans' moves to seek government intervention in regulating the industries largely failed, while polarizing sympathies further.[75]

Despite these dissentions within the business world of Calcutta, a large number of British managing agencies survived the Depression, the war, independence of India, and continued to be profitable in the 1950s. Curiously, few diversified their businesses away from jute, tea, and coal, and took part in the new world of opportunities then opening up. A.M. Misra asks why the business opportunity offered by a protected import-substituting regime after 1947 was exploited almost entirely by Indian groups rather than the British managing agency firms, some of whom had been better-placed than the former in the heavy and capital goods industries that were being promoted by the new regime.[76] Her answer is that the 'broadly nationalistic attitude' of some of the leading houses of India made them more open to risk-taking on a grander scale. 'Culture' in this case means a quasi-political ideology, which accounted for risk-taking.

It is necessary to draw in these varied notions of culture into one integrated story. Surely, conservatism of the colonial European firms weakened them. But what killed them was also a decisive change in

---

[74] *The Logic of Collective Action: Public Goods and the Theory of Groups*, New Haven: Yale University Press, 1971.

[75] S.R. Sen, *Restrictionism during the Great Depression in Indian Tea Jute and Sugar Industries*, Calcutta: Firma KLM, 1997.

[76] '"Business Culture" and Entrepreneurship in British India 1860-1950', *Modern Asian Studies*, 34(2), 2000, pp. 333–48

the balance between the two fields, and the intrinsic impossibility of ethnic cartels to achieve anything. By 1950, the Indian groups were firmly in possession of means to control, raid, and loot the European firms through stock-market takeovers and buyouts, with overt or covert political help. One personality in Calcutta's long schizophrenic business culture had overwhelmed the other by 1960.

CONCLUSIONS: CASTE OR GUILD?

Returning to a theme the chapter began with, I have traced the history of a kind of merchant collective that do not quite fit the word 'guild', even though that word has been used in this context. If the defining features of a 'guild' are the existence of statutes applicable to the members and the presence of a royal charter upholding the right of the association to frame its own statutes, then Indian merchant groups were not guilds in the strict sense of the term. And yet, the difference did not matter until the eighteenth century. Birth and marriage could secure the same purposes that guilds served—compliance, negotiations, and property rights—just as well as a formal guild could, and the rulers respected the autonomy of the community.

The community became unstable from the eighteenth century due to the cleavages and contradictions between individual interest and the interest of the community, and inadequate monitoring of individuals who inhabited both the formal and the informal worlds of business. We can roughly date the former in 1750–1850, and the latter in 1850–1950. The former contradiction reflected new entrepreneurial opportunities opened by trade and industrialization. The moral basis of community organization came under strain from conflicts between the old and the new rich. The availability of redress under English laws brought intra-community and intra-family disputes out into the open.

In the nineteenth century, the growth of a formal world of corporations, governed by new laws, gave community-bound entrepreneurs an institutional choice, to stay informal or to become formal. The leading industrialists in the nineteenth century chose to do both, even as the two worlds were growing steadily further apart. Even as their businesses were funded by public money, leading business families could keep parts of their dealings hidden from the public by taking recourse to the bazaar or social networks. This flexibility became a source of wrongful, and yet not necessarily illegal, deals that community members in Calcutta and Bombay struck with each other and with others for a long time to come.

Merchant communities supplied the clearest illustration of the endogamous guild. Modes of association among artisans did not develop in an exact parallel, despite similarities, as we see in the next study.

4 Artisans
Guild for training

Organizationally speaking, the world of the craftsmen was quite variable in pre-colonial India. Not all artisans functioned from within well-defined communities. Most rural craftsmen did not. Artisans needing large-scale operation, such as iron-smelting, usually worked in groups, but these groups supplied only crude labour collectively and not the regulatory services associated with guilds. The situation was different among the skilled urban artisans. Here, guilds were common. Technical knowledge and expertise, apprenticeship, knowledge of markets and clientele, and usually also a sense of distinctness from the local society, were shared among people who saw themselves as a homogeneous social unit. Members of different communities transacted in goods, but individual artisans rarely recruited business partners or apprentices from outside the community. The precise constitution of the social club was variable, and this chapter will identify a major difference between northern and southern India in the constitution of these communities. Taking South Asia as a whole, we observe a variety of associational models at work—endogamous guild, 'brotherhood', and professional guild.

Some of these forms were nineteenth century innovations. New commercial imperatives led to diversity in the nature of the collective, made all old clubs adapt in own fashion to serving long-distance trade, led to decline in some of them as outsiders infiltrated new contracts, and altered craft clubs into caste associations.

THE SEVENTEENTH CENTURY
Scholarship on industry in the seventeenth century suggests a separation between the agrarian subsistence economy and the towns where the political elite and the great temples were located. The rural

world of manufacturing in north India, for example, rarely supplied goods to the rich urban consumers.[1] There was little social and intellectual intercourse between the rural and the urban artisans. The organizational side of rural craft production in pre-colonial India remains largely unknown.

Illustrations of formal or informal collectives usually come from the towns. The urban artisan was organized, and the nature of the organization was partly shaped by the clientele they served. Whereas the rural artisan apparently worked with family labour, urban artisans worked within collective bodies such as communities or master-apprentice teams where the respective positions of the masters and the apprentices were clearly defined. It would appear that the master artisan was much more than a skilled individual; the master was also the channel of negotiation and contract, if contract is the right word, between the elite consumers and the artisan communities. The master was a 'craftsman-contractor', to borrow an expression from Vijaya Ramaswamy.[2] Furthermore, the exclusive privileges of the community and that of the master within it were maintained by the state or the temple that frequently hired their services.

Our knowledge about urban crafts in Mughal India derives from accounts of European travellers like François Bernier or Francisco Pelsaert, and that of the court functionary, Abul Fazl. Fazl mentions the presence of 'guilds of artificers', and guild masters, in whose appointment the town administrator had a say. The picture of work organization that we receive from these accounts suggests that these guilds worked as adjuncts to another powerful institution, the *karkhana*. Karkhana today means factories. In this context, the term did not necessarily mean factories, but included factories along with stores and some administrative departments. The main north Indian seats of power developed a hierarchy of karkhanas owned by courtiers and individuals close to the court, though much more is known

[1] Irfan Habib, 'Potentialities of Capitalistic Development in the Economy of Mughal India', *Journal of Economic History*, 29, 1969, pp. 32–78; K.N. Chaudhuri, 'Some Reflections on the Town and Country in Mughal India', *Modern Asian Studies*, 12, 1978, pp. 77–96.

[2] 'Vishwakarma Craftsmen in Early Medieval Peninsular India', *Journal of the Economic and Social History of the Orient*, 47, 2004, pp. 548–82'.

about the imperial karkhanas.[3] Two features of this institution are noteworthy. First, by means of karkhanas urban north India became culturally at home with the idea of collective work. Karkhana supplied the context in which master-apprenticeship relations crystallized into an institution.

Second, while the karkhanas did not necessarily rule out private production for the bazaar, they did represent a subversion of the market. The extent of subversion varied. It was, however, important enough to find mention in all major studies on the karkhanas. The subversion happened in three ways. There was implicit or explicit control of the courts on purchase of inputs. The output was rarely marketed but retained for consumption, gifts, even provincial revenue-payments, and exports. And the karkhanas recruited the best workers. Buyers of craft goods, a few hundred powerful families that commanded a large part of the net tax resources, did not represent a 'market' worth the name. Whole industries functioned in a relationship of *dependence* on public authority. The courts did not depend on them. They were not a source of tax-revenue for the courts as their European counterparts were. They were employees or quasi-employees of the court.[4] Markets, of course, existed in urban north India both for local consumers and for long-distance trade in fine craft goods. However, the frequent joining of political power and purchasing power shaped forms of transactions, turning these into quasi-political rather than economic markets.

For example, an urban artisan hierarchy took shape as a result of such transactions. Bernier distinguished between two types of urban artisan. At one extreme was the bazaar artisan who was nominally independent, that is, not an employee of the rich and powerful, and yet a perpetually poor man, lowly skilled, and subject to extortion by merchants or agents of the rich. At the other end was the elite among the artisans, the super skilled artist, who was an employee of the karkhana. Thus, '[t]he artists ... who arrive at ... eminence in their art are those

---

[3] Tripta Verma, *Karkhanas under the Mughals*, New Delhi: Pragati Publications, 1994.

[4] In this sense, Indian skilled craft tradition can be seen to belong primarily in what Hicks has called the Revenue Economy, rather than a commercial economy, even though markets formally existed in both, J.R. Hicks, *A Theory of Economic History*, Oxford: Clarendon Press, 1969, pp. 22–4.

only who are in the service of the King or of some powerful Omrah, and who work exclusively for their patron.'[5] As for the rank and file, 'virtually every relevant feature of the economy, society and the state was designed to hold the artisan firmly down to his lowly place ...'.[6]

Neither guild nor caste was needed for market regulation in a production context such as this. The master's power reflected that of the patron. Since there was no effective market, the guild did not have any commercial interest to serve or protect. For the same reason, nor was there much entrepreneurial resource to protect. And yet, precisely because the crafts in demand were particularly intensive in craftsmanship, training was a vitally important issue. So was regulation of competition in the labour market. The guild, such as there were in urban north India, was either a body that maintained the hierarchy of craftsmen, or a quasi-administrative body engaged in facilitating transactions conducted by the courtiers.

Material on southern India and the Deccan suggest again the presence of strong artisan collective bodies. But in south India, these bodies represented castes and lineages, that is, endogamous guilds formed of a cluster of intermarrying families. From before the time of this study, three professional groups—weavers, blacksmiths, and the Vellala peasant clans—experienced a rise in their social and ritual status relative to other working people.[7] Notably, the weavers supplied expensive textiles to the courts, the temples, and organized merchant groups; the smiths made guns; and the peasant lineages were the backbone of the fiscal system. The weavers were organized in strong collective bodies, which one historian of Vijayanagar termed 'caste-guild'. The guilds did not fight professional battles. They fought caste battles. They were platforms for collective bargaining and bargained and battled for privileges that would accrue to a cluster of families. The separation between rural and urban artisans was maintained by social legislation that prohibited intermarriage, and thus prevented the rural

[5] F. Bernier, *Travels in the Mogul Empire A.D. 1656–1668*, London: Humphrey Milford, 1916, p. 256, emphasis added; see also pp. 228–9 on patronage.

[6] T. Raychaudhuri, 'Non-agricultural Production', in T. Raychaudhuri and Irfan Habib, eds., *The Cambridge Economic History of India*, 2 vols., Cambridge: Cambridge University Press, 1983, vol. I, p. 214.

[7] Vijaya Ramaswamy, 'Artisans in Vijayanagar Society', *Indian Economic and Social History Review*, 22(4), 1985, pp. 417–44.

artisans from encroaching on the preserves of the urban artisans.[8] The presence of a deep hierarchy separating the rural carpenter serving the peasant from the urban carpenter serving the temples has been noted for medieval south India.[9]

The situation outside the two great empires remain obscure. Important historical studies on merchants and artisans in medieval south India do mention the term 'guild', but supply rather little information on the internal structure of these collectives, so that their similarity or otherwise with respect to European guilds remain open to interpretation.[10] Nandita Sahai, who has studied artisan groups in eighteenth century Jodhpur, seems justified in cautioning against the use of the word 'guild' in the context of Indian artisan collectives, a point raised also by M.N. Pearson in his review of Meera Abraham's work.[11] Historians have noted the general scarcity of trade associations in the Deccan, with the significant and noticeable exception of Ahmedabad. When in 1675 the British in Bombay tried to revive goldsmiths and silversmiths' guild in a bid to prevent debasement of metals, the attempt had to follow British statutes and conventions rather than any existing Indian custom.[12]

One of the important functions of the artisan collective in pre-colonial India was to organize industrial training. Transmission of skills followed master-apprenticeship in the north Indian urban crafts. But a more universal system was hereditary transmission of skills. The two modes of transmission became indistinct when apprentices were

[8] Ramaswamy, 'Vishwakarma Craftsmen'.

[9] Ibid.

[10] See especially Meera Abraham, *Two Medieval Merchant Guilds of South India*, New Delhi: Manohar Publications, 1988, and also Vijaya Ramaswamy 'The Genesis and Historical Role of the Master Weavers in South Indian Textile Production', *Journal of the Economic and Social History of the Orient*, 28, 1985, pp. 294–325; and 'Vishwakarma Craftsmen'.

[11] N. Sahai, 'Crafts in Eighteenth Century Jodhpur: Questions of Class, Caste and Community Identities', *Journal of the Economic and Social History of the Orient*, 48, 2005, pp. 524–51; M.N. Pearson, 'Review of *Two Medieval Merchant Guilds of South India* by Meera Abraham', *Journal of Asian Studies*, 49, 1990, pp. 953–4.

[12] H. Fukazawa, 'Non-Agricultural Production: Maharashtra and Deccan', in Raychaudhuri and Habib, eds., *Cambridge Economic History of India*, vol. 1, 1983, pp. 311–12; this remains the only significant reference to 'guild' in the *Cambridge Economic History of India*, the benchmark study on medieval India.

recruited from the extended family or kin group. There is no doubt that hereditary transmission allowed for 'routinisation of craft operations', long apprenticeship, and thus, could lead to superior craftsmanship. In Marx's colourful language, 'It is only the special skill accumulated from generation to generation and transmitted from father to son, that gives to the Hindu, as it does to the spider, this proficiency'.[13] But insular systems of transmitting knowledge had a cost.

It could leave markets for inputs and tools undeveloped. The system involved a division of communities rather than a division of labour. As a result of community control on knowledge, there was substantial integration of the processing of raw materials, tools, and inputs with final goods production within each community. The point was noted by H. T. Colebrooke, 'every manufacturer and every artist working, on his own account, conducts the whole process of his art from the formation of his tools to the sale of his production'.[14] This description, in fact, is somewhat exaggerated. More specific descriptions of tools exchange in the nineteenth century suggest that market exchange did exist in the sphere of industrial tools and between castes, but in a custom-bound way. Artisan castes did not buy tools and did not sell raw materials freely. Evidence of a serious trade, even commission-contract kind of transaction, in industrial equipment and major manufactured raw materials in early modern India remains relatively scarce, if not unknown, and restricted to highly specialized goods.

Tools exchange conformed with traditional patterns of reciprocity among artisan communities. When the British engineers in the nineteenth century contemplated procuring iron from the central Indian smelters Agarias, they were reminded that the Agarias traded only with the blacksmiths. They 'will not take to new customers, and Lohars, who have influence over them, will do all they can to retain the monopoly'.[15] Anthropological surveys of rural artisan castes

[13] Karl Marx, *Capital*, vol. I, (the English tr. of the third German edition by Samuel Moore and Edward Aveling), edited by F. Engels, Moscow: Progress Publishers, 1958, p. 340.

[14] Cited in Walter Hamilton, *The East India Gazetteer; containing particular Descriptions of the Empires, Kingdoms, Principalities, Provinces, Cities, Towns, Districts, Fortresses, Harbours, Rivers, Lakes, &c. of Hindostan and the Adjacent Countries beyond the Ganges and the Eastern Archipelago*, London: John Murray, 1815, p. 121.

[15] Sabyasachi Bhattacharya, 'Cultural and Social Constraints on Technological

in the early twentieth century also found immense variety in tools and processes in the manufacture of the same good, between sub-castes and between villages. The diversity points again to the limited transaction between craft communities in the sphere of knowledge. Because it was difficult for members of one community to join another, the knowledge base of each evolved in relative isolation, illustrating J.D.M. Derrett's point that 'India affords evidence for the theory of the genetic transmissibility of acquired characteristics in humans'.[16]

THE EIGHTEENTH CENTURY
The lines we can draw from the organization of seventeenth century urban industry to the organization of industry among those artisans who participated in the eighteenth century export trade in cotton textiles cannot be either clear or straightforward. Three conclusions can still be drawn about organization in Indo-European trade. First, much of the European demand was supplied by large villages that contained clusters of weaver families. In the major regions supplying this demand, Bengal, Coromandel, and Gujarat, textile production had been mainly rural. Second, the households conducted business by means of 'headmen', who were artisans themselves in almost all cases. If the rural artisanal world had been relatively less collectivized, it became collectivized through Indo-European trade. And third, perhaps reflecting the newness of these structures, the intermediate authority was consistently embroiled in disputes.

Prasannan Parthasarathi notes the presence of 'powerful networks of solidarity' in the Coromandel weaver villages, organized around jati, that is cemented by rules on marriage, and additionally by collective contributions to temple and ritual activities.[17] Parthasarathi's work contains a valuable description of the weaver 'corporate structures', which much resembled the pattern visible with the merchants (Chapter 3), and were quite different from artisan organizations in the north, the east, and the west. Furthermore, a significant part of

Innovation and Economic Development : Some Case Studies', *Indian Economic and Social History Review*, 3(3), 1966, pp. 240–67.

[16] 'Rajadharma', *Journal of Asian Studies*, 35(4), 1976, pp. 597–609.

[17] *The Transition to a Colonial Economy, Weavers, Merchants and Kings in South India, 1720-1800*, Cambridge: Cambridge University Press, 2001, pp. 31–5.

that institutional heritage persisted into the twentieth century.[18] In the eighteenth century, an important and almost invariant element in weaver corporatism was the internal hierarchy at the top of which was located a headman.

In the eighteenth century, the private European merchants and Company officers purchased cotton textiles through the intermediation of the headmen of local weaving communities. On the Coromandel Coast, the headman was known as the *careedar*, and enjoyed certain commissions on sales of the community. The headman and the caste organization that he represented, Joseph Brennig suggests, became the channel of negotiation with the Companies, and possibly sheltered the weaker members of the community from extortion.[19] S. Arasaratnam's work describes a hierarchy in the weaving villages of the Tamil country at the end of the seventeenth century composed of weavers who did not possess looms, weavers who possessed looms, caste-heads and village leaders, weaver-traders, and traders by caste.[20] The weaver-traders and traders by caste both mediated between the merchants and the weavers; but the former additionally hired other weavers at times and functioned like master-craftsmen as well as social leaders. The intermediary was expected to ensure supply of work. The privilege implicitly granted to them was that the principal would not contract directly even when there was excess supply of workers in the market.

These systems of mediation served the principals poorly, for the mediator could take advantage of information asymmetries between the employer and the contractor. Agency in the textile trade was rife with complaints that became particularly bitter when buyers competed for the same pool of suppliers. Delivery time was never predictable, for suppliers routinely contracted with more buyers than they could satisfy. Goods were diverted from contract sales to other bidders, from contract to spot markets, from the Company to private traders, and in Bengal, the Dutch and the English were played off against one

[18] Mattison Mines, *The Warrior Merchants: Textiles, Trade, and Territory in South India*, Cambridge: Cambridge University Press, 1984.

[19] 'Textile Producers and Production in Late Seventeenth Century Coromandel', *Indian Economic and Social History Review*, 23(4), 1986, pp. 333–56.

[20] S. Arasaratnam, 'Trade and Political Dominion in South India, 1750–1790: Changing British-Indian relationships', *Modern Asian Studies*, 13(1), 1979, pp. 19–40.

another.[21] 'The problem of bad debts...', writes Om Prakash, 'plagued all commodities the Europeans procured in India.'[22] Historians of the textile trades of Coromandel and Bengal describe how the Company shifted from contracts with merchants to contracts with weaver-headmen in trying to take closer control of production, a move Arasaratnam called 'a substantial revision in the Company's approach', although Bengal and Coromandel differed much between themselves upon the precise design of enforcement systems.[23]

The weaver-headman entailed more specific problems that stemmed from the nature of the relationship between the headman and the actual producing community. The headman could become an instrument of oppression and opportunism vis-à-vis the artisans when the headman had the backing of the Company behind him. This unstable and potentially violent role of the weaver-headman has been explored in particular detail by P. Swarnalatha. Her account suggests that headman authority tended to be more contested when the headman was from outside of caste, as in the case of the colourful figure of Chinnum Jagappa. When such contests broke out, 'despite all the obstacles of illiteracy, lack of power, and resources, the ability of weavers to successfully obtain and maintain community support across space and time stand out'.[24] On the other hand, when the headman's own interests were integrated with that of the other members, 'solidarity' could become a weapon in bargaining, negotiations, and organization of protests against the actions of the principals.[25] The need for a radical institutional change was in the minds of those who had a stake in this trade.

---

[21] A recent paper concludes on the organization of the textile and opium businesses—'Enforcement problems appear to be widespread: producers default on advances often by engaging in outside sales, and buyers renege on price commitments often by manipulating quality criteria'. R.E. Kranton and A.V. Swamy, 'Contracts, Hold-up, and Exports: Textiles and Opium in Colonial India', *American Economic Review*, 98(3), 2008, pp. 967–89.

[22] *European Commercial Enterprise in Pre-Colonial India*, Cambridge: Cambridge University Press, 1998, p. 171.

[23] Ibid.

[24] P. Swarnalatha, 'Revolt, Testimony, Petition: Artisanal Protests in Colonial Andhra', *International Review of Social History*, 46(1), 2001, pp. 107–29.

[25] Parthasarathi, *Transition to a Colonial Economy*, explores the dynamics of resistance in detail.

In Bengal, a key point of transition in the relationship between the headman, the merchant, and the artisan came with the assumption of revenue collection rights by the East India Company (1765), which gave the Company more bargaining power with local notables. Thereafter, Company merchants used company authority to coerce weavers. Om Prakash describes the institutional shift '...from market-determined to coercion-based'.[26] Whereas historians suggest that the new regime of coercion was made possible by politics, it is necessary to remember that the business had long been conducted in an environment in which third-party enforcement of contract was just not available. The very desire to control or influence local politics can be interpreted as an indirect response to pervasive risks, persistent problems with contract enforcement, the ever-increasing amounts of money tied to this business, and the inherent weakness of indigenous law to serve impersonal exchange between communities.

The end of the eighteenth century and the beginning of the nineteenth saw decline in artisan enterprise in cotton textiles. On the one hand, in varying degrees in all regions, the power of patrons with almost limitless purchasing power began to decline, even though patronage on a smaller and more localized way persisted in the princely states of the nineteenth century.[27] On the other hand, the Industrial Revolution destroyed a large part of the traditional craft industry in India. A recent revision suggests that this dual process, known as 'de-industrialization', was perhaps less catastrophic upon the artisan tradition than historians once imagined. Trade adversely affected only a segment of the artisanate, and the segments that did not suffer competition from mechanized goods could potentially *gain* from trade by obtaining access to imported raw materials and distant markets. These latter segments, at times, utilized new opportunities of

[26] 'From Negotiation to Coercion: Textile Manufacturing in India in the Eighteenth Century', *Modern Asian Studies*, 41(6), 2007, pp. 1331–68. See also for a similar argument in the context of Bengal, Hameeda Hossain, *The Company Weavers of Bengal: The East India Company and the Organisation of Textile Production in Bengal 1750-1813*, New Delhi: Oxford University Press, 1989; and of Madras, Parthasarathi, *Transition to a Colonial Economy*.

[27] A.K. Bagchi, 'Deindustrialization in India in the nineteenth century: Some theoretical implications', *Journal of Development Studies*, 12(2), 1976, pp. 135–64; Irfan Habib, 'Colonialization of the Indian Economy, 1757–1900', *Social Scientist*, 3, 1975, pp. 23–53.

capital accumulation, which process induced changes in technology and industrial organization, and eventually contributed to the evolution of modern small-scale industries in the region.[28] How did the collective cope with this transformation?

NINETEENTH CENTURY: NEW FORMS

Whatever collectives there were before, had to become market-oriented. As before, collective bodies were prominent and powerful, but they had also diversified. The broad distinction between the organizational forms runs along caste and teams. But the degree of formality also varied. And the primary objective of the association also shifted somewhat. Ahmedabad trade guilds came closest to being formal associations, but restricted themselves to regulation in the product market. Master-artisan collectives in northern India were mainly interested in devising rules to regulate the labour market. Other collectives in southern India involved more explicit play of castes and communities to serve regulatory ends.

[28] See on various aspects of the transition in artisan industries, Douglas Haynes, 'The Logic of the Artisan Firm in a Capitalist Economy: Handloom Weavers and Technological Change in Western India, 1880–1947', in Burton Stein and Sanjay Subrahmanyam, eds., *Institutions and Economic Change in South Asia*, New Delhi: Oxford University Press, 1996; and 'Artisan Cloth Producers and the Emergence of Powerloom Manufacture in Western India 1920–1950', *Past and Present*, 172, 2001, pp. 170–98; Tirthankar Roy, *Artisans and Industrialization. Indian Weaving in the Twentieth Century*, New Delhi: Oxford University Press, 1993; *Traditional Industry in the Economy of Colonial India*, Cambridge: Cambridge University Press, 1999; 'Acceptance of Innovations' in Early Twentieth-century Indian Weaving', *Economic History Review*, 55(3), 2002, pp. 507–32; and *Rethinking Economic Change in India: Labor and Livelihood*, London: Routledge, 2005; Sumit Guha 'The Handloom Industry of Central India: 1825–1950', *Indian Economic and Social History Review*, 26(3), 1989, pp. 297–318; Peter Harnetty, 'Deindustrialization Revisited: The Handloom Weavers of the Central Provinces of India', *Modern Asian Studies*, 25(3), 1991, pp. 455–510; Haruka Yanagisawa, 'The Handloom Industry and its Market Structure: The Case of the Madras Presidency in the First Half of the Twentieth Century', *Indian Economic and Social History Review*, 30(1), 1993, pp. 1–27; Konrad Specker, 'Madras Handlooms in the Nineteenth Century', *Indian Economic and Social History Review*, 26(2), 1989, pp. 131–66. The point of artisanal roots of present-day Indian industrialization has been made especially in Haynes, 'The Logic of the Artisan Firm', and 'Artisan Cloth Producers'; and in Roy, 'Acceptance of Innovations', and *Rethinking Economic Change*.

Figure 4.1: Bengali silk weaver in Mushidabad region, c. 1900. Source: Nityagopal Mukherji, *A Monograph on Silk Industry in Bengal*, Calcutta: Government Press, 1903

The strength of trade guild in Ahmedabad is evident from its survival into the nineteenth century. W.W. Hunter's *Imperial Gazetteer* (1885)observes that:

the system of caste or trade unions is more fully developed in Ahmedabad than in any other part of Guzerat. Each of the different castes of traders, manufacturers and artisans, forms its own trade guild. All heads of households belong to the guild. Every member has a right to vote, and decisions are passed by a majority of votes. In cases where one industry has many distinct branches, there are several guilds.[29]

For examples, among potters, the gazetteer reports the existence of separate guilds among makers of bricks and tiles, and makers of earthen jars. In 'the great weaving trade', silk weavers and cotton weavers belonged in different guilds. The objects of the trade guild were, 'to regulate competition among the members, and to uphold the

[29] W.W. Hunter, *The Imperial Gazetteer of India*, vol. I, London: Trubner & Co., 1885, pp. 87–8.

interest of the body in any dispute arising with the other craftsmen'. One interesting instance of collective bargaining occurred in 1872. The cloth merchants decided to reduce the charges customarily paid to the sizers. The sizers struck work. Both actions were possible because of the existence of associations. The dispute lasted six weeks, before an agreement was signed on stamped paper. One common instance of regulation of competition was the agreement to work short time. In 1873, the Ahmedabad bricklayers experienced a sudden increase in competition from among daily-wagers. Given the allegation of rising unemployment, the guild met, and decided that none should be allowed to work extra time. 'The guild appoints certain days as trade holidays, when any member who works is punished with a fine. This arrangement is found in almost all guilds'.

The decisions of the guild were enforced by fines. But often there were cases of refusal to pay. When the members of the guild belonged to one caste, 'the offender is put out of caste. If the guild contains men of different castes, the guild uses its influence with other guilds to prevent the recusant member from getting work'. These fines and a steep entry fee from anyone wishing to start trade in the town formed the income of the guild. The entry fee was correlated with required skill—'[N]o fee is paid by potters, carpenters and other inferior artisans'. Further, for a son succeeding a father in the license to carry on an independent business, the entry fee was waived. 'In other cases the amount varies, in proportion to the importance of the trade, from £5 to £50'. The guild spent its money mainly on community feasts and on rarer occasions, charity. The guilds also maintained community hotels.

Although institutionalized forms of association such as the Ahmedabad guilds were rare in north India, a variety of clubs do find mention. The common local term was panchayat, which implicated a fraternity. These clubs were almost always present in craft towns of the western Gangetic plains, especially when artisans-cum-merchants handled expensive raw material. A nineteenth century example is the smelting of precious metals. To maintain purity, smelting used to be done in Lahore, Delhi, and Lucknow in common premises monitored by bodies like town councils. The maintenance of the furnace was done for a fee imposed on all members of the silver or *jari* merchant community. In the 1880s, it was found that the fee had no legal force.

'Renegades' took advantage of this, and eventually, the payment ceased, weakening the very institution itself.[30] Further examples of a similar nature from the interwar period come from Benares—'A distinct set of goldsmiths called *sodhas* handle gold and silver bars for converting these to wire. They are prohibited from dealing directly with the gold and silver merchants until the bar passes through the panchayats of the *sodhas* who guarantee the weight in payment of a fee from both the merchants and the goldsmiths.'[31]

From the same town, among the silk *kamkhwab* weavers—'There is no union or trade guilds but customs are observed like laws, and so there is no lack of discipline. A few years ago, a disciplinary committee was formed and constitutions were made ... But the committee failed due to the manager's embezzlement of the common money.'[32]

There was more scope for free-riding in a formal rather than the informal association. The desire to move towards a formal guild might itself signify weakening of customary regulation.

A more amorphous sense of the collective appears in the material when the master artisan is seen to regulate capital, labour, and skills. Interestingly, the master was often called *karkhanadar*. How did the north Indian karkhana survive the eighteenth century? The history of shawls in Kashmir suggests that the karkhana became a private firm catering to merchants in overland trade with Europe.[33] In those industries where long-distance trade developed early, karkhanas must have altered their nature earlier. But such early transition was not the rule. By and large, the concentrations of skilled artisans in the eighteenth century tended to be cities with powerful regimes. The fundamentally non-market character of karkhanas might have diminished, but could not have withered until the nineteenth century. Around 1900, royal karkhanas affiliated to regional courts still existed, but they were not the principal employers of skilled artisans of the

[30] E. Burden, *Monograph on the Wire and Tinsel Industry in the Punjab*, Lahore: Government Press, 1909, pp. 9–10.

[31] S.N. Majumdar Choudhury, 'Extracts from a Survey of the Small Urban Industries of Benares' in United Provinces', *United Provinces Provincial Banking Enquiry Committee 1929–30*, vol. 2 of 4, Allahabad: Government Press, 1930, pp. 371–91.

[32] Ibid., p. 387.

[33] John Irwin, *Shawls*, London: HMSO, 1954.

towns. Most artisans worked for the market in very different systems.

By 1900, the word karkhana had bifurcated into two distinct sets of meaning. Outside northern India, in the handloom weaving towns of Bombay-Deccan, karkhana referred to any small factory and the karkhanadar to the generic owner of the factory. In the early nineteenth century Kashmir shawl, the term karkhanadar referred to *owners* of karkhanas, who in turn hired masters. In this wider usage, the words had lost the political and social character that they once represented in the urban artisanal tradition of the Gangetic plains.[34] In its homeland in the upper Gangetic plains, karkhana retained shades of the older meaning. Here again karkhana referred to a workshop, but the karkhanadar was not necessarily the generic owner, but also a master and a contractor. They were not just any capitalist or employer, but individuals engaged in the regulation of master-apprenticeship relations and protection of knowledge. The north Indian karkhanadar retained a little of the older heritage, and was the leading representative of a community of skilled artisans.

To illustrate this point, consider three sets of studies of karkhanadars of Benares (silk), Lucknow (embroidery), and Moradabad (brass). In these three examples of established urban crafts that survived into the modern times, the karkhanadar played multiple roles. There was a simple management function of avoiding fraud. In Lucknow, 'orders in bulk are not generally trusted to the ordinary workman until he can show some standing as a karkhanadar.'[35] There was, secondly, a more complex management function—coordination. In United Provinces generally, the karkhanadar coordinated between processes, kept accounts, guaranteed quality, supervised artisans, and trained artisans.[36] Supervision and training were widely believed to be the important roles, and in some situations dominated the other roles of coordination and trust. In Benares brasswares, 'the karkhanadar's position is that of a foreman in a factory ... The karkhanadar has little connexion with the business side of the industry. The karkhanadar

[34] Ibid.

[35] Ardhendu Bhattacharya, 'Extracts from a Survey of the Small Urban Industries of Lucknow in United Provinces', *United Provinces Provincial Banking Enquiry Committee 1929–30*, vol. 2 of 4, Allahabad: Government Press, 1930, pp. 392–411.

[36] United Provinces, *United Provinces Provincial Banking Enquiry Committee 1929–30*, vol. 1 of 4, Allahabad: Government Press, 1930, pp. 362–4.

is only responsible for the work by the workmen. Usually he permits a few apprentices to be taken in by the workers'.[37] Karkhanadars, thus, were men 'higher in status than the workmen. Every workman, therefore, aspires to become a karkhanadar ... several workers sometimes combine to run karkhanas on a profit-sharing basis (for example, brass workers of Benares)'.[38] Since the karkhanadar was not strictly a capitalist, the worker working under him was 'neither strictly a wage-earner ... nor precisely a home-worker. He is a combination of the two and perhaps more of the former'.[39]

Karkhanadars tried to regulate the progression of workers into their own ranks. Anyone with some money and a reasonable reputation could in principle set himself up as a karkhanadar. But in practice, the incumbents insisted on rules governing time of service. In Lucknow embroidery—'It seems to be an unwritten law with the karkhanadar that until a man can show some six years' work in the city he is not to be given the full wage. And the worker, whatever efficiency he may have obtained, submits to the rule, for the refusal to accept underpayment may mean starvation for him'.[40]

In Benares brassware and cotton carpet manufacture, 'apprenticeship is restricted within the caste'.[41] In Moradabad brassware, there was a rule that if any karkhanadar trained one from outside the community, he was 'outcasted'.[42]

And yet, commercial opportunities always attracted men (and occasionally women) from outside the caste to enter production and sub-contracting. In Moradabad brassware, a training school was established so that 'the barrier, even when it exists, is slowly and steadily declining'.[43] When demand declined or quality became a less serious consideration than before, merchants often dealt directly with artisans rather than with karkhanadars. And, in one interesting example, in Lucknow embroidery, a whole craft tradition slowly passed from skilled male artisans to women inside households. 'The

[37] Ibid.
[38] Ibid.
[39] Bhattacharya, 'Extracts from a Survey', p. 394.
[40] Ibid., p. 396.
[41] Majumdar Choudhury, 'Extracts from a Survey', p. 378.
[42] United Provinces, *Provincial Banking Enquiry Committee*, p. 379.
[43] Ibid.

spare-time workers ... are satisfied with almost any remuneration...'. Women rarely combined, questioned the authority of the dealers, or negotiated with them, and therefore the merchants/artisans dealing with women did not need the backing of a guild.[44] Extending the same principle, in the 1920s, the craft moved further away from city women to rural women '...in the villages around Lucknow who are content with even lower wages than their sisters in the city.'[45] In new and relatively more mechanized trades, such as manufacture of knitted textiles, the karkhanadar felt less threatened by the worker. Individual craftsmanship was a less important resource here than was capital. The masters themselves opened training classes in which anyone could join.[46]

The master–apprentice relation was governed by a set of rules that had enough force in the interwar period to ensure that new entrants followed the rules. The clearest expression of these rules comes from the cities of northern India, mainly, Lahore, Amritsar, and Agra. The artisans were mainly Muslims, who recruited apprentices from outside their immediate families.

A 1940 description of artisans of Lahore offers a detailed picture of the corporate body that the skilled masters tried to develop.[47] The report surveyed conditions of carpenters, blacksmiths, metal-workers, and bricklayers mainly. Lahore, like other commercial–industrial cities of the time, had experienced a construction boom in the 1920s fuelled by profits made during the First World War. The four types of artisans surveyed were directly or indirectly connected with the building trade. At the time of the survey the industry was recovering from the worst effects of the Depression, when all construction activities had stopped. This unusual situation coloured the description to some extent.

Some of the main features of employment practices need to be stated:

(a) There was a deliberate attempt to keep family and apprenticeship distinct; even when the father was an artisan, it was customary

---

[44] Ibid., p. 380.
[45] Ibid.
[46] Majumdar Choudhury, 'Extracts from a Survey', p. 387.
[47] Punjab, *Artisans of Lahore*, Lahore: Government Press, 1941.

to have the son trained by another master (*ustad*), or face the stigma of being called a *be-ustada* or self-trained.

(*b*) On completion of training, the ustad issued a *sanad*, or license. Some artisans were 'of the opinion that all the earnings of an artisan would be *haram* (unlawful) unless he got a *sanad*'[48]. But this statement hints at the existence of such unlawful practices in some quarters.

(*c*) The apprentice paid only a token fee to the ustad at the time of joining, which consisted of a turban, a scarf, and sweets. He was expected to render service not only in the workshop, but also at the master's home. This description referred to a period when the demand for apprentices was brisk, and the apprentices themselves on occasion received some money.

(*d*) The period of apprenticeship varied between one and ten years. When the apprentice came from an artisan family and had already been trained well, the training period could be very short. For someone without previous exposure to the craft, the training period could be long. In the construction trade, long apprenticeship was common because new entrants came from farming background.

(*e*) While entry from peasanthood to artisan occupations was relatively easy in some cases, exit from artisan occupation could be difficult. 'According to some Muslim tarkhans [carpenters] their family traditions were such that they could not give up carpentry and take to a new trade; to do so made one an object of ridicule in the *biradari* and even deprivation of its privileges, such as inter-marriage'[49].

(*f*) Attainment of masterhood had meaning not only inside the trade, but also in the wider market for high-quality skills. For example, railway workshops, when they hired a construction supervisor or a contractor, looked for persons with the ustad status.

(*g*) A 'licensed' artisan was not necessarily the same thing as being reputed in the trade. Fresh graduates of the apprenticeship system followed individual masters in the early days of their

[48] Ibid., p. 6
[49] Ibid., p. 8

careers, until they themselves were known enough to receive independent contracts.

(h) The term 'guild' does appear in this description in one context. Raj was the name given to the *ustad* in the building trade 'by the ancient "guild" of brick-layers'. No details are available on this institution. If it ever existed, its disappearance was easily explained by the entry into the building trade from rural classes, an effect of the 1914–29 economic boom in Punjab. A more informal collective was the biradari. Its significance appears to have been confined to imposing some form of social sanction for breaking an undefined set of rules.

From elsewhere in the urban crafts of interwar India, glimpses of a similar set of practices can be found. One example was the cotton carpet industry of Patna city, where 'the work generally is done by hired labourers (under the guidance of one who may be called master worker or Malik of the Karkhana) who are all Muslims'.[50] There is a mention of biradari among artisans of urban north India in one source on silk weavers.[51] But, as Yusuf Ali, the author of this work qualified, nowhere did biradari mean formal rules and regulations. 'Organized guild' in that sense 'are unknown'.

The brotherhood concept spilled over to the merchants too, who in Benares silk weaving, rose from the ranks of the artisans themselves. 'There is a compact sense of brotherhood among the different members of the panchayats'.[52] In this case, the commitment was used to protect advances made to individual workers. If anyone disappeared with the money, the panchayat made sure that the person did not take a job with another member.

When we move to south India, artisan panchayats had a much clearer association with caste, caste association, and endogamous guild. By contrast with urban north India, Hindu artisans in southern India by and large worked in family units. Recruitment occurred along hereditary lines rather than a formal master–student system. In one of

---

[50] B.N. Mukherjee, 'Dari Industry of Patna', in Patna College Chanakya Society, *Annual Report*, Patna, 1936–7.

[51] Abdullah Ibn Yusuf Ali, *A Monograph on Silk Fabrics produced in the North-Western Provinces and Oudh*, Allahabad: Government Press, 1900, p. 102.

[52] Ibid., p. 371.

the more well-known examples of the caste-collective from south India, the craft association and the kinship community were indistinct. The Sourashtras were a small group of silk and cotton weavers and dyers based in textile towns of south India, the most important settlement being Madurai. Numerous reports from the colonial period suggest how the economic growth of Madurai owed 'to the Saurashtra merchants and silk weavers, who have ... come to a foremost place among the ranks of [the town's] citizens'.[53] Part of their commercial success owed to innovations made in the use of dyes while maintaining guild-like exclusiveness in sharing the new knowledge.

Madurai silk derived its historic reputation mainly from a red dye. In the late nineteenth century, when the dye material changed from a local plant to the mineral-based dye then imported, the adaptation of the dye to the particular style of weaving posed a problem. A solution was found through collaboration between German dye-makers and Sourashtra technicians-cum-entrepreneurs. Once the new technology was found usable, it spread quickly among the community. But it needed specialized factories to enable standardization and economies of scale in handling raw material. 'Red factories', consequently, mushroomed. Fifteen years from the first experiment, '...the suburbs of Madura are now almost entirely covered with drying yards'. In 1921, half the Madras Presidency's import of synthetic dyes went to just one town.[54]

The period between 1880 and 1920 witnessed not only this economic transition, but also the deployment of an explicit sense of community to restrict access to the new knowledge and to diffuse class formation within the group. A number of contemporaries attributed the spread of the new knowledge and yet its restriction to one town and one group to the role of 'caste' as a craft guild. What mattered was not only that the owners of the dyeing factories knew the specific formulae, but that they could secure cooperation from the workers not to work for or divulge these formulae to outsiders. Skill-retention and training are described by observers in terms that almost depict a formal guild. Indeed, in some

[53] Edgar Thurston, *Castes and Tribes of Southern India*, vol. VI, Madras: Government Press, 1909, p. 165.

[54] The cited text from N.G. Ranga, *Economics of Handlooms*, Bombay: Taraporevala, 1930, p. 60; All India Handicrafts Board, *Report on Hand Printed Textile Industry in Madurai (Madras)*, New Delhi: Government Press, 1964.

of these writings, the word 'guild' *was* used.[55] And yet, no formal guild actually existed. What did exist was a correlation between community and skill, and attempts to perpetuate it. The following are two examples, fifty years apart. In 1925—'Closest secrecy is maintained in preserving [the Saurashtras'] trade secrets.' Even in the employment of non-Saurashtra labour in the dyeing process, this point is as a rule strictly followed. Only Saurashtra workmen are engaged in the steaming process. In fact, wherever an element of brainwork is wanted, the Saurashtra *maistries* [master-artisans] alone are wanted'.[56] And as recently as 1976, 'there are some trade secrets pertaining to the work of textile printing. These secrets are never divulged to any body, particularly a non-Saurashtrian. The non-Saurashtri labourers are engaged in textile printing, but they are not shown any secret of the trade'.[57]

The other side of such exclusion was 'strong *esprit de corps*', a constant theme in the context of Madurai's quality of work. It can also be found or invoked in other contexts, like the rarity of violent disputes, and diffused class-formation. Even as capitalism grew roots in Madurai, Sourashtra production remained confined in families. Wage labour was conspicuous by its absence. To a large extent, this was made possible by an informal agreement among the employers not to employ outsiders in this business. Indeed, new entry was so difficult that it appeared as 'virtually a closed industry so far as the labour force is concerned', the stated reason being the historic association between Sourashtra labour and high-quality work.[58] The unity was also seen in matters of trust—'[T]hey are very keen to stick to truth in their dealings'.[59] And they 'seldom borrow from other than their castemen'.[60] The turn of the century also saw significant attempts to consciously recreate a Sourashtra identity. Linguistic-literary movements, and institutions associated with

[55] A.J. Saunders, 'The Sourashtra Community in Madura. South India', mimeo, Madura, c. 1920–22; K.R.R. Sastry, *South Indian Gilds*, Madras: Indian Publishing House , 1925.

[56] Sastry, *South Indian Gilds*.

[57] I.R. Dave, *The Saurashtrians of South India*, Rajkot: Saurashtra University, 1976, p. 65

[58] J.D.K.S. Singh, *The Handloom Industry in Madurai City*, Madurai: Madurai Kamraj University, 1981.

[59] Dave, *Saurashtrians of South India*.

[60] Saunders, 'The Sourashtra Community', p. 116.

identity-formation and assertion of common identity, had their origin in these decades.

The community was useful as always in sharing scarce resources, but these resources had changed meaning. From capital, credit, and craftsmanship, the critical productive resource had become education in the early twentieth century (and in the late twentieth century, government jobs reserved for 'backward' castes). Increasingly, we see the Sourashtra magnates invest in education and welfare, much like the merchants we have encountered in the previous chapter.

The Sourashtra example notwithstanding, the message of the north Indian cases seems to be the progressive weakening of authority. By and large, the attempt by masters, headmen, panchayats, and guilds to restrict access to technical knowledge was as persistent as it was futile in modern India. The collective did not become redundant, for it performed business roles and contracting roles. But retaining a monopoly over knowledge was already a subsidiary and unimportant function. In some cases, masters themselves started schools or admitted recruits from a larger social pool. In some cases, merchants found groups (such as the women *chikan*-makers of Lucknow) outside the reach of traditional authority willing to learn the business. An industrial system based on tacit knowledge and exclusive apprenticeship, thus, transformed itself into a system based on open-access learning. This trend did not occur in the manner of a sudden revolution. And arguably, this opening up would have taken place without Western agency, but colonial education policies and colonial obsession with printed information undoubtedly speeded it up.

CONCLUSION

In north Indian towns in the seventeenth century, the karkhanas sponsored by courtiers were the most well-developed business organization among the artisans. In pre-colonial south India, by contrast, the endogamous guild was the more common form. In imperial cities, both collectives received significant direct or indirect protection from the court. As powerful buyers disappeared and commercial imperatives took hold, these collectives changed their form and purpose. The collective did not stop being useful in sharing resources, commanding labour, or bargaining. But the source, the scope, and the nature of its authority had shrunk. In all regions, community and masterhood were mainly focused upon training of labour and quality control. But even this engagement was changing. As with the Sourashtra case, community spawned more or less formal caste associations that shifted the accent of collective effort from narrowly artisanal industrial training to general education in the twentieth century. The move appears more visible in contexts where caste and community associations had already been entrenched; in some ways it reflected no more than a change in the goals of the caste collective. It was considerably weaker in urban northern India and the master-apprenticeship world, under constant attack from interlopers.

If the employers were organized in collectives, we would expect supply of labour to be collectivized as well. The next chapter finds this proposition to be true, and shows how a truncated version of the community worked as an early form of trade union among migrant workers.

5 Workers
Collective bargaining

B etween 1800 and 1920, millions of people left their homes and jobs to work in new enterprises inside India and overseas. Circulation of working people in the Indian subcontinent had, from a long time past, been an essential part of the cycle of life punctuated by famines, land hunger, wars, movements of grain and grain taxes, trade, artisan settlements, and the rise and fall of states.[1] But few examples of large-scale migration or circulation before the eighteenth century involved wage work. The employment of wage workers grew enormously in scale and diversity in the colonial period. What kind of systems of employment did these movements leave behind? What kind of new systems of employment did they entail? The present chapter will try to answer these questions.

Scholarship on recruitment of labour in eighteenth century port cities suggests a dualistic world; neighbouring villages populated by service producers sold services to urban consumers who belonged in another social world. The former world consisted of families divided into castes and communities, but permanent and long-term wage relationships were rare. By contrast, the nineteenth century migrant labourers formed nothing like a traditional social unit. They were predominantly males, who had left their villages and families behind. They were wage workers foremost; there was no question of going back to one's own relations at the end of the day's work. Nevertheless, they

[1] For some examples, Ian J. Kerr, 'On the Move: Circulating Labor in Pre-Colonial, Colonial, and Post-Colonial India', *International Review of Social History*, Supplement, 51, 2006, pp. 85–109. On artisan migration, see Douglas E. Haynes and Tirthankar Roy, 'Conceiving Mobility: Weavers' Migrations in Pre-colonial and Colonial India', *Indian Economic and Social History Review*, 36(1), 1999, pp. 35–67.

needed to recreate a social world, not only for the sake of a comforting feel in an alien setup, but also for the sake of safety, security, and bargaining. They recreated this world not from scratch, but by using elements of community administration, one element in particular, the headman. Teams in the plantations and textile factories formed around headmen. The team concept suited the employers, who used it to institute supervision and training. But the informal team carried its own cost.

This transformation is studied using four illustrations—eighteenth century port cities, indentured workers to Mauritius in the early nineteenth century, Assam tea workers in the late nineteenth century, and cotton mill labourer in Bombay in the interwar period.

URBAN LABOUR IN THE 1700S

Historical scholarship on colonial port cities—Madras, Bombay, and Calcutta—suggests two broad patterns of change in employment relations in the eighteenth century. These towns, described as 'hybrid' or 'city of villages' were sites on which fortified foreign merchant settlements had been erected in the middle of a rural surrounding.[2] The villages located all around the forts provided the new settlements with food, services, and manufactures. When migrants moved in to settle, they settled as families to create a new village. These villages retained their distinct identity defined by caste and occupation. Thus, in the 1700s or the 1800s, the port city formed out of Indo-European trade was basically a market-place in which consumers of goods and services and the suppliers of these goods and services transacted while retaining their respective territorial and cultural distinctiveness. The villages themselves did not remain unchanged by the new transaction opportunities. As Susan Neild shows for Madras, the availability of urban employment weakened customary obligations and ties in the villages. Successful neo-rich merchants bought land and forced their way into rural elitehood. In the end, the villages were incorporated

---

[2] Susan Neild, 'Colonial Urbanism: The Development of Madras City in the Eighteenth and Nineteenth Centuries', *Modern Asian Studies*, 13(2), 1979, pp. 217–46. For a more detailed history of the spatial configuration of the city, see Meera Kosambi and John E. Brush, 'Three Colonial Port Cities in India', *Geographical Review*, 78(1), 1988, pp. 32–47.

into the city limits shorn of the power and authority of the older
landed elite.

Despite these changes in the structure of political authority and
despite urban expansion through incorporation of the villages,
the latter retained their distinct caste-occupation correspondence,
contributing to 'the social fragmentation and rural atmosphere' of
the city. These were villages that themselves consumed little of the
goods and services they produced, selling instead all of their output.
The increasing diversity of caste composition, far from leading to
more social and economic exchange between castes, apparently had
the opposite effect. Caste affiliations extended across the city, caste
conflicts were more rather than less pronounced than before, and
occupational distinctiveness maintained through spatial isolation and
choice of settlement.

Ravi Ahuja's work on eighteenth century urban labour revises this
picture of two worlds—the recreated caste-village on the one side
and the colonial centre on the other—transacting at arm's length.[3]
When moving from commodity to labour market, a picture of deeper
engagement emerges. The colonial authority, Ahuja suggests, tried
taking firmer control of urban labour markets. The isolation of the
two worlds, service suppliers and service consumers, was not as neat
as one would imagine. Paradoxically enough, the attempt to secure
stable and disciplined labour on a large scale hardened the autonomy of
the community. The universal response to the need for more frequent
negotiation and more inclusive contracting was to seek the help of the
headman-intermediary more than before. Colonial labour regulation
consisted in making the headmen liable for the performance of those
whom they controlled. Outside of law, where did headman authority
derive from? How was the headman chosen? Ahuja suggests that the
city authorities tried to construct caste panchayats. This view assumes
that the administrative and moral authority to create whole new
institutions among workers was already available. A more modest
alternative would be that the castes of workers and artisans responded

[3] Ravi Ahuja, 'The Origins of Colonial Labour Policy in Late Eighteenth-
Century Madras', *International Review of Social History*, 44, 1999, pp. 159–195. See
also Michael R. Anderson, 'Work Construed: Ideological Origins of Labour Law
in British India to 1918', in Peter Robb, ed., *Dalit Movements and the Meanings of
Labour in India*, Delhi: Oxford University Press, 2003, pp. 87–120.

to the city's increasing social diversity by trying to strengthen their own fragmented governance structures.

The nineteenth century labour history confronts us with a very different world. Permanent sites hiring hundreds of workers at a time began to appear in the eighteenth century port cities. In these cities, hiring of workers did not always involve long-distance migration. Indigo factories in the 1830s and 1840s, and mines and tea plantations a little later, recruited workers who came from villages far away. And from the end of the century, industrial cities recruited workers from hundreds of miles away. India also contributed in the same period to the formation of a global proletariat. Between 1846 and 1940, workers from the Indian subcontinent going to Burma, Mauritius, Guiana, Fiji, Trinidad, Jamaica, Natal, Malaysia, Ceylon, and East Africa numbered five million at least. Initially, all were wage-earners. More than a million others had been born outside their places of work, and working in manufacturing, mines, and plantations inside India. These figures do not include the considerable flow of short-distance and seasonal movements of agricultural labourers, which too had grown in size, composition, and distances covered. Nothing like the scale of movement that characterized the nineteenth century had occurred before in so short a time.

Before we consider the institutional dimensions of this vast change, it is necessary to look at the available accounts of labour supply more generally.

TWO ACCOUNTS OF LABOUR SUPPLY

Economists hold that labour supply relates positively to real wage. Since Arthur Lewis, a variety of dual economy theories have modelled rural–urban labour transfer with reference to wage and the probability of getting a job in the urban labour market. The existence of a rural non-farm sector and an urban informal sector complicates the story, but does not necessitate major changes in the essential structure of the rational choice model of labour supply. During much of the nineteenth century, however, real wage in those occupations that employed mobile people did not see significant change, and older and newer occupations saw little wage-disparity between them. Why were so many people moving in search of work, then?

There can be two accounts of labour supply in the nineteenth century—immiseration and institutional change. A variety of 'push factors' are highlighted in the Marxist-nationalist account of economic change in the nineteenth century. New property rights in land, decline of handicrafts, and high risks associated with grain exports led peasants into debt trap, artisans into unemployment, and both into wage-labour. Early statements of the immiseration thesis processed census occupational data to show a significant increase in the proportion of agriculture in work-force, matched by a fall in the proportion of handicraft industries in the work-force, and an increase in wage-labourers in the agricultural work-force.[4] The pessimistic reading of these ratios was challenged, however. One critic argued that landlessness as such did not increase in rural India, but older forms of landlessness associated with caste gave way to a market-dependent form associated with high rents and low wages.[5] Research on national income showing that average rural incomes increased in the pre-war 50 years questioned the theory of rural crisis. Regional agrarian history revealed rather limited extent of dispossession of the peasantry from land. Historians of industrial labour showed that many workers in the cotton textile mills were in fact land-owning peasants, and closer to the rural elite than to the proletariat. Careful scrutiny of the census data itself found the evidence on proletarianization to be weak with male workers, and strong with female workers.[6]

Some of these revisionist points hint, not at crisis, but at institutional change. A useful point of entry comes from a study that sees 'the problem faced in earlier ... times [to have been] to find a mechanism

[4] See S. J. Patel, *Agricultural Labourers in Modern India and Pakistan*, Bombay: Asia Publishing, 1952. See also Utsa Patnaik, *Agrarian Relations and Accumulation: The 'Mode of Production' Debate in India*, Bombay: Oxford University Press, 1990.

[5] Dharma Kumar, *Land and Caste in South India: Agricultural Labour in Madras Presidency in the Nineteenth Century*, Cambridge: Cambridge University Press, 1965.

[6] Alice Thorner, 'The Secular Trend in the Indian Economy, 1881-1951', *Economic Weekly*, 14, 1962, pp. 1156–65; Daniel Thorner, '"Deindustrialization" in India, 1881-1931', in D. and A. Thorner, *Land and Labour in India*, New York: Asia, 1962, pp. 70–81; J. Krishnamurty, 'The Growth of Agricultural Labour in India', *Indian Economic and Social History Review*, 9(4), 1972, pp. 327–32.

to shift from a "backward-bending" to a "forward-sloping" labor supply curve', a problem that cannot be addressed without reference to 'those institutions that influenced or determined the nature and limits of collective behavior'.[7] India in the nineteenth century was hardly a special case. What were the relevant institutional factors in India? How did collective decisions change in the labour market?

A new household allocation of labour constitutes one part of the answer. The seasonality of monsoon agriculture imposes long periods of idleness in peasant households. While urban jobs allowed peasants to utilize their idle time better, peasant households responded to new income earning opportunities by allocating the labour of men to these jobs whereas the women stayed back to look after the farm. The practice of early marriage pushed a disproportionate number of rural women into agricultural wage-labour, or to join factory labour only when their husbands worked in another department of the same mill and neighbours and older siblings were available to look after young children. Factory women in interwar India were nearly all married.[8] The majority of those women who remained behind reported themselves to the census as agricultural workers. The release of surplus labour in this fashion imparted a stabilizing effect on wages.

In order to explain the labour supply decisions of landless households we need to consider another institutional transition—contractual change that lowered barriers to entry into agricultural labour.

Outright slavery was rare in Indian agriculture. Yet, like all labour-scarce agrarian societies, and especially one with pronounced seasonality, peasants needed to secure labour supplies at times by means of systems that restricted freedom. The closest equivalent of slavery was a caste-based obligation to perform labour, and the presence of implicit restrictions on ownership of land. The association between caste and labour tended to be close in labour-intensive paddy cultivation where seasonal labour-tying was a necessity. In these densely populated areas, land was fertile but scarce. There

[7] Stanley L. Engerman, 'Cultural Values, Ideological Beliefs, and Changing Labor Institutions: Notes on their Interactions', in John N. Drobak and J.V.C. Nye, eds., *The Frontiers of the New Institutional Economics*, San Diego: Academic Press, 1997, pp. 97, 102.

[8] Tirthankar Roy, *Rethinking Economic Change in India: Labour and Livelihood*, London: Routledge, 2005.

was landlessness and yet acute shortages of labour could develop in certain seasons. Caste and class correspondence was relatively weaker in the dry zones, where land was harder to cultivate and seasonal labour-tying was not so much a necessity because of low levels of seasonal labour demand.[9] Late nineteenth century evidence suggests that a universal form of labour-tying was the farm servant contract whereby the head of a family pledged his labour, sometimes his family's labour, for one, two, or three years, to a specific employer. From the late nineteenth century, however, as the labour market entered a state of flux throughout India, farm servant contracts began to decline or the average duration of employment contracts tended to fall. The availability of migrants reduced the employers' need for labour-hoarding. The availability of jobs elsewhere led the rural labourer to assert more often his/her freedom to choose the employer. Now, the farm servant contracts in agriculture had been traditionally male-biased. Women rarely entered such arrangements. As attached labourers were replaced by those hired from the casual wage-labour markets, the entry of women in rural labour markets increased.

Such was the role of the family in transforming a possibly inelastic labour supply into a more elastic one. When we observe the worker at the work-site, we see the other driver in institutional change, formation of teams. The earliest large flow of wage-workers in the nineteenth century was made up of indentured labourers.

INDENTURED WORKERS: 1830–1900
In the 1830s, famines and the rumour of jobs available in Calcutta drove groups of landless men out of their villages and on the roads. They came from remote tribal villages in the uplands of Chota Nagpur, where fertile soil and surface or subsoil water were scarce. Labour contractors called *arkatis* waited on their routes, and persuaded them to sign indentures to go to Mauritius or British Guiana.[10] The

[9] For a discussion, see David Ludden, 'Introduction', in Ludden, ed., *Agricultural Production*, Delhi: Oxford University Press, 1994, pp. 1–35.

[10] Formally, indenture was a contract to serve for a fixed term, usually several years. Informally, because workers were often non-literate and ill-informed, the contract could resemble slavery. Historical scholarship on South Asia debates its resemblance to slavery. It needs stressing that the indenture had been an established form of labour recruitment when Indian emigration began. It was not

abolitionist rhetoric then raging in Britain blurred the distinction between indenture and slavery, and made this traffic controversial. When the government in Bengal barred some of these contractors (but allowed the trade after a short-lived ban), arkatis, now tough and dangerous men from the small towns along the way with a smattering of Europeans among them, conducted the business secretly in the nights. Some individuals signed the contracts with a reasonable knowledge of what they were committing themselves to. Many signed without a clear knowledge or understanding.

The labour contractor almost always found an intermediary within the group to negotiate terms with. This figure, commonly called the *sardar* (leader), and in some contexts *maistry* or *kangany*, was entrusted with the accounts and eventually with some supervision tasks at destination. In some later reports the sardar occasionally appeared as a collusive agent, one who mysteriously disappeared at the last minute when the ship set off. In most cases, however, the sardar continued on the journey, and reinvented himself as a foreman at destination.

Where did headship come from? It is easy to speculate that sardari authority or agency was invented by powerful employers of colonial India as a means of control over the labour of individual workers whom they did not know well. The evidence showing that headship was a colonial creation is not necessarily strong, however. There is plenty of evidence that clearly marked headship existed among the potential migrants before organized recruitment took hold. It is equally plausible that the prior presence of sardars had made some

---

an institution devised as the next best thing to slavery. David Galenson's work on indentured workers who went from Europe to the Americas in the seventeenth and the eighteenth centuries suggests that the contract originated in farm service, that mainly literate craftsmen and tradesmen dominated the migrant population, and that the contract left scope for individual negotiation and bargaining rather than being imposed by the employers. The Indian indenture engaged peasants, and quite substantially, tribesmen who depended on farming and forest resources. Historical scholarship as well as the sources remains strangely silent on the scope of individual negotiations. It would seem that initially at least migration from India was more driven by push factors, such as low levels of agricultural surplus, rather than by the attraction of better wages in the case of the New World. See Galenson, *White Servitude in Colonial America: An Economic Analysis*, New York: Cambridge University Press, 1982.

Figure 5.1: The indigo factory, north Bihar, c. 1870. Source: James Inglis, *Sport and Work on the Nepaul Frontier*, London: Macmillan, 1878

groups better able to cope with the new forms of recruitment than other groups. Contracting for labour services via a chief or a headman was common in the eighteenth and early nineteenth century northern India. Bishop Reginald Heber, through his travels came in contact with groups of manual workers, all of whom worked under designated leaders. 'According to the strange usage of Bengal, … nobody can do any thing without a leader, the "sirdar", or master of the gang, without whom they would not work, and whom they allowed (voluntarily, since there is nothing but custom which makes them do so) to receive their wages, and draw poundage on them in consideration of his superintendance.'[11] A detailed survey of the Bihar districts in the 1830s found that 'a great many' hill tribes and forest-dwelling communities had their own 'chief men' and 'leading men'.[12]

The very first official documents prepared by the government on emigration referred to the migrants by their castes. Migrants moved in

[11] *Narrative of a Journey through the Upper Provinces of India, Calcutta to Bombay, 1824-1825*, vol. 1, London: John Murray, 1828, p. 110.

[12] Montgomery Martin, *The History, Antiquities, Topography and Statistics of Eastern India*, vol. 1 of 3, London: W.H. Allen, 1838, p. 178.

groups. The overwhelming majority were Ahir, Kurmi, Kahar, Dusadh, Chamar, whose main occupation was agricultural labour and tenancy, and the three major semi-nomadic tribes, Santal, Munda, and Oraon. The phrase 'Hill Cooly' gradually took over the descriptions.

The Hill Coolies inhabit the ranges of mountains bordering upon the western bank of the Ganges, from 200 to 300 miles distant from Calcutta. These people are every year compelled by paucity of food to resort in great numbers to the plains. In the province of Lower Bengal a large proportion of them are employed in the indigo factories; and lately large drafts have ... been engaged for the Assam tea plantations. The Hill Coolies in their own country, are necessitated to subsist upon the products of the chase, reptiles, and insects; in short ... all sorts of disgusting food.[13]

Forest-dwellers living on semi-arid hill slopes appeared to be more sensitive to new wage-earning opportunities than the settled peasants who were averse to leaving their land. By hill coolies, the shippers and their agents commonly understood the particular caste or profession known as Dhangars (later called Oraon). Dhangars indeed were prominent among those who left for overseas work, though they were possibly outnumbered by all the other castes together. They were also prominent among the migrants headed for the tea estates in Assam and Dooars.

Historians of migration have traced the nineteenth century flow of indentured workers from India to the tropical colonies to increasing economic distress in India caused by British policies.[14] There is some truth in this picture, especially when we consider Chota Nagpur. Between 1830 and 1860, the majority of the migrants came from Chota Nagpur, the eastern projection of the central Indian plateau. The region consisted of the old administrative district Chota Nagpore in the centre, Ramgarh in the north, Gnagpur and Singhbhum in the south, Surguja in the west, and Jungle Mahals in the east. The whole

---

[13] India, *Correspondence relative to the Introduction of Indian Labourers into the Mauritius*, London: HMSO, 1842.

[14] See, for example, Walton Look Lai, *Indentured Labor, Caribbean Sugar: Chinese and Indian Migrants to the British West Indies, 1838–1918*, Baltimore and London: Johns Hopkins University Press, 1993, pp. 19–26; Brij V. Lal, *Girmitiyas: The Origins of the Fiji Indians*, Canberra: Australian National University, 1983, p. 2; David Northrup, *Indentured Labor in the Age of Imperialism 1834–1922*, Cambridge: Cambridge University Press, 1995, p. 60.

uplands region, for its common geographical characteristics, came to be referred to as Chota Nagpur.

Before the nineteenth century, the whole uplands were mainly forested, without major roads and highways, and difficult of access on all sides. Commerce was of little consequence in this area. Although it was rich in minerals, and iron-making was present everywhere, the major part of the output was locally consumed. Transportation was rudimentary. The major rivers in the region were not navigable even in the dry seasons, and had no known bridges before the railways in the late nineteenth century. The population of the uplands lived on agriculture that concentrated in the river valleys. With some exceptions, the region had rocky soil, poor supply of water, and low yield of paddy, all of which did not permit either prosperous or risk-free cultivation at any time. And yet, the very poverty of land resources, combined with inaccessibility, had left the region more or less untouched by imperial expansion in the late-Mughal period. Half-hearted attempts at conquest notwithstanding, the Mughal kings never tried to create a strong fiscal state in the uplands. The communities living here (whom colonial sources called 'tribes') remained distant from the imperial state. The communities included the Munda and the Oraon, interspersed with Kherias, Hos, Birhors, and others. Mundas and Oraons together were referred to as Kols, and the land where they had been settled Kolhan.[15]

Being isolated from a state that had an interest in fostering private property rights in exchange for the right to collect taxes, these communities developed forms of joint property on land, defined by village and territory rather than by individual plots. In many places village headmen allocated lands for cultivation to families. Proprietary rights did exist, but attached not to the person paying taxes, but to the person clearing a patch of land. Work, and not obligation to the state, defined who should have property right.[16] From the late eighteenth century, the situation began to change. The desire to raise more

---

[15] The classic description of the Kols and their region of ancestry is E.T. Dalton, 'The "Kols" of Chota-Nagpore', *Transactions of the Ethnological Society of London*, 6 (1868), pp. 1–41.

[16] J. Hoffmann, 'Principles of Succession and Inheritance among the Mundas', *The Journal of the Bihar and Orissa Research Society*, 1915, pp. 5–19.

taxes drove the Company government in Bengal to consolidate and encourage zamindaries in the plains region bordering these uplands, and the zamindars in turn gave grants of taxation rights in the uplands to outsiders and capitalists. With the Company's might behind them, these new right-holders could collect taxes better than before. In the struggle for resources that ensued, the join rights of the settlers proved relatively weak. Many members of the settler communities faced loss of territorial rights, a fact they resented very deeply. The 1831 Kol rebellion, which unleashed a surprising potential for violence among the forest communities, was the first of a series of uprisings attributed to these developments.

In other words, a specific form of dispossession from property had been ongoing for some time in the region that sent out a large number of people abroad. And yet, attributing emigration to 'distress' would be a simplistic view. Outsight dispossession happened on a rather limited scale, for the new masters of land needed the settlers to cultivate it. Counteracting laws that recognized village rights were framed soon. With or without dispossession, wages and levels of living in the uplands had always been very low. In the interviews of the returnees from Mauritius in 1840, there was no mention of a particular crisis leading to a loss of wages or livelihood before people moved.[17]

More than outright dispossession, the collective property rights in the uplands made the uplands communities mobile in a different way. Unlike the plains peasants, who were fiercely attached to the plots of land that they legally owned, the holders of a vaguely legal village right had less reason to be so attached even without a threat from the outsiders. And land was simply not a valuable asset here. Migrants from this region not only went to Mauritius, but also to the

---

[17] There were, by contrast, particular 'push' factors active with the first large batches that left the Madras coast. The decade of the Guntur famine (1833) was generally bad for agriculture on the Andhra coast. The region suffered, in addition to several years of acute scarcity, a violent cyclonic storm and tidal waves on November 16, 1839. In the 1840s, there was mention of the business of punjam cloth being depressed, forcing some weavers to join the migrants from India, *Correspondence between the Government of India and the Court of Directors relating to the Hill Coolies*, Calcutta: Government Press, 1841, p. 34, Collector of Rajahmundry. However, weavers and spinners were a small number by comparison with landless labourers among migrants from all regions.

tea plantations, indigo factories, and indigo plantations in Bengal. Being thus familiar with wage-work in the plains, having regularly circulated between seasonal factory labour and field labour, some of the upland people understood well the financial difference that going to Mauritius would mean for them.

Migration, thus, was a combination of two factors: a locally shaped propensity to circulate, and knowledge of new opportunities for wage earning. The nineteenth century created what David Northrup calls 'a new imperial economy'.[18] For India, the economic space was defined by the expanse of the British Empire. By 1860, India was a piece among other 'fragments of empire', and this integrated world, along with the much reduced hazards and increased speed of the voyages, presented anyone otherwise willing to join the labour pool with the choice of a wide world of wage labour.[19] The Anglo-French convention of 1860 agreeing to source labour mainly from India was a significant point in the evolution of this transnational labour market. By then, hundreds of thousands knew and understood what it meant to go overseas.

As mentioned before, the wage rates remained strangely flat despite movements of people,

The average rate of wages paid to Hill Coolies and others at European factories and establishments in Bengal, Tirhoot, Assam and Goruckpore is three and a half rupees to five rupees a month; less than three rupees is rarely paid; and they very often receive four rupees. These wages, when received by Dhangas or Hill Coolies, are sufficient to enable them to save money to return periodically and every year to their families.[20]

Mauritius paid not much more than the upper bound of these wages at 1838. Sugar estate work was year-round. The indigo planters preferred these groups, and this preference carried over to the European shippers of indentured workers in Calcutta and onward to the planters in Mauritius. All that said, one of the more powerful incentives for these groups to leave home and join the migrant labour pool was the attraction of easier social and economic mobility in the

---

[18] *Indentured Labor.*

[19] Madhavi Kale, *Fragments of Empire: Capital, Slavery, and Indian Indentured Labor in the British Caribbean*, Philadelphia: University of Pennsylvania Press, 1998.

[20] India, *Correspondence*, p. 7.

sugar estate. Precisely because changing occupations was so difficult in a collective-dominated production system, those in the greatest need of doing so had a propensity to leave the system altogether. But those who managed to leave still needed the protection of a collective themselves. All early bands of migrants had headmen when they moved. In later reports there was an explanation why this was so, and the explanation again revolves on the institutional specificity of the uplands:

The land system of the Sonthal Parganas is one which lends itself with peculiar advantage to co-operation amongst the cultivators of the soil. The unit is the village. At the head of almost every village there is a headman. The headman is the representative of the village through whom the villagers as a body deal with the proprietor. The proprietor is merely the rent receiver, and has no part in the management or internal economy of the village.[21]

Headship, thus, was a carry-over from autochthonous, communal, jointly held property rights. The worker groups that came from villages which carried a sense of communal ownership and control over resources, including labour, formed cooperative communities naturally. The institution of a headman was inseparable from that of the community. A cooperative community needed a representative in dealing with the market outside it. The headman was this channel of negotiation between the community and the market. Even when the headman himself did not join migrant groups, the concept travelled in a modified form.

A second, and quite different, example of endogenous root of headship occurs in south India. Almost all recruitment to Ceylon tea estates was done without indenture by the kangany system, which was seen as recruitment of a 'purely patriarchal character', giving rise to a labour force '...subdivided into a number of smaller groups, each under its patriarch ... ; and the family principle is manifested in the groups which are under these minor headmen.'[22] The group was more a family than an association. It held its earnings together, and had joint liability for advances made to any member. The headman-

[21] India, *Report of the Indian Irrigation Commission 1901–1903*, Part–II—Provincial, London: HMSO, 1903, p. 175.

[22] Ceylon Labour Commission in 1908, cited in India, *Report of the Committee on Emigration from India to the Crown Colonies and Protectorates*, London: HMSO, 1910.

cum-group principle gave financial security to individual members. The head kangany in an estate was in charge of the wage-bill of the workers in an estate. The fact that the kanganies received from their employers or at least some of them, a commission for each day their recruits worked, gave '...the introducer of the labourer ... a financial interest in the welfare of his protégés'.[23] Money cemented these bonds in a more systematic way than in the other prominent examples of the foreman. Shades of debt bondage have also been found in the relationship.[24]

Not all sardars were headmen. Hill coolies, first of all, did not form the majority among emigrant groups. Kanganies could be found only among Tamil labourers who moved in specific destinations, principally, Ceylon, Malaya, and the Straits Settlements. Some of them were individual migrants without a team. Reports of raids on illegal labour depots in the 1830s suggest the picture of a chaotic human mass, rather than an organized and hierarchical one with a clear leader among them. It is likely that in certain situations the institution could be moulded rather more by the worker groups themselves with or without reference to a notional tradition. Why would workers need a headman?

In some cases from the 1840s, the groups appear to have elected leaders. The journey to the port of embarkation needed one person to keep accounts, and receive and distribute food rations, and was again conducive to the emergence of headmen. Of groups that were found travelling in Arcot in search of work, it was written—'The people were in small parties, according to their villages, families or other circumstances; to each party there was one man, who received money for the individuals composing it ..., and acted as a sort of chief'.[25]

In the return journey, sardars performed an important function—to keep charge of the savings brought home by the individuals. If

[23] India, *Proceedings of the Assam Labour Enquiry Committee in the Recruiting and Labour Districts*, vol. I (Evidence), Calcutta: Government Press, 1906, T. H. Hill, Protector of Labour, Federated Malay States.

[24] For example, R.K. Jain, 'South Indian Labour in Malaya 1840-1920: Asylum Stability and Involution', in Kay Saunders, ed., *Indentured Labour in the British Empire 1834-1920*, London and Canberra: Australian National University Press, 1984, pp. 158–82, on Malaya.

[25] India, *Exportation of Hill Coolies*, Calcutta: Government Press, 1841, J.D. Bourdillon, Joint Magistrate, Arcot.

the onward journey reported individuals who were on their own, almost all individuals belonged in a group on the return journey, and followed a headman. The logic of this organization had to do with keeping money in safe custody. Was the money safe from the headman? Perhaps it was, during the length of the journey, seeing that the headman had reason to fear his wards in the confined space of the ship. But such dependence might lead to opportunism when headman authority was backed by the employers.

The need for protection and the threat of extortion increased sharply during the voyage. Of the 200-odd returnees who were interviewed by the police and port officers at the Calcutta port in the winter of 1841–2, almost every individual brought with him a sum of money. The sardars kept the money or kept accounts. Sardars had a reason to keep trust. They were potential returnees, and one tainted by allegations of fraud had less chances of returning. On board a ship, the sardars could face serious problems if something went wrong with the money. Sardars were also the means of negotiation in the distribution of food and water rations. The Muslims were left to cook on board, but the Hindus came in two classes—those who cooked on board in a shared kitchen, and those who refused to share kitchen. The last group was given parched rice (*chira*) for food ration. These segregations began to break down when the ship had been a few days at sea. Members of the parched rice group, then, began to enlist at the boiled rice kitchen.[26] To control gate-crashing and impersonation, a sardar was appointed for each batch of 10–20 people.

In view of reports of frequent thefts and the operation of a thriving underground economy in the lower deck, a variable mixture of *sardari* authority and team-work was crucial to the safety of everyone. Sardars, artisans, and townsmen had more money in hand than the others; there was a shortage of water on board; luxuries like bhang, opium, and sweetmeats were needed to survive the stress; and for some, the food rations were not enough. A great deal of trade, therefore, happened on board. The ship's cook clandestinely passed on some part of the supplies, especially liquor, to the workers' quarters, and generally had good relations with the sardars with whom they had drinks together.

---

[26] India, *Exportation of Hill Coolies*, p. 18, evidence of James Rapson, ship-owner.

Women were scarce in the crowded darkness between decks, and those who travelled almost invariably were embroiled in small or large disturbances. In the mutinous Edward, the harassment of a woman by the Chief Officer led to a major disturbance. Language, experience, negotiation, and authority, all mattered in how these disturbances were settled. In the Edward case, the captain and the officers spoke no Hindustani. The captain took the officer's version of the event for granted, which angered the sardars.

Both before and after reaching Mauritius, individuals without the backing of a collective were exposed to varied forms of exploitation. At the port of embarkation, the commission on migrants was so high that an underworld was always predating on newcomers. The first major enquiry into 'abuses' of the recruitment system recorded a number of such cases. A woman was intoxicated, shut up in a box, and taken to the ship.[27] The man Ameen was intoxicated in Calcutta and carried on board. Rajcomar, a boy from Arrah, had met a man who hired him to accompany a party of new recruits to the docking place at Calcutta, but was himself forced into the ship. Bibee Zuhoorun was enticed into the ship with promise of service with a family.[28] At the plantation, similarly, individuals were vulnerable to the brutal treatment of the employer. The detailed statements recorded of four returnees presented a strong indictment of the plantation system in Mauritius. They had not been paid wages, were held prisoners, had their food rations cut, were beaten up, and eventually sent home, by the planters, their agents, and the police.[29] Curiously, such witnesses tended to be 'vagrants', single women, or young boys looking for a job alone. Rarely did they belong in an identifiable group. Conversely, complaints were rare with groups working under sardars.

Thus, the security and safety of the workers were important motivations behind the informal collective in the 1830s. As the nineteenth century moved on, however, we begin to see other drivers at work in shaping the collective and modes of authority within it. At the work-site, the sugar estates in this case, the supervisory functions were more visible. The employers, their agents, or sub-agents needed

[27] Ibid., p. 26.
[28] Ibid., p. 46.
[29] Ibid., pp. 35–6.

several qualities at once—an interpreter, one who could keep charge of money and make payments, and one who had enough influence on the group to make them work well and to minimize chances of desertion. The communication angle is illustrated in later examples. Knowledge of English, which usually meant previous service under a European or in the army, made some migrants suitable for the job.[30] Even in groups that did not necessarily have sardars, the employers chose one man to do the job. In a linguistic melting pot, communication was an important function for the workers too. It was for this reason that the original batches often continued intact under a sardar. Keeping accounts is one function that recurs with remarkable consistency in nearly all reports of the sardar-cum-supervisor from the nineteenth and the twentieth centuries

When at the gardens these coolies work directly under their sardars, who get a daily or monthly allowance from the garden for every head they produce for labour, and, at the same time, are allowed to draw the pay of their gang, and distribute it according to the muster rolls they prepare...[31]

This particular function appears in mines, plantations, small-scale industry, and in a modified manner, in the mills.

Demographic changes played a role in changing the nature of sardari authority. Net immigration reached a peak in 1854, and from 1861, Indo-Mauritian population began to outpace immigrants. Increasingly, the sardar was an 'old immigrant', rather than a headman among a fresh batch of recruits. Sugar milling being a seasonal activity, and there being a ready pool of settled workers now available, the mode of hiring shifted towards casual labour by the late nineteenth century, with the result that some old immigrants now became labour contractors. In other examples of migrant communities too, we observe this transition in dynamics—from headman to contractor.

---

[30] As in the case with which Northrup begins his book, see, *Indentured Labor*, p. 1.

[31] British Parliamentary Papers (House of Commons), *Copies of Government of India Despatch, dated the 22nd day of June 1889, with its Enclosures, including reports by Mr. Tucker and, of Memorial of the Indian Association of Calcutta, dated the 12th day of April 1888 in continuation of House of Lords' Return (No. 14), 5th March 1889,* London, 1888–9, p. 36.

Among early immigrants, through the five or six years they lived in Mauritius, there were instances of individual mobility. People set up small businesses, moved from the sugarcane estate to household jobs, some older immigrants were given land, which eventually became the foundation for a large small-planter society, and thus became the foundation for a process that Prabhu Mohapatra calls 'villagization', and some were promoted to headship.[32] Strong patronage relations between the sardar and the European overseer could become an avenue of mobility.[33] These tendencies loosened the team. In formation of hierarchies among the migrant communities, old immigrants who could speak Creole, and returnees, were placed in an advantageous position.[34] Their superior knowledge of working conditions and where jobs were available was indispensable information for potential migrants, whereas on their power of persuasion the employers relied for fresh recruitment of good workers. As Carter has shown in the context of Mauritius, returnees played a significant historical role in increasing information in the public domain, and in transforming the overseas destinations from an unknown to a known world to potential migrants by the last quarter of the nineteenth century.[35]

Throughout this transformation of the sardar from a social leader to a foreman, sardari authority also derived from a persistent worry about quality of workers. Ironically at the same time, questions of efficiency of the sardari recruitment system itself were being raised. In some colonies the law on the infringement of the indenture had to be invoked too often. Some quite vocal returnees 'gave the colony a bad name'.[36] The problem partly was that from the more successful settlements, in the Caribbean, Fiji, and East Africa especially, where a section of the settlers progressed from unskilled manual labour to

[32] "'Following Custom'? Representations of Community among Indian Immigrant Labour in the West Indies, 1880–1920', *International Review of Social History*, 51(2), 2006, pp. 173–202.

[33] B.V. Lal, 'Labouring Men and Nothing More: Some Problems of Indian Indenture in Fiji', in Kay Saunders, ed., *Indentured Labour in the British Empire, 1834-1920*, London: Croom Helm, 1984, pp. 126–57.

[34] J. Houbert, 'Mauritius: Independence and Dependence', *Journal of Modern African Studies*, 19, 1981, pp. 75–105.

[35] Marina Carter, *Servants, Sirdars and Settlers: Indians in Mauritius, 1834–1874*, New Delhi: Oxford University Press, 1995.

[36] India, *Report of the Committee on Emigration*, p. 19.

trade and skilled manual labour during the nineteenth century, the scale of return was smaller compared to Mauritius where avenues of mobility were limited. But these points do not explain away the persistent and long-standing complaints about quality.

When we gather together these complaints across different temporal and spatial contexts, the definition of quality can be shown to shift. There were four senses in which quality of worker or similar terms were used, and these were—vagrancy, shirking, industriousness, and mobilization. The mid-nineteenth century employer in the tea districts was worried about vagrancy. His counterpart in the sugar plantations elsewhere in the world was concerned about shirking and industriousness. The mill managers in Bombay of the 1930s were more concerned about hidden trade union elements. In official view, among the different classes of people who migrated in the nineteenth century, some were better able than others to withstand the discipline and rigour of agricultural labour in the plantations. Some had escaped the law or the harshness of life and livelihood in their places of origin, and these were more prone to shirking and complaining. A certain number of 'priests, barbers, jewellers, and men of that kind' did voluntarily enlist with the agents, and they were, official accounts believed, the complaining type.

The sardar was closely connected with the perceived problem of quality. Throughout the nineteenth century, any returnee sardar could earn handsome amounts by sending fresh recruits. In the views of the employers some took unfair advantage of the offer. 'They [the returnees] also send back before their indentures are over persons of the wastrel and loafer class of whom the colony wishes to rid itself'.[37] In order to get a handle on the problem, which would mean being better-informed than the sardar, employers tried to reduce industriousness to a few social markers. This was a long-standing preoccupation in colonial records, even though the constant grappling with social markers of good work did not necessarily improve the system. In the early nineteenth century, the 'junglies' or forest-dwellers were preferred to peasants, and the commission in recruitment reflected these preferences. In the second half of the nineteenth century, when the tribal element among migrants had fallen in response to

[37] Ibid.

high mortality among this class, 'Madrassies' and north Indians were similarly classified, in a manner that reflected a preference for the upper castes.[38] Yet, Brahmans were frequently clubbed with undesirables when it came to industriousness.

By the late nineteenth century, then, the headman was reinvented as a tool of management, in response to perceived or real problems of quality. We see another example of the same transformation in Assam.

DISCOVERING THE SARDAR IN ASSAM

The number of workers in the Assam tea estates increased from less than a hundred thousand in 1870 to almost 600,000 in 1900. Recruitment systems differed between the three major plantation clusters in north-eastern India, the Dooars in northern Bengal, Surma Valley in easternmost Bengal, and the Upper Assam. The two former regions were more accessible than Upper Assam, and faced much less difficulty in recruitment. Both these regions consequently could afford to experiment with the system of recruitment. In both, free or non-indentured labour played a larger role. For Upper Assam, however, problems of supply were more serious.

In 1905, Sir Bampfylde Fuller, Chief Commissioner of Assam, in a circular addressed to the Indian Tea Association, asked why tea garden labour had become 'markedly unpopular', and the labour force recruited were 'both intractable and inefficient'.[39] Two factors seemed responsible. First, the labourers were engaged on four-year contracts, running away from which invited arrest and trial. And second, labourers were recruited by agents who did not correctly inform them of the conditions in the plantations or the terms of employment. This view was far from exceptional at the turn of the century. Influential voices among planters in Assam, Dooars, and Surma Valley acknowledged the 'serious abuses' that the labour recruitment system entailed, and at the same time found it impossible to reform the system.

Sir Bampfylde spoke at a time of transition in the gardens of Upper Assam. About the middle of the nineteenth century when plantations in Assam and Dooars began to grow, the region was sparsely popu-

[38] Lai, *Indentured Labor*, pp. 112–15.
[39] India, *Proceedings of the Assam Labour Enquiry*, p. ix.

lated, had bad communications, and no local labour pool. Indeed, the difficulty of communication was legendary, as the following description of transporting tea in Assam around 1845 shows:

In the rains, tea chests could be taken in canoes down the small streams flowing into the Brahmaputra, but in the cold weather these streams dried up and as bullock carts scarcely existed in Assam at that time, chests had to be carried by coolie or by elephant. [Both elephants and labour were scarce at that time]. Even when the tea had been brought as far as the Brahmaputra, the difficulties of transporting it to Calcutta were great. The normal method of transport between Calcutta and Assam was by means of country boats, [which] were generally dragged along the bank by ropes when ascending the river...The journey between Calcutta and Gauhati seems to have taken anything from two and a half to three months.[40]

Not surprisingly, finding labour for such destinations as these posed a huge challenge. Large flows of overseas migration from Chota Nagpur had by then begun. And it was inevitable that the planters would consider a system very similar to the one already in place in the case of Mauritius.

In the 1840s, recruitment was done by professional labour agents or arkatis.[41] The agents practiced misinformation as a form of art. Many workers signed an indenture on a wrong understanding of what the job entailed, where they were going, and what their chances were of returning. A general and acute labour scarcity, met with workers who felt cheated even before arrival, gave rise to demands for securing labour more firmly to land. The response was a long (five years to start with) indenture contract at the plantations end. The distinctive feature of the Assam contract was that it was drawn between individual workers and the planter, rather than between the contractor and the planter, as in the case of Madras and Ceylon. Liability of fulfilling the contract fell on the individual worker, and to secure this obligation an Act was passed that made it possible for employers to penalize and bring back the deserting worker—the Workmen's Breach of Contract

[40] Percival Griffiths, *The History of the Indian Tea Industry*, London: Weidenfield and Nicholson, 1967. In this case, the transportation problem was solved by a combination of railway, steamboats, and bullock carts, and not railway alone.

[41] The best general account of the agent in the tea gardens is Griffiths, *History of the Indian Tea Industry*, pp. 267–96.

Act, better known as the Act XIII of 1859. On the other side, the Inland Immigration Act of 1863 made it mandatory for all contractors to be licensed.

Shortage continued. By the third quarter of the nineteenth century, increasing competition for labour had made the traffic more difficult. Development of railway construction and mining in the 'catchment' areas increased the local demand for labour. The contractors had to travel further to obtain workers. Landowners were generally against emigration. Some charged unauthorized commission for allowing recruiting agents into their territories. Others spread rumour with the help of the police.[42] To allow an alternative to indenture, an Act passed in 1882 enabled 'free' recruitment by unlicensed contractors. In practice, most free labourers were also put on a contract directly when they reached Assam. The so-called free labourers did not often see the difference, and the recruiters did not try too hard to explain it to them. These labourers were free until they reached depots in Dhubri or Dibrugarh, river-ports where the contracts were signed after considerable haggling over commission between the garden agent and the contractor's men, and before they were taken to the gardens.

In 1900, going to Assam had acquired an adverse image in lower Bengal and Bihar. The recruiters needed to be both tough and wily to do their business. The business attracted such people.[43] The free recruiters told the prospective worker that he or she would be employed in the coal mines located in the same larger region. On such promises, the party came to Raniganj, a mining town in the Burdwan district of Bengal, which contained a 'depot' or waiting station for prospective emigrants. At this stage, the party had to appear before a magistrate and the worker was required to state that he/she was going to Assam willingly. Upon learning the truth, sometimes the labourer tried running away. The manager and the sub-agent tried to force the person back to the court-room. If the labourer gave evidence at this

[42] '[A] common story [in Jubbulpore] is that oil is extracted from the bodies of coolies', India, *Assam Labour Enquiry*, p. 57.

[43] According to one professional agent, 'most of the people free recruited under the present system have been *phuslaoed* [tricked] by the recruiters', India, *Assam Labour Enquiry*, p. 5.

stage that he/she had been forced, the manager could be prosecuted. But prosecution was rare because the labourer's will gave way at some stage in these proceedings, especially in a situation in which the underworld was patently interested.[44]

And yet, reports of recruitment probably exaggerated the involuntary nature of the migration. During famines and epidemics, Assam received a large number of migrants who wanted to escape starvation. Neither wage nor the quality of life was actually worse in the plantations.[45] The evidence of desertion does not suggest that desertion was as serious a problem as claimed. In 1877, deserters as proportion of the mean labour force formed 5.7 per cent; in 1901, the percentage was 3 (the proportion rose again later, in anticipation of the end of the Act XIII).[46] By comparison in the mills, the incidence of 'absenteeism' was far worse, at 10–15 per cent of the work-force on an average day.[47] At the end of the nineteenth century, actual instances of punishments under the specific provisions of the 1859 Act were as low as 0.1–0.2 per cent of total garden labour force.[48]

The adverse reputation of Assam had built on two connected problems—the notion of the region as a land-of-no-return, and scarcity of single women in the plantation society. The problem was not that a large number made a serious attempt to escape. The problem rather was that very few did. To people back home, those who renewed their contracts vanished permanently. Upper Assam in this way 'tied one down.'[49] The demographic profile was a major cause of stress. The gar-

---

[44] A European Magistrate of Ranchi remarked that 'the recruiters keep up connection with local badmashes [miscreants]'. As one contractor explained, 'if I tell the ways [of enticing a coolie without inviting the Magistrate's suspicion], I may suffer in consequence'. Ibid., p. 8.

[45] Ibid., p. 10.

[46] R.K. Das, Plantation Labour in India, Calcutta: R. Chatterjee, 1931.

[47] 'Absenteeism', usually a result of some workers leaving for their villages without taking leave, was the principal example cited by the mill owners to show that the quality of labour was inadequate. The reliance on the jobber rested on this feature. What is not clear, however, is whether absenteeism was the cause or the effect of the dependence on the agent.

[48] India, Assam Labour Enquiry, p. 238.

[49] 'The Dooars are more popular than Assam because people can come back when they like', E.M. Whitley, S.P.G. Mission, Ranchi, before India, Assam Labour Enquiry, p. 13.

dens employed a large number of women. Nearly all were married when they arrived. Few among the single male migrants could find a wife. Few could return home easily to marry. Few had the bride-price in hand. Single women rarely volunteered for enlistment. After free recruitment began in 1882, single women needed to furnish a witness certifying that they were going of their own volition. Women accompanied by male relatives were hired, but upon paying a commission to those relatives. Single women migrants were often desperate individuals who 'only wanted to get away'.[50] Others were tricked by predators.[51]

Around 1880, the feeling among planters was that, whereas the professional contractors were good at supplying large numbers quickly, their methods ended up gathering 'the sweepings of the bazaars'.[52] With its bad reputation behind, Assam had become the 'bankruptcy court, the divorce court and the poor-house of the down-country districts'.[53] Planters were routinely left with individuals who had no prior experience with cultivation. There was little a planter could do to coerce the contractor to minimize the risk of shirking. 'My chief objection to the contractor system was that the contractors recruited for Assam as a whole and not for individual concerns, the result being that ... unless we took the bad with the good, they used to refuse to supply us'.[54]

By contrast with the contactor-recruited single male homesick to an extraordinary degree, the 'sardari coolies', or workers hired by foremen, belonged in groups made up of friends, relatives, and women. By 1880, an ideology of the 'headman' took roots in the European planter circles. 'The best way of working with the natives of the coolie class is to deal with them through headmen who understand their likes and dislikes in a way which no European could'.[55] Sardari recruitment,

[50] Ibid., p. 5.

[51] For one example, India, *Assam Labour Enquiry*, p. 4. On women's migration to Assam, see also S. Sen, '"Without His Consent?": Marriage and Women's Migration in Colonial India', *International Labor and Working-Class History*, 65, 2004, pp. 77–104.

[52] India, *Assam Labour Enquiry*, p. 23–4.

[53] Ibid., p. 77.

[54] India, *Assam Labour Enquiry*, p. 171, A.B. Hawkins, Assam Oil Company.

[55] India, *Assam Labour Enquiry*, pp. 46, 50.

in this way, solved many problems at once—that of getting labour, getting stable labour, training labour, the challenge of creating a new society, and facilitating communication. The example of the kangany system also influenced this perception. Who were the garden sardars? They were senior workers, who sometimes rose from the ranks, and sometimes were established headmen. In all cases the sardar was 'the working head of his own settlement of coolies and he would see to their welfare'.[56] The expectation from the new rules was that a sardar, sent back home with a license and monetary incentives, would recruit from immediate relations and friends. Sardari workers were cheaper to obtain. The contractor spent money on search, but the sardar did not have to. Based on somewhat idealized descriptions of the sardar, the *Assam Labour Enquiry* 'made a recommendation—which runs quite contrary to all received thought on the subject—that estates should work through headmen and gangers'.[57]

In 1915, the sardari system was the only legalized system of recruitment for Upper Assam. The change was such a thorough one that even the employer 'cannot himself legally engage labour in a recruiting district; he must do so through the agency of his garden sardars'.[58] Equally, a labourer who wanted to voluntarily join the garden had to go though a sardar. A labourer who left home could not return to Assam without a sardar. With all competition blocked, and labour demand still brisk, the sardar turned into a contractor. The triumph of the new sardari system, thus, brought on the collapse of the 'true sardari system' as it existed in the late nineteenth century. 'Such men' as the new sardars 'are obviously professional recruiters and not genuine labourers. Not infrequently they are sent to districts other than their home districts'.[59] In one case of inspection in Basti, United Provinces, it was found that a large number of recruitments had taken place at the railway station. Search costs were still very high, and so was the commission offered, so that the sardars had incentive to switch effort from training relatives to recruiting from far and wide. The new law that prohibited entry of anyone into an estate

[56] Ibid., p. 46.
[57] Griffiths, *History of the Indian Tea Industry*, p. 280.
[58] Ibid., p. 52.
[59] Ibid.

unaccompanied by a sardar virtually killed the labour market in the gardens of Upper Assam.

The 'true sardari system' died because it was incapable of reducing search costs. Sardars could recruit only on a very limited scale. After all, '[T]he *sardar* is an amateur whose operations are confined to the neighbourhood of his own village. The recruiter is a professional whose field is the whole district'.[60] The usual practice was to call in a worker who was about to retire, and send the person home in search of workers. Some treated the occasion as a paid holiday, a luxury in the tea garden world.[61] Equally, a planter often treated a demand for a holiday as a chance to recruit new people. Some never returned. Some returned to join another garden on a false identity. The sardars thus sent home did not try too hard to search for people. Interviews of retired sardars at the Royal Commission verified what planters and officers often complained, that the old-style sardar succeeded in getting not more than two to three people on average in a lifetime consisting of three visits home. The old-style sardari had by then exhausted its potentials. 'My sardars failed because they had recruited all their relations and friends and so had exhausted their connections'.[62]

While the old system died, the new sardari system brought back the old problem of selection. Once again, recruitment began to 'result in a considerable number of undesirables being brought right up to the gardens'.[63] But by the early interwar period, the connotations of quality had changed. Desertion was a problem on a smaller scale. Assam did not evoke the fears that it had two generations before, at least partly because returnees had increased in number, and as with Mauritius, 'every migrant on his return became an apostle of migration'.[64]

The emerging problem, rather, was sardar power. Each sardari worker was bound by social ties to one sardar, and loyalties were not easily transferable. The wages of ordinary workers, therefore, barely

[60] India, *Assam Labour Enquiry*, p. 41.

[61] Ibid.

[62] India, *Assam Labour Enquiry*, p. 151, E.W. Pickard-Cambridge, planter.

[63] India, *Royal Commission on Labour in India, Vol. VI, Part II, Evidence recorded in Assam*, Calcutta: Government Press, 1931, J.H. Copeland, Manager, Cinnamara Tea Estate.

[64] J.C. Jha, *Aspects of Indentured Inland Emigration to North-East India 1859–1918*, New Delhi: Indus Publishing, 1998

rose between 1910 and 1930, even as sardari commission remained high. Workers who appeared before the Royal Commission on Labour in India (1929–31) testified to the persistence of low wages.[65] Managers admitted that the low wages worked as disincentive to work.[66] Debts secured the sardar's control over the workers. The sardar discriminated between 'his own men' and the others he was asked to supervise, and cultivated the belief that runaways could be beaten and arrested.

The estate worker did not handle machinery; the mill worker did. The authority of the headman in the industrial setting derived not only from the recruitment role but also from a training role.

THE 'SARDAR' AND INDUSTRIALIZATION

If the eighteenth century port city was a 'city of villages', in the late nineteenth century, the urban identity of the metropolis was stronger and had submerged community identities and spaces within it to a great extent. Increasingly, single male migration dominated the urban labour force, as migration was now induced no longer by the limited consumption of services by the European residents, but by industrialization, public utilities, export trade, and large-scale construction. These migrants could not afford to live in the communal quarters. The territorial distinctness of the working class, thus, was fading away.

Interestingly enough, even as the correlation between caste and space weakened, caste and community as such did not. Recruitment and hiring operated on a much larger scale than before, and under the rubric of breach of contract laws. The headman was not necessarily the only kind of recruiting agent. But if old needs disappeared, new ones arose. Training and apprenticeship, discipline, keeping labour at the work-site for long hours, were important functions inside a mill, relegated again to the intermediary. In exchange for securing a stable, reliable, disciplined labour force, the headman was allowed considerable freedom to hire and fire individual workers under him. Even as more individuals moved in to the cities, it was never easy for

[65] India, *Royal Commission on Labour, Vol. VI, Part II*, pp. 114–18, workers at Boloma Tea Estate.

[66] India, *Royal Commission on Labour, Vol. VI, Part II*, p. 113, C.K. Bezbaruah, Manager, Boloma Tea Estate.

" Indian Textile Journal."

The Jobber and his Tenters.

Figure 5.2: Jobber watching over his tenters, c. 1920. Source: Arno Pearse, *The Cotton Industry of India*, Manchester: International Federation of Master Cotton Spinners and Manufacturers, 1930

the individual migrant in Bombay or Calcutta to secure a job without the help of the intermediary.

The counterpart of the sardar inside the Bombay cotton textile mills was the jobber, and inside the Calcutta jute textile mills the sardar, in a milieu that had a considerable presence of workers from Chota Nagpur. In both these contexts, the labour-agent was rather more indispensable as supervisor than in the plantations context.

The jobber was a senior worker who began as a labour contractor, evolved into a supervisor or head of work-teams, and throughout, was given over significant powers to hire casual labourers and fire them as well, on a token permission from the immediate superior.[67] Unlike

[67] For discussions on the Bombay jobber, see Morris, *Emergence of an Industrial Labour*, pp. 129–142; D. Kooiman, *Bombay Textile Labour: Managers, Trade*

the manager, the jobber was 'one of the workers', a counterpart of the headman of worker gangs or a master artisan. The element of an informal collective in the jobber-worker relationship is illustrated by the fact that in some situations, when the jobber left the job, the team lost theirs too, or followed their captain.[68] Part of this custom was recreated. But there was also involved here a notion of work-team that can be seen at work in its clearest form in artisanal textile factories, and that also recur in sardari recruitment in the plantations. Merchants established factories producing carpets or cloth in northern India, but did not recruit workers. They did not even know who the workers were. They hired masters to do the work by piece-rate, which the latter did by bringing in their own apprentice teams.[69] The jobber and the sardar evolved from similar norms. They were neither workers nor managers. Rather, they were masters in command over their own men.

The early history of the Bombay jobber remains obscure. While mill construction began in the 1850s, the growth of the industry was shaken by the 1860s cotton famine and subsequent crash at the end of the civil war in America. Between 1880 and 1900 Bombay was short of labour. A solution had been envisioned by Jamsetji Tata, who vigorously campaigned among other mill-owners and among provincial administrators for concerted action on importing

---

Unionists and Officials, New Delhi: Manohar Publications, 1989; D. Mazumdar, 'Labour Supply in Early Industrialization: The Case of the Bombay Textile Industry, Economic History Review, 26(3), 1973, pp. 477–96; and Chandavarkar, The Origins of Industrial Capitalism, pp. 195–207. There were differences and similarities between Bombay and Ahmedabad in recruitment and supervision in the nineteenth century. For a picture of the Ahmedabad jobber that overlaps with that of his counterpart in Bombay, see Salim Lakha, 'Character of Wage Labour in Early Industrial Ahmedabad', Journal of Contemporary Asia, 15(4), 1985, pp. 421–41.

[68] 'A.: If a jobber moves from a mill he will take the labour with him. ... Q.: Does he take the labour with him because of their affection for him or because of bonds of other kinds? A.: Bonds of other kinds ... there is no affection about it'. Evidence by R. Blackwell, J. Parker, J. B. Green, Bombay European Textile Association, India, Royal Commission on Labour in India, Vol. I, Part II, p. 332.

[69] T. Roy, Traditional Industry in the Economy of Colonial India, Cambridge: Cambridge University Press, 1999.

labour from the densely populated United Provinces.[70] The 1880 Famine Commission had already underscored the need to encourage emigration from this region. About the same time, Tata had purchased the ill-fated Dharamsi mill. The mill was located nine miles away from the centre of Bombay, in a place (Kurla) then notorious for being a den of the underworld. Some of the labour contractors of the closed mill had started up in gambling, and allegedly intimidated former workers from joining the mill. Agents were sent to Broach to recruit workers, but the attempt did not produce results. Having failed to create a steady and disciplined labour force, Tata persuaded the Bombay Mill Owners Association to write a letter to the administrator of the United Provinces in 1888 seeking administrative help with recruitment in that region. The Lieutenant Governor responded coldly reminding the Association of 'the law of supply and demand'. In the next decade, migration from the region did increase greatly.

Description of this episode suggests two lessons about the formation of labour force in the period of rapid mill building in the city. First, the jobbers already performed two functions for the employers—to recruit, and to supervise workers. The 'gambling jobbers had under the old regime become masters'. And second, the workers came from a much differentiated pool. Indeed, without the help of the jobbers, the employers had no effective means to control the 'fierce and fighting Mahrattas' or the 'exceedingly riotous and mischievous' Julaha weavers.

When older insiders looked back to the nineteenth century around 1900, they saw the early jobber as a recruiter of labour who brought fellow villagers into the city. If the jobber did not play a major function in management in the first phase of the industry, the transformation of the recruiting agent into a dual role of recruiter-supervisor happened soon after. Morris D. Morris suggests that the jobber became transformed from a recruiter to an agent of command because of a linguistic, cultural and communication gap between the managers and the workers.[71] A senior worker who spoke the language

[70] D.E. Wacha, *The Life and Life Work of J. N. Tata*, Madras: Ganesh and Publishers, 1914.

[71] Morris D. Morris, *The Emergence of an Industrial Labor Force in India: A Study of the Bombay Cotton Mills*, Berkeley and Los Angeles: University of California Press, 1965, pp. 129–53.

of the ordinary worker and came from the same social background, and yet could communicate with the managers, bridged the gap.

By around 1900, the jobber had become a unit of management. But they were not necessarily controlled by the management. Jobbers were prominent figures in workers' neighbourhoods in the early twentieth century, and some of them functioned as channels through which collective bargaining and urban politics could join together. They played a positive role in looking after the interests of the ordinary workers in the early stages of the growth of the mill industry. Pioneering figures in labour mobilization and organization emerged from jobber background. Workers had reasons to look up to them for fair treatment from the employers, and moral support.

One of the functions the jobber was increasingly called upon to do was supervision of machinery. A 'Retired Mill Manager', wrote at the turn of the century: 'The whole of the frames department is put under a head jobber with an assistant under him ... They have to repair all the breakages in the machinery, change the counts when required, prevent singles, and generally to see that all is going on straight under the direction of the foreman'.[72]

Despite being in charge of the machinery, the jobber was not exactly a technical man, but a medium between the workers and the technical men. They belonged in a segment of the hierarchy that was distinct from the segment represented by the Parsi or European foremen. The Royal Commission on Labour in India hinted at a horizontal divide within the working class. The workmen and the supervisors were distinguished by possession or otherwise of literacy.[73] In England, the distinction did not exist, permitting workmen to graduate into supervisors. In India, literacy and unbridgeable class difference acted as a barrier to this progression. There were two apparent consequences of this divide. First, the supervisory positions, occupied by Europeans initially, were later 'Indianized' with people who did not rise from the ranks, but were products of universities and polytechnics. They did not speak the language of the workers and did not belong to the same social class. Second, an intermediate layer of supervisors rose

[72] *Indian Textile Journal*, 'Hints on the Management of Cotton Mills', 14, 1903, p. 81.
[73] India, *Report of the Royal Commission on Labour in India*, Calcutta, 1931, p. 31.

from the ranks to monitor workers. The jobber was answerable to the 'Lancashire managers and their Parsee assistants' for keeping the machines in good condition, performing tasks in time, and supervising work-teams under him. At the same time, the jobber, or his female counterpart the *naikin*, was also in charge of completing tasks, and hiring extra hands in case of shortness in order to complete tasks.

Interestingly, the jobber was becoming redundant as a recruitment agent in the 1920s. For, between the 1870s and the 1920s, a great casual labour market had emerged in the city. The early-interwar period saw increasing rural crisis and unemployment in the cities. Real wages in Bombay mills were more than double that an artisan would earn in a small town, and significantly above the annual average incomes in farming. The cost of moving to the city had decreased, and the knowledge of living conditions increased. Workers in search of casual work would present themselves at the mill gate every morning. It was not the manager, but the jobber who selected casual labourers from this pool. The daily task of the head jobber was to select those extra hands to be employed for the day, and start the machines before the department heads entered the mill premises.[74]

These hands were selected as *badlis* from crowds gathered at the mill gate. The jobber, who usually kept a subsidiary muster of his own, did the selection. Any senior or skilled worker could also hire substitutes, and enjoyed some of the powers that the jobber did. Once the managers agreed to take in a large number of badlis to meet a shortfall, the jobbers said—'They will create trouble ... go on strike ... the best men will leave the mill unless a certain proportion of the men are allowed to work, at least for half the month or something like that'.[75] However, who would stay and who had to leave was a decision that depended on the price of job security in the internal labour market, which was partly controlled by the intermediaries.

Why was the jobber needed for recruitment any more if the labour supply had shifted? The jobber was valuable, Chandavarkar explains, as a recruiter because of variations in the demand for casual labour,

[74] India, *Royal Commission on Labour in India, Vol. I, Part I, Written Evidence recorded in Bombay Presidency*, Calcutta: Government Press, 1931, p. 296, Bombay Textile Labour Union.

[75] N.G. Hunt of Greaves Cotton, *Proceedings of the Bombay Strike Enquiry Committee*, vol. III, p. 1071.

in turn attributed to fluctuations in market and availability of raw cotton.[76] The jobber knew the men individually and understood the difference in quality, was the answer advanced by millowners.[77] But neither view is completely convincing, for the Bombay mills were not models of work-effort, and mills 'up-country' had installed personnel managers to serve these functions.[78]

The persistence of the recruitment function can be interpreted also as the reward offered to the jobber for another task that he was expected to serve. One of the implicit goals of the system was endogenous provision of quality, including skill and reliability. The managers and owners could wash their hands off training and education of workers because the jobber was by default in charge of these functions. In 1908, when the Indian Factory Labour Commission investigated the question why the work-day was very long in the Indian mills, it was apparent that the mill owners had hardly any serious thought on the point of organization of work. This was attributed to 'the fact that the owners themselves had not been brought up to the practical working of a mill'.[79] In 1903, the retired mill manager cited above suggested that this work-organization where the jobber was supervisor-cum-boss was not only a long-standing feature but also carried hazards especially when scarcity appeared, 'the jobber can baffle the foreman or manager who is utterly unacquainted with the class of hands working in Bombay mills'.[80] Inevitably, training of workers became a part of the commercial and hierarchical transactions that tied the senior workers and jobbers with the workers.

The system led to poor work effort. Not all jobbers and worker-bosses were technical experts. Indeed, few were. Given their authority over the workers, the jobbers could still potentially arrange on-the-job training if they wanted to. But they had no incentive for doing so. The commission collected from a worker for providing him or her with a job was higher for the less skilled, because the latter would find

---

[76] Chandavarkar, *Origins of Industrial Capitalism*, p. 196.

[77] Morris, *Emergence of an Industrial Labor Force*, p. 136.

[78] India, *Royal Commission on Labour in India, Vol. I, Part II, Oral Evidence recorded in Bombay Presidency*, Calcutta, 1931, p. 431.

[79] India, *Indian Factory Labour Commission, vol. II, Evidence*, Simla, 1908, p. 111.

[80] *Indian Textile Journal*, 'Hints on the Management', p. 81.

it harder to get a job. The return from creating a really skilled worker accrued to the mill. The return from recruiting raw hands accrued to the jobber. There was incentive, therefore, to under-train or not to hire the best quality. Mills in Bombay always kept more people on the rolls than were needed. The mill-owners' standard complaint was that absenteeism reached high levels. But they did not investigate why there were high levels of absenteeism. The jobber had an incentive, namely the commission, to hire larger numbers than were needed.[81]

Not only did the jobber find it profitable to hire more heads than necessary, the jobber and the senior workers came into frequent conflicts. The former lived on commissions, and any worker who believed he/she had the prospect of getting a job elsewhere refused to pay the commission demanded.[82] In short, if a senior worker was given the power to fire other workers, the first people to go would be the potential competitors, namely the good quality people. A great deal of these abuses was publicized by the Textile Labour Union. The Union was caught up in its own dilemma. The divisions within the work-force—with its jobbers, skilled workers, the rank and file, apprentices, badlis, migrants and settlers, castes and communities—made the task of forging class consciousness an impossible challenge. Paradoxically, they could not succeed in this challenge without using the persuasive power of the intermediaries themselves. In this situation, they could hardly afford to open another front by raising the training and quality implications of the system.

The managers tolerated this practice as long as the jobber took care of delivering a job in time, and as long as wages were low enough. The situation did not demand a remedy when competition was mainly from Lancashire, where wages were more than seven times that of the Bombay wages at 1920. But a threat developed with Japan's entry into the world cotton textile market. Wages in Japan were only 15–20

---

[81] This syndrome was widely discussed in late-interwar Bombay. See Bombay, *Report of the Textile Labour Inquiry Committee*, vol. II (Final Report), Bombay: Government Press, 1940, p. 338. See also Morris, *Emergence of an Industrial Labour Force*, pp. 129–30.

[82] The most detailed description of commissions, including these practices, is available in the representation of the trade unions. See, in particular, Bombay Textile Labour Union, *Report of the Indian Tariff Board (Cotton Textile Industry Enquiry) 1927*, vol. III, (Evidence of Local Governments, and so on.), Calcutta: Government Press, pp. 438–9.

per cent higher. The mill owners had two choices—rationalization or wage-cuts—and a few chose the latter, leading to strained industrial relation. From the first major strikes in 1924 and 1925 to the time when the Great Depression struck, the work organization in Bombay came under serious scrutiny for generating too much inefficiency.

CONCLUSION

Formation of groups and the transformation of the group-leaders into agents of some kind were tendencies present in industrialization throughout the world. India supplied models of hierarchy from its own tradition. The early nineteenth century headman guided a group through difficult and unfamiliar forms of market negotiation. From these origins, the collective later absorbed managerial roles. The nineteenth century collective represented a form of partnership between the headman and the manager ensuring reliable supply of effort, in exchange for some freedom granted to the former to recruit and retrench workers. Critics felt that it had already become an exploitative device which some employers and headmen colluded to keep going, and yet the workers did not need any more. In the twentieth century history of the cotton mills of Bombay, we see this syndrome develop.

The community among workers was a far cry from the community among merchants. Marriage played no visible role in the making of a worker group. The workers shared neither a strong emotional capital nor valuable resources like money, information, or craftsmanship. Often hailing from the same villages or kin and caste groups, they did share a bond, but a bond contingent on immediate needs of security and communication. Optimists among planters believed the sardar would recreate a social world around the workers. The truth was—the sardari authority reflected the individual worker's vulnerability.

From the capitalists' side, negotiating with a headman saved on training and supervision costs, but entailed loss of control on incentives and discipline. In situations that demanded the capitalist try to raise labour productivity, agency became a burden. Skill formation had always been a serious problem in interwar Bombay, and addressed badly by the employers and intermediaries alike. There was a historical antecedent to the skill problem. Traditional artisans who had a well-developed apprenticeship tradition had joined the mill to a rather limited extent in India. Predominantly, the mill work-force was composed of peasants, who had no distinct institutional heritage on training. The ethnically diverse composition of the work-force, and the heavy dependence of the employers on recruiting agents for communication with and supervision of workers, led to a curious joining of two distinct kinds of headmanship in one person—social leadership and skill leadership. In turn, the confusion undervalued skill leadership, and therefore training and apprenticeship, and the two roles were often in conflict.

Peasants are the subjects of the final study. Rural society throughout the world tends to be identified with traditionalism, meaning dominance of family and commune. Colonial India conforms to this picture, but also shows that traditionalism had modern roots.

6 Peasants
Property and market

This chapter explores how changes in peasant property rights and peasant participation in markets in the nineteenth century reshaped the role of the collective. Peasant property rights on land, before the eighteenth century, derived from the position of the peasant community in the fiscal system. The community was strong among other reasons because tax obligations were usually fixed upon groups, and sometimes associated with militarily powerful clans or groups that could command the labour resources adequate to breaking new land. Agricultural growth in pre-colonial times was a group effort. Growth occurred by means of extension of cultivation, a process that depended on partnership between chiefs or military tribes in charge of tax collection, and dominant peasant lineages in charge of production. For the same reason, peasant revolts targeted officers and agents of the state, and were organized by communities rallying around their chiefs.

In the eighteenth century, even as imperial control collapsed, substantially the same arrangement continued. Some of the local rights of tax collection became saleable in the course of commercialization and decentralization of authority, but there were few instances of actual sale. The big change came about between 1793 and 1857, when British Indian reforms demilitarized the armed local elites while creating an unencumbered ownership right in land. Continuity was respected, intentionally or otherwise, in the design of these reforms. Ownership rights went to groups already in possession of superior rights in the old regime, and the new owners needed to befriend dominant peasants for the reason that the latter commanded productive resources and the fiscal system and law books in some regions respected joint property of clan and kinship.

Still, the new world silently chipped away at the power and relevance of the peasant collective. It did so partly by privileging superior right-holders in the market for commodity and credit, partly by inviting numerous lawsuits disputing the rights of clans, and partly by intensifying trade disputes that took on a class character. The new disputes occurred between peasants and capitalists, rather than between the peasants and the state. The state was drawn in as a third party responsible for making deterrent laws. These laws, in turn, reduced the power of the capitalist, allowed peasants to lead credit and sale transactions, and speeded up the differentiation process.

PEASANT PROPERTY BEFORE THE EIGHTEENTH CENTURY

Burton Stein classified pre-colonial property 'rights' on land into three classes—'prebendal' or state-issued rights, private property rights, and communal rights.[1] The sphere of private property rights was narrow, being restricted to land grants made to individuals with exceptional, usually religious, merit. Nearly all the rest involved either the influence of state offices, or that of a kin, lineage, and village network. None of these rights was easily saleable, for the first was conditional on loyalty and power, the second was conditional on merit, and the third was conditional on an agreement between members of a collective.

In pre-seventeenth century northern India, 'there was little question of the peasants claiming property rights over any parcel of land'.[2] For, peasants shared the right to use land with the local chiefs. In matters of detail, the system could differ between different regions of South Asia. But the fundamental principle changed little; intermediaries collected the dues from the peasants, retained a portion, and delivered the rest to the treasury. Their right upon land consisted in a right to collect taxes. Their obligation was to supply soldiers when called upon to do so. In some cases, the intermediaries were located in the village. In the Mughal *jagirdari* system, they represented a military-administrative

---

[1] Burton Stein, 'Eighteenth Century India: Another View', in P.J. Marshall, ed., *The Eighteenth Century in Indian History. Evolution or Revolution?*, Delhi: Oxford University Press, 2003, pp. 62-89

[2] Irfan Habib, 'Agrarian Economy', in Tapan Raychawdhuri and Irfan Habib, eds, *The Cambridge Economic History of India*, vol. I, Cambridge: Cambridge University Press, 1982, p. 54.

hierarchy whose authority was technically non-hereditary, rather than peasant headmen whose authority was usually hereditary.

There was in any case a 'welter of rights' that bound each plot of land. Along one axis, the 'welter' would refer to the incomplete and segmented nature of every property right. Rights consisted of rights to collect taxes, rights to own the produce, rights to control cultivation, and rights to the commons.[3] Along another axis, the 'welter' would refer to shared nature of every property right.

Land sales were permitted and could occur. Historians have found evidence of sales and sale deeds, in medieval south India and in Mughal north India.[4] All evidence of sale points to a dependence of sale upon consent of the community and the officers, which would make sales primarily a form of intra-communal exchange. S. Naqvi, for example, mentions 'the existence of the right of alienation of land and of sale' in Mughal north India, but 'not without the consent of fellow landowners'. On the other hand, sale to members of the community were considerably easier to effect.[5]

How did agricultural growth occur in this regime? In the prevailing institutional set-up, agricultural growth could not conceivably take the form of private investment working to raise land yield. The welter of rights would make neither measurement nor capture of the incremental yield an easy matter for anyone. In no known episode of large-scale extension of cultivation did land market or land improvement play a key role. Peasants were not known to just buy their way into new territories.

And yet, the agrarian order was hardly a static one. Although early Company administrators described the Indian village as a peaceful, harmonious, changeless, if inefficient, economic and social order,

[3] See Dharma Kumar, 'A Note on Land Control', in Peter Robb, ed., *Rural India: Land, Power and Society under British Rule*, New Delhi: Oxford University Press, 1989, pp. 62–77 for an insightful discussion on 'land control'.

[4] Irfan Habib, 'Aspects of Agrarian Relations and Economy in a Region of Uttar Pradesh during the 16th Century', *Indian Economic and Social History Review*, 17(1), 1980, pp. 205–32; John F. Richards, 'The Seventeenth Century Crisis in South Asia', *Modern Asian Studies*, 24(4), 1990, pp. 625–38; B.A. Prakash, 'Agricultural Backwardness of Malabar during the Colonial Period: An Analysis of Economic Causes', *Social Scientist*, 16(6/7), 1988, pp. 51–67.

[5] 'Marx on Pre-British Indian Society', *Indian Economic and Social History Review*, 9(1), 1972, pp. 380–412.

a historiography that helped them to identify the representatives of the village tradition to negotiate revenue contracts with, historians recognize that there never was a changeless village order in pre-colonial India. Kings, chiefs, and peasant clans constantly redefined relationships and renegotiated terms, people moved from old to new tracts, hills to forests, forests to plains, and created new zones of agrarian expansion as well as decline. David Ludden's conception of agriculture consisting of territoriality and 'moving elements' captures this fluid nature of the village.[6]

Fluidity did not mean randomness. Sponsored resettlement of peasant communities, as opposed to private investment in buying or improving land, were more powerful forces behind the dynamics of agricultural growth and decline. 'Entrepreneurship' took the form of extensive growth or breaking new land frontier. Burton Stein calls such moves, in the context of the dry uplands of Vijayanagar, 'developmental investment'.[7] When colonizing new lands or trying to expand the agricultural frontier, the kings did not hire workers to do the job. If agricultural growth was not significantly market-mediated, nor was it totally state controlled. When rulers and their officers needed to raise tax resources, they usually forged a partnership with agents who were rooted in land and understood cultivation. They offered the latter low assessment for a number of years in exchange for organizing a land extension project. Land extension and fiscal stability required gifting secure rights to communities of peasants or headmen and chiefs among these communities. Some notion of hereditary rights of the original settler, thus, became ingrained in the land law of every region.

Who were these agents? Two broad categories would figure prominently in almost any answer to this question—military tribes and peasant clans. The land extension steps described before were always extremely labour-intensive, and required a reliable authority structure on the ground. Such authority and such scale of labour could only come from pre-existing hierarchical groups. A successful fiscal system rested on three types of enterprise—brute power, record-

[6] *The New Cambridge History of India IV. 4: An Agrarian History of South Asia*, Cambridge, Cambridge University Press, 1999.

[7] 'Eighteenth Century India: Another View', in Marshall, ed., *Eighteenth Century*.

keeping, and the command of labour. These tasks were sometimes performed by the same families, as with the Rajput lineages in north India. In Mughal north India, especially Awadh, administrative units (*pargana*) and Rajput lineages who had been soldiers and dominant peasants or tax collectors, tended to coalesce.[8] Rajput bands were again agents in land extension in seventeenth century Malwa.[9]

In most parts of India, however, the coalescence of military, administrative, and peasant power tended to be weak, or to become weak in the late eighteenth century. There was division of labour between these roles and an attempt to take over one or more of these functions by the paid officer of the state. In the uplands of western Maharashtra in the seventeenth and eighteenth centuries, superior rights vested with families that were credited with having started cultivation in a village, and also with families that had served the state as soldiers, but these two identities did not necessarily coincide. In Khandesh, for example, the overlap between administration and military tribes was weak. The dominant lineages in the village were of peasant stock. And the class of dominant cultivators tended to be organized in a corporate body. With the collapse of the Mughal Empire in northern India, migrant clans of Jats and Gujars occupied agricultural lands, usually with the consent and backing of ambitious local chiefs. The break-up of the Vijayanagar Empire saw powerful peasant 'headmen' occupy landed estates in the drier regions of south India.

In Mughal northern and eastern India, a hierarchy formed along the lines of long-settled groups that had broken the land, and migrant or late-comers. *Khud-kasht raiyats* (resident tenants) were collectively responsible for payment of land revenue. In return, they enjoyed lower tax rates and control over common property resources. Those who enjoyed more secure ownership rights on land and lenient revenue terms were also entrusted with the duty of tax collection and payment at the village level. Being collectively responsible for the financial

---

[8] Stewart Gordon and John F. Richards, 'Kinship and Pargana in Eighteenth Century Khandesh', *Indian Economic and Social History Review*, 22(4), 1985, pp. 371–97.

[9] Stuart Gordon, 'The Slow Conquest: Administrative Integration of Malwa into the Maratha Empire, 1720–1760', *Modern Asian Studies*, 11(1), 1977, pp. 1–40.

affairs of the village enabled their 'acting as a corporate body'.[10] In deltaic Tamil Nadu and parts of Bombay–Deccan, superior right-holders enjoyed *miras* rights, which were in principle rights over shares of the village produce, but in practice rights of land control vested in dominant peasant lineages. The miras rights were technically saleable, but sales were not common.[11] In Malabar, superior tax-payers had not been cultivators themselves. Superior rights to the produce of land were shared and specified in terms of caste. The real cultivators were the agrestic serfs.

PEASANT PROPERTY IN THE EIGHTEENTH CENTURY

Large states collapsed into smaller ones in the eighteenth century. The general consequence almost everywhere, and certainly in large parts of northern and eastern India, was a fragmentation and collapse of executive power, and consolidation of local groups and agents. In some cases these agents were peasant clans, in some cases, they were military elites. I have suggested earlier a picture of breakdown of customary law and customary justice among merchants and artisans. The agrarian order was not very different. Cohn's studies of the Benares region show how the authority of the state courts crumbled away in the eighteenth century, 'with litigants buying decisions' and judicial positions being 'looked upon as forms of private income for political favorites of the rulers'.[12] Kum Kum Banerjee, in a study of grain trade in the Bihar towns in the eighteenth century, suggests that rudimentary profession-based institutions of regulation in the urban trades disappeared in the eighteenth century.[13] Ravinder Kumar suggests that the autonomous juridical institutions of the Deccan village on the eve of British takeover were strong, and 'served to heighten

[10] Richards, 'Seventeenth Century Crisis'.

[11] Tsukasa Mizushima, 'Mirasi System as Social Grammar—State, Local Society, and Raiyat in the 18th-19th South India', *http://www.l.u-tokyo.ac.jp/~zushima9/pdf(for%20hp)/1-28.doc.*

[12] B.S. Cohn, 'From Indian Status to British Contract', *The Journal of Economic History*, 21(4), 1961, p. 615; 'The Initial British Impact on India', *The Journal of Asian Studies*, 19(4), pp. 418–31.

[13] 'Grain traders and the East India Company: Patna and its Hinterland in the Late Eighteenth and Early Nineteenth Centuries', *Indian Economic and Social History Review*, 23(4), 1986, pp. 403–29.

the isolation of the village'.[14] One of the routes by which former tax elites could now become de facto owners of land was the juridical one. The zamindars, for example, could now try small criminal and common law cases without challenge from any other administrator.[15] Tax collectors tried to become 'little kings'. Simultaneously, a market developed in tax collection rights.

The right to collect taxes had shown evidence of commercialization from the seventeenth century onward.[16] These rights were heritable and saleable to an extent. But sales were not common occurrences. Failure to pay taxes invited punishments, and did not usually lead to expropriation, because these rights had been connected with a promise to supply soldiers during battles. But now these rights began to change hands more frequently.

The fundamental source of this upheaval was the existence of a large number of states with weak, crumbling, and ad hoc fiscal administration, and wholly insufficient resources. There was pervasive government failure. The rulers were forced to offer terms that made the revenue rights more marketable. Merchants and financiers became closely associated with tax farming in exchange of loans advanced to fiscally weak successor states. '[M]oney [became] a crucial component of agrarian relations' in the eighteenth century.[17] In turn, this process could lead to 'growing intensity of conflicts between rights', as tax farmers tried to convert rights acquired from the state into something like private property rights, often in conflict with communal rights.[18] Reshuffling at the top of the order pushed tax farmers to make new kinds of land grants, and create new kinds of right on land.[19]

[14] 'Rural Life in Western India on the Eve of the British Conquest', *Indian Economic and Social History Review*, 2(3), 1965, pp. 201–20.

[15] Muhammad Basheer Ahmad, *The Administration of Justice in Medieval India*, Aligarh: The Aligarh Historical Research Institute, 1941, pp. 173, 279.

[16] Tapan Raychaudhuri, 'The State and the Economy: The Mughal Empire', in Tapan Raychaudhuri and Irfan Habib, eds., *The Cambridge Economic History of India*, vol. 1, Cambridge: Cambridge University Press, 1983, p. 177

[17] C.A. Bayly, *Rulers, Townsmen and Bazaars: North Indian Society in the Age of British Expansion 1770–1870*, New Delhi: Oxford University Press, 1983, p. 163.

[18] Stein, 'Eighteenth Century India', p. 79.

[19] For a study of a region in eastern India, Meena Bhargava, 'Perception and Classification of the Rights of the Social Classes: Gorakhpur and the East India Company in the late Eighteenth and Early Nineteenth Centuries', *Indian Economic*

Further below merchants and tax farmers, among the peasantry, a crystallization of property rights did begin to happen as a result of growing commodity trade. Sumit Guha notes the presence of an informal peasant property right in the Deccan towards the end of the eighteenth century.[20] Actual sales were neither common nor easy to effect. Rights were after all still heavily tied up in eighteenth century Deccan.[21] The best scholarly work available on Maratha law stated that 'from the Miras Patras which have hitherto been brought to light, it will be seen that the sales of immovable property were very rare and took place only under unavoidable circumstances'.[22]

Furthermore, the eighteenth century transition also offered a chance for dominant peasant lineages to consolidate themselves. Commodity trade opportunities, more competition among tax collectors, and collapse of imperial control, all point at the same direction. To the extent the dominant lineages succeeded in securing control on land, rights would become less saleable than before and the resistance to sales would grow too.

PEASANT PROPERTY: 1793–1857

When the East India Company officers began a discussion on how best to overhaul the archaic and crumbling fiscal system in territories under their control, they encountered a society that had been hierarchized along settler clans, tenants-outsiders, and labourers. An anonymous writer on agriculture in the western Gangetic plains stated the situation thus:

When we occupied the country, we found two classes of tenants—one with a right of occupancy, and one mere tenants at will. ... [I]n most estates of the Provinces there were certain tenants who had hereditary rights. They held their fields subject to payment of a rent which was not liable to arbitrary increase. ... They were, in some cases, men who had once held proprietary rights in the estate; in others, they were relatives of the proprietor; in others, they were merely tenants of very long standing, who had probably helped to bring the estate into cultivation. They were seldom men of inferior caste,

---

and Social History Review, 30(3), 1993, pp. 215–37.

[20] 'The Land Market in Upland Maharashtra', *Indian Economic and Social History Review*, 24(2), 1987, pp. 117–44.

[21] Kumar, 'Rural Life in Western India'.

[22] V.T. Gune, *The Judicial System of the Marathas*, Poona: Sangam, 1953, p. 2.

Figure 6.1: Jat peasant, c. 1820. Source: Tashrih-al-Aqvam. © British Library

and were protected in their rights more by public opinion than by legal enactments.[23]

In other words, an association between economic inequality, social inequality, and inequality in taxation rights and privileges informed the big picture of the agrarian world drawn by colonial administrators. Powerful clans in the western Gangetic plains controlled rights to use land, and commanded irrigation and livestock resources. They belonged in a few identifiable castes and communities. Although the officers sometimes 'reified' these distinctions and/or misunderstood the rights and duties of particular segments, neither the presence of a hierarchy, nor the insular nature of the clans with the firmest control on land, was fictional.[24]

The key point of the new property rights regime introduced by the Company in India was to recognize ownership rights at the expense of all other rights on land. Strategic land gifts were reduced in the new regime. Tax rates were fixed, and tax collection became a state office.

[23] A District Officer, *Notes on North-western Provinces of India*, London: W.H. Allen, 1869, pp. 147–8.

[24] On misreading, see Bhargava, 'Perception and Classification'.

The expected economic gain from the move was that land could now become a source of private investment. The return on land could be in principle calculated and compared with other uses of capital, attracting moneyed people including peasants to transact in land. Land should, via market, end up in the hands of the efficient user of land. The expected political gain was the demilitarization of the village. A locally entrenched armed elite, whether peasant chiefs or military clans, was considered dangerous to the regime, especially a regime run by foreigners, as well as a source of fiscal leakage.

How revolutionary was this step after all? The answer to this question depends on whose name appeared on the new title deed. Despite regional diversity and local experiments, property reform was a marriage of convenience between the dominant groups and the state almost everywhere. There was great deal of reshuffling among the rural tax-collecting aristocrats, especially in north India. But within the village, established norms generally won, and led to continuance, even consolidation, of the dominant peasants.

In Bengal and British Malabar, legal titles went to former tax-payers who did not actually cultivate land. The Bengal reform was called the Permanent Settlement or the zamindari system and involved giving land titles to zamindars. In western and southern India, and sporadically elsewhere, under the ryotwari settlement, land titles were given to peasants. In parts of the western Gangetic plains, land titles were given to dominant peasants.

In Bengal, revenue farming in the eighteenth century had strengthened sections of the rural aristocracy, who received legal title for no other reason than that the new regime had little information, and even less control, on the actual tillers of the land. In Malabar, the British reforms awarded land titles to the priestly and the warrior castes which earlier paid the taxes. The agricultural backwardness of Bengal and Malabar has been attributed by present-day historians as well as a section of the colonial officialdom to the decision to award titles to non-cultivating elites, who in turn exploited the tenants.[25]

---

[25] B.A. Prakash, 'Agricultural Backwardness of Malabar during the Colonial Period: An Analysis of Economic Causes', *Social Scientist*, 16(6/7), 1988, pp. 51–67.

Figure 6.2 Peasants of the Doab, c. 1870. Source: Louis Rousselet, *India and its Native Princes*, London: Bickers and Sons, 1883

The Bengal case should not be overdrawn. Any assumption that in zamindari areas, the way to get more output from land was to coerce the tenant should be discarded in the face of a well-known interpretation of the Permanent Settlement, which has argued that peasant power was in fact entrenched in lower Bengal and that there was path dependence in the new alliances that the zamindars needed to strike.[26] Indeed, in principle, it is equally plausible that the way to get more from land in a scenario where the owner did not understand cultivation was to offer incentives to the dominant peasants. Such strategies were present in Bengal. Rent-paying peasants had been differentiated, and a section

---

[26] Ratnalekha Ray, *Change in Bengal Agrarian Society, c. 1760–1860*, New Delhi: Manohar Publications, 1979.

of the tenantry—the *jotedars* and their counterparts—were powerful from very early times. In the eighteenth century, revenue farming had led to a coalition form between the peasant headmen and the revenue farmers, and consolidated the political and economic dominance of the former.[27] These peasants were organized in collectives, and negotiated terms with the zamindars as a group.

In the Bihar districts, new tenant groups organized themselves in caste collectives, using caste as a bargaining platform and as a means to 'combine powerfully against the zamindar'.[28] The dominant peasants owned or controlled key resources like land, credit, water, implements, and animals. Real work in the village, therefore, was impossible without their consent, cooperation, and control. Peter Robb makes the important point that in zamindari villages in Bihar, interdependence could be present in all economic decisions. 'Even within each basic production unit, the allocation of tasks among family members or between them and employees or patrons might be subject to restrictions and agreements'.[29] Survival as a peasant in this environment did not depend on private and economic resources, but on being able to get along with the coalition of dominant cultivators.

In ryotwari areas, the property right reform itself had the effect of consolidating the dominant lineage and group. Groups with access to land but unwilling or unable to cultivate land, were more likely to sell their way out of the village, as part of a larger strategy to shift from landed to literate occupations. Members of the pre-colonial rural elite, both military and service kinds, were among the principal sellers of land. All kinds of moneyed people bought land in the nineteenth century, but the groups likely to buy land titles were peasants and labourers. The decline or withdrawal of the non-cultivating elites and the consolidation of the peasantry left asset inequality broadly unchanged.[30] The general character of land transfers, in other words,

[27] Ratna Ray and Rajat Ray, 'Zamindars and Jotedars: A Study of Rural Politics in Bengal', *Modern Asian Studies*, 9(1), 1975, pp. 81–102.

[28] Peter Robb, 'Hierarchy and Resources: Peasant Stratification in Late Nineteenth Century Bihar', *Modern Asian Studies*, 13(1), 1979, pp. 97–126.

[29] 'Peasants' Choices? Indian Agriculture and the Limits of Commercialization in Nineteenth Century Bihar', *Economic History Review*, 45(1), 1992, pp. 97–119.

[30] Dharma Kumar, 'Land Ownership and Inequality in the Madras Presidency: 1853-54–1946-47', *Indian Economic and Social History Review*, 12(3), 1975, pp. 229–61.

was not from the poor-to-the-rich, nor from peasant-to-lender, as neo-Marxist historians suggested in the 1970s, but contained a significant element of rich-to-the-poor, peasant-to-peasant, and elite-to-peasant shifts.[31]

The initial steps in a ryotwari exercise involved finding out who the original cultivators were, to whom private rights were to be delivered. In a rural world where collective ownership and use of assets had been common, the task was not going to be an easy one. The local administration needed informants, which agents, willingly or otherwise, exploited the ignorance of their principals.[32] Because the dominant peasants could manipulate this process better, the ryotwari title holder was more likely to be the prominent cultivator or kin group in the village.

In the Bombay Deccan, *thulwaheeks*, 'founding families' or original settlers as distinct from *uprees* or lease-holders, gained from this process. The former were responsible for tax payments and in exchange enjoyed inalienable rights to cultivate.[33] In deltaic Tamil country, mirasi or *kaniyatci* rights meant that the harvest of the fields in a village was jointly owned amongst a group of coparceners. These co-sharers of the output of land consisted of the Vellala peasant caste in the early nineteenth century. Although the revenue officers who studied the system exaggerated the traditionalism of Vellala peasanthood, they were probably right in their assessment of the barriers to entry into the collectives then in existence not only of outsiders, but even of non-resident Vellalas.[34] Mirasidars received the legal title to land. The Company administration, however, was caught up in a long-standing dilemma, whether to allow a freer entry for labourers and tenants into land ownership, that is, allow a freer bidding for tax. The peasant

[31] On the Marxist literature on peasant differentiation, a selection of relevant essays can be found in Utsa Patnaik, *Agrarian Relations and Accumulation: The 'Mode of Production' Debate in India*, Bombay: Oxford University Press, 1990.

[32] For an interesting study of this problem, see Neeraj Hatekar, 'Information and Incentives: Pringle's Ricardian Experiment in the Nineteenth Century Deccan Countryside', *Indian Economic and Social History Review*, 33(4), 1996, pp. 437–57.

[33] Ravinder Kumar, 'Rural Life in Western India on the Eve of the Brtish Conquest', *Indian Economic and Social History Review*, 2(3), 1965, pp. 201–20.

[34] Eugene R. Irschick, 'Order and Disorder in Colonial South India', *Modern Asian Studies*, 23(3), 1989, pp. 459–92.

collective, itself partly a product of these policies, was simultaneously respected and held in suspicion by the administration. In the dry areas of Madras Deccan, by contrast, hierarchy among original right-holders and late-comers had already been weak. Peasant society here was more equal, and so were the rights, both being levelled down to a broad uniformity by the small amount of surplus that one could get out of land. In these zones, the dominant peasant was not a prominent feature of the agrarian order.[35]

'DIFFERENTIATION' VIA TRADE AND CREDIT: 1857–1947

The new regime of property, thus, strengthened ownership, while ownership rights were at the same time captured by old families—tax-paying ones in Bengal and Malabar, dominant peasants almost everywhere else. If we read from this description that there was more continuity than change in the authority and integrity of peasant community, we would make a mistake. Economic history suggests that the cornerstone of the pre-colonial land system, joint rights of peasant lineages, weakened everywhere and a process was initiated that the Marxists used to call 'differentiation'.[36]

Differentiation in this context would refer to the creation of means by which individuals and families within a formerly more homogeneous group could become unequal in income and wealth. The neo-Marxist literature considered the land market and land transactions to be the most important of such means. As a matter of fact, outright transfers of ownership rights occurred to a very small extent in all regions of India. According to one estimate, between 1882 and 1945, secure cultivation rights that changed hands formed no more than 0.5–1 per cent (average annual) of total area under such rights in Bengal.[37] In a south Indian district in the first decade of the

[35] On regional differences in institutional structure within Tamil Nadu, see Arun Bandopadhyay, *The Agrarian Economy of Tamil Nadu, 1820–1855*, Calcutta: K.P. Bagchi & Co., 1992.

[36] For a discussion of the category in the context of comparative history, see Henry Bernstein, 'Agrarian Classes in Capitalist Development', in Leslie Sklair, ed., *Capitalism and Development*, London: Routledge, 1994, pp. 40–71.

[37] Nariaki Nakazato, 'Regional Patterns of Land Transfer in Late Colonial Bengal', in Peter Robb, Kaoru Sugihara, Haruka Yanagisawa, eds., *Local Agrarian Societies in Colonial India: Japanese Perspectives*, New Delhi: Manohar Publications, 1997, pp. 250–79.

twentieth century, percentage of land to change hands was 1.5–2.2.[38] Mortgaged area is usually a good predictor of net sales. In Punjab in the early twentieth century, net mortgaged area (the difference between mortgages entered into and those retired) was usually less than one per cent of total area.[39] Why the land market was apparently paralyzed is an interesting question, to which I return further on.

Three other means of differentiation deserve more attention than land market transaction. These are—land law, which privileged the family over community; commodity trade, which privileged the large over small land-owner; and the credit market, which privileged the land-owner rich enough to have money to lend to other peasants. These three forces chipped away at the cohesion of the caste or communal group in the village.

Of these three forces, the role of commodity trade and credit is well-researched. The property rights reforms were followed by a long period of commercialization led by inland and overseas trade in such goods as indigo, wheat, rice, cotton, jute, groundnut, and sugarcane. Agricultural exports in real terms about doubled between the middle of the nineteenth century and the First World War. Cash crops like wheat or cotton needed finance because being traded over long distances under prior contracts, these involved more investments in time and money. The extended monetization of rent and tax, combined with the disparity between seasons of tax-collection and harvests, required credits. Through a process of mobility, migration, and resettlement of members of trader-moneylender groups, credit relations penetrated more deeply into rural India. The new relationship between the debtor and the creditor in the Indian village became controversial.[40] The credit market was imperfect, so that the lender could control the terms of credit. Accounting and legal literacy

[38] D. Rajasekhar, 'Commercialization of Agriculture and Changes in Distribution of Land Ownership in Kurnool District of Andhra (c. 1900–50)', in S. Bhattacharya et al, eds., *The South Indian Economy*, New Delhi: Oxford University Press, 1991, pp. 78–119.

[39] Neeladri Bhattacharya, 'Lenders and Debtors: Punjab Countryside, 1880–1940' in Sugata Bose, ed., *Credit, Markets and the Agrarian Economy of Colonial India*, Delhi: Oxford University Press, 1994, pp. 197–247

[40] See Sugata Bose, ed., *Credit, Markets and the Agrarian Economy of Colonial India*, New Delhi: Oxford University Press, 1994, for a selection of relevant essays.

was loaded in favour of the creditor. The peasant could get entrapped in a cycle of debt. Historians have used the term 'dependence' in the context of increasing indebtedness.[41] Of these worries, the one that took precedence over others was the threat of the peasant losing land to a non-cultivating moneylender.

As the land transfer data confirm, actual transfers occurred to a limited extent. Lenders lent money not because they hoped to take possession of the property of the poor, but because they had a reasonable chance of making money from the interest income. In a normal season, the interests of the debtor and the creditor were aligned rather than being in contradiction. The debtor expected to make money after paying back the loan, and the creditor hoped the debtor would repay rather than fail to repay the loan. Two types of lending satisfied that condition. In Punjab, a great deal of lending was made to relatively prosperous peasants. Credit symbolized creditworthiness. And increasingly, credit was tied to commodity trade. Interest rate was implicit in the low prices fixed on delivery of crops by the debtor to the creditor. Both such contexts point to the presence of peasants, who were richer than their neighbours, and some of whom took part in grain trade and credit business at the same time. These people found it profitable to rent *in* land and hire poorer peasants, thus stimulating market exchange in land and labour services.

That the new market-property-fiscal regime created opportunities for such peasants to grow richer is amply demonstrated in the literature. In the context of early nineteenth century Tamil Nadu, David Ludden writes—'Mahajan mirasidars and headmen used their control of land, labour, and various commercial assets to accumulate the financial resources that enabled them to contract for village revenues. Mirasidars formed the local keystone of the revenue arch'.[42] In the dryland Deccan, although social structure was relatively 'flat' to begin with, an in-equalizing tendency did emerge in the nineteenth century.

[41] For example Shahid Amin, 'Small Peasant Commodity Production and Rural Indebtedness: The Culture of Sugarcane in Eastern U.P., c. 1880–1920' in Sugata Bose, ed., *Credit, Markets and the Agrarian Economy of Colonial India*, Delhi: Oxford University Press, 1994, pp. 80–135.

[42] 'Agrarian Commercialism in Eighteenth Century South India: Evidence from the 1823 Tirunelveli Census', *Indian Economic and Social History Review*, 25(4), 1988, pp. 493–519.

Bruce Robert writes—'Sat-Shudras were, on the average, holders of better land, comprised a higher proportion of middle to large farm holdings, and accounted for the bulk of rural credit transactions in the pre-independence period. These, along with political influence and personal farming abilities, enabled Sat-Shudras to gain the economic and political leverage necessary to consolidate their position in the village'.[43] David Washbrook shows, again in Madras-Deccan, that a small elite of rich peasants captured the gains from commodity and factor market transactions.[44] The story was similar in nearly every example of agrarian commercialization, whether new frontiers such as the canal zones of Punjab and Sind, old agrarian zones in the Gangetic plains, the wheat belts in Narmada valley, or the cotton belts in Gujarat, Berar, and Deccan.[45]

The story in Bengal, however, is complicated by an additional factor—new tenancy laws.

'DIFFERENTIATION' VIA TENANCY LAW: 1857–1947

The new property rights regime empowered ownership rights at the cost of other customary rights, including rights to the commons and rights of tenancy.[46] In Permanent Settlement tracts the move had serious implications, for here the owner was not a peasant and all peasants became tenants by the new law. Sections of the administration felt the peasantry needed stronger forms of protection. A series of tenancy acts (1859–1928) were the concrete expression of that desire for intervention. These acts recognized and strengthened the occupancy rights of tenants, or the so-called 'raiyati' rights of peasants settled on a land for generations.

[43] 'Structural Change in Indian Agriculture: Land and Labour in Bellary District, 1890-1980', *Indian Economic & Social History Review*, 1985, 22(4), pp. 281–306.

[44] David Washbrook, 'The Commercialization of Agriculture in Colonial India: Production, Subsistence and Reproduction in the 'Dry South', c. 1870-1930', *Modern Asian Studies*, 28(1), 1994, pp. 129–164.

[45] I discuss the regional evidence on the rise of the rice peasant in *The Economic History of India 1857-1947*, New Delhi: Oxford University Press, 2006, Chapter 4.

[46] On the commons, see M. Chakravarty-Kaul, *Common Lands and Customary Law. Institutional Change in North India over the Past Two Centuries*, 1996, New Delhi: Oxford University Press.

Tenancy reform induced differentiation in two senses. First, it set in motion a process of erosion of zamindar power. In the middle of the nineteenth century, landlords had succeeded raising rents and turned occupancy rights into lucrative investment for moneyed people.[47] But the equation began to change from the late nineteenth century. Nearly all studies of zamindar-peasant relation about a hundred years after the Permanent Settlement began, acknowledge that the balance of power turned in favour of entrepreneurial peasants with protected tenancy, as prices increased faster than rents, the zamindars were constrained from raising rents, the courts were busy settling rent disputes, and the interventionist bias within the bureaucracy became stronger.[48] In Bengal, tenant property right became more valuable after 1880, while correspondingly zamindari right lost in value.[49]

There was another effect of tenancy reforms upon inequality. By strengthening cultivator rights, tenancy reforms encouraged mortgages and increased the value of such rights.[50] The law deepened the already existing cleavage between 'superior' rights and a whole class of inferior rights. With the superior tenant receiving legal protection, tenancy reforms could turn one segment of land-users now in possession of a deed into a small-scale landlord, and encourage the rent market further below. A proliferation of subleases was inevitable. Tenancy Regulation tried to keep up with this trend, but never quite managed to do so. In effect, a large number of these leases were unregulated. In some regions, protection of superior tenants had a similar effect on the land market, that is, push market in lease rather than in ownership rights.[51] Contemporary official documentation in Bengal called it

[47] Robb, 'Hierarchy and Resources'.

[48] Chitta Panda, *The Decline of the Bengal Zamindars: Midnapore, 1870–1920*, New Delhi: Oxford University Press, 1996; Jacques Pouchepadass, *Land, Power and Market: A Bihar District under Colonial Rule, 1860–1947*, New Delhi: Sage Publications, 2000; Peter Robb, *Ancient Rights and Future Comforts: Bihar, the Bengal Tenancy Act of 1885 and British Rule in India*, Richmond: Curzon, 1997.

[49] B.B. Chaudhuri, 'Agrarian Relations: Eastern India', in Dharma Kumar, ed., *The Cambridge Economic History of India*, vol. 2, Cambridge: Cambridge University Press, 1983, pp. 86–176.

[50] Jacques Pouchepadass, 'Land, Power and Market: The Rise of the Land Market in Gangetic India', in Peter Robb, ed., *Rural India*, New Delhi: Oxford University Press, 1992.

[51] Crispin Bates, 'Regional Dependence and Rural Development in Central

'subinfeudation'.[52] In principle such a regime can reduce land market transactions. It would limit demand by raising the price of land, and limit supply by raising expected future earnings from scarcity rent.

Towards the end of the interwar period the world market in peasant exports collapsed, and terms of trade between agriculture and manufacturing began to move against the peasants, reversing a fifty-year pre-war trend in the opposite direction. When a commercial depression joined increasing scarcity of good lands and strong rights, rent became more important than profit. Profit became uncertain and rent more certain, the scope of agrarian entrepreneurship was squeezed, and peasants faced incentives to turn into rentiers. In studies on the Bengal rural economy, rapidly sliding into an economic crisis that broke out in a huge subsistence crisis in 1943, this process has been called 'depeasantization'.[53]

'DIFFERENTIATION' VIA OWNERSHIP LAW
While strengthening ownership rights, land law left the definition of the owner open. In one interpretation, the new 'rule of property' in 1793 tried to remodel Bengal in the image of landed society in England, by elevating individual property ownership.[54] Later interpretation departs from this assessment, however. It is now clear that there was something quite the opposite of individuation working in land law reform. In Punjab, the kinship group and community custom received legal recognition as owner in preference over the individual; elsewhere the fictional joint family received priority over the individual. Both these models opened up large fields of property disputes.

David Washbrook argues that, whereas property rights reforms were driven by an ideology of individualism, an ideology of conservation of social structure saw the collective rights of joint families becoming

India: The Pivotal Role of Migrant Labour', in Ludden, ed., *Agricultural Production*, p. 324.

[52] For example, Bengal, *Report of the Land Revenue Commission Bengal, Vol. I*, Calcutta: Government Press, 1940, p. 34.

[53] B.B. Chaudhuri, 'The Process of Depeasantization in Bengal and Bihar, 1885–1947', *Indian Historical Review*, 2(1), 1975, pp. 105–65.

[54] Ranajit Guha, *A Rule of Property for Bengal: An Essay on the Idea of Permanent Settlement*, Paris: Mouton Publishers, 1963.

more secure.[55] In fact, two, in principle distinct, conservative elements in law joined hands—the attempt to give the fiscal system local sanction and stability, and a reading of Hindu and Muslim codes that privileged a collective of individuals over the rights of the individual. These two things could lead to different kinds of results.

In parts of Punjab the fiscal imperative favoured the old style peasant community organized around kinship. The classic example was the system adopted in present Haryana whereby a clan or lineage of proprietors was made responsible for tax payment. In this region, a form of common law stipulating that all co-sharers had to agree before an outsider was admitted into the community of cultivators had been designed as a means to keep strangers out of the 'village community' or 'brotherhood'.

The legal imperative did not, however, strengthen the community, but a substantially new idea, the joint family. The Sanskrit and Persian law books relied on by the administrators suggested to them the sanctity of a unit consisting of a line of agnate descendents. This unit, where it could be found, enjoyed property rights. The succession to property followed, in a Hindu joint family, the *Mitakshara* text in most parts of India, the *Dayabhaga* in Bengal and Assam, *Mayukha* in western India, and *Nambudri* in Kerala. These texts laid out degrees of relations who could claim shares in a joint family, and restricted the freedom of the head of the estate to make bequests. The major difference between regional practices concerned the degree of inclusion of female successors into the definition of coparceners; the more restrictive system being the *Mitakshara*, and the more liberal the *Mayukha*.

Ownership by joint family or the coparcener group partly explains why land sales were difficult to effect. Land sales were not unknown in pre-colonial times, but sale without political agency had been rare. By making tax collection an office of the state, the British reforms removed that element of political agency, thus reducing one type of transaction cost. And yet, by tying up ownership with family and community the new regime increased another kind of transaction cost. The courts deciding a disputed title frequently refused to

[55] 'Law, State and Agrarian Society in Colonial India', *Modern Asian Studies*, 15(3), 1981, pp. 649–721.

recognize land deeds issued by the revenue department, and took an inordinate time to settle disputes over any landed property. Even if buying new land had become easier than before, taking possession of land was never easy for an outsider. Merchants and moneylenders were unwilling and unknown to involve themselves in land ownership on a large scale for this reason.[56] These difficulties in transfer of landed property were cited by the major banking community in Tamil Nadu, the Chettiars, to be the reason for shifting their extensive rural credit business outside India.[57] Because they incorporated local customs to a great extent, the laws and procedures tended to be written in a mixture of English, Persian, Sanskrit, and vernacular, were frequently unreadable and open to constant reinterpretation by judges.

Precisely because it was something of a legal fiction, the right of the family and the community was also fiercely contested. In the market place and in the court-room in the middle of the nineteenth century, collective right to land was being challenged just as resolutely as the judges tried to uphold it. A large part of the customary jurisprudence had concerned the family. 'And it is this central doctrine which is in fact being gradually weakened by modern tendencies...'.[58] Systematic conflicts arose between individual rights and rights of the community, between equity/fairness and the claims of the family to self-preservation. Land legislation was an important context for such conflicts between collective and individual property rights.

In Punjab, that all succession in such cases involved coparcener claims left open the interpretation of coparcener rights. Was this an alienable right? Could a coparcener sell his or her customary entitlement without the others' consent? Was this right in principle distinct from the right to property accumulated or owned by the head

[56] Vasant Kaiwar, 'Property Structures, Demography and the Crisis of the Agrarian Economy of Colonial Bombay Presidency', in Ludden, ed., *Agricultural Production*, 1994, p. 64.

[57] C.J. Baker, 'Colonial Rule and the Internal Economy in Twentieth Century Madras', *Modern Asian Studies*, 15(3), 1981, pp. 565–602.

[58] S. Vesey-FitzGerald, 'The Projected Codification of Hindu Law', *Journal of Comparative Legislation and International Law*, 3rd Ser., 29(3/4), 1947, pp. 19–32. The text continues: 'Hindu law is dominated by a single great ideal, the continuity of the patriarchal family striding on from father to son through innumerable generations. This ideal explains not only its law of inheritance, but its theories of adoption, of the property rights of women and of the family'.

of the household? Until mid-nineteenth century, judges followed the principle that coparcener rights were alienable subject to consent of other coparceners. And yet, this rule of thumb was unworkable in practice, and case laws moved in the opposite direction. The principle came under pressure with rising land values and growth of agriculture in Punjab. 'The common village bond has been broken by the introduction into the proprietary body of persons of different independent tribes whose lands all intermix, or where many uncontested alienations have taken place in the presence of agnate relatives or the alienors'.[59] Members of these lineages resorted to the courts the more to prevent entry into or exit from the lineage. As land values increased in Punjab, *jat* peasants and sub-castes became drawn into disputes that linked adoption (to acquire a male heir) and inheritance. Adoption was long governed by 'custom' that prescribed certain rules making adoption valid in the eye of the court. These rules were broken, out of a need for more flexible rules, and these acts were challenged by rival claimants to property.

Disputes over Acts of sale and pre-emptive actions against sale were so numerous that a series of case laws enacted between 1880 and 1900 ruled that no Act of transfer of property would be effected solely with reference to custom and without registration under the Transfer of Property Act (1882), and also that a registration was by itself valid with or without the sanction of custom.[60] In moving in this direction, judges implicitly recognized that coparcener rights to pre-empt sale was a 'tribal' custom which tended to interfere with the operation of an efficient land market.

As former 'tribes' and pastoralist communities settled down as peasants in Punjab, members of these groups went to court over succession rules. The disputants wanted to be treated either as a religious group or as a caste category, depending on the particular circumstances of the parties.[61] Acts of sale or gift of land by individual proprietors was routinely challenged by relatives claiming to be

---

[59] Fazil vs Sadan, 1910, see T. Sanjiva Row, *The All India Digest, Section II (Civil) 1811–1911*, vols. I–, Madras: The Law Printing House, 1912, col. 986.

[60] See W.H. Rattigan, 'The Influence of English Law and Legislation upon the Native Laws of India', *Journal of the Society of Comparative Legislation*, New Ser., 3(1), 1901, pp. 46–65, for discussion.

[61] Jowahir Singh vs Yakub Shah, P.H.C., 1906.

co-sharers of the land according to the custom among peasant communities. When rural artisans (such as *lohars*, rural blacksmiths) took up cultivation, the courts had to decide whether they should be allowed their own custom in respect to inheritance and succession, or be subjected to religious law.[62] Incorporation of norms into statutes, thus, presented an impossible dilemma in Punjab, at a time when and because the Punjab economy was changing so rapidly.

The problem afflicted courts in all regions in varying degrees. Attempts to formalize custom encouraged a contest of assertion between religions and castes. Whereas earlier custom had a precise content settled by the community heads, now the empty pages of the statute book created an opportunity to frame an advantageous version of custom. The new regime, in other words, created a choice where none existed before. In turn, the existence of a choice led to more disputes; disputant parties expressed their preferences in the courts. In this way, laws became 'a luxuriant jungle'.[63]

SHIFTING CONTEXT OF PEASANT DISPUTES: FROM COLLECTIVE TO CLASS

Commercialization of agriculture created a new space for conflicts over terms of trade. South Asia had seen uprisings, insurgency, and revolt by peasants before the nineteenth century. But these revolts almost always involved failure of agreements drawn between peasants and agents of the state. They were disputes over tax, tithe, and rent. In the nineteenth century, a whole new field of dispute was opened up between peasants and capitalists. Whereas formerly peasant revolts had been led by headmen and chiefs and were organized around communities, the very nature of the disagreements now made peasants form alliances that cut across communal boundaries. The response of the state in some of these conflicts was to institute new laws restricting the capitalist, implicitly favouring credit and trade relations within the peasantry. Conflicts carrying potentials for large-scale violence were rare occurrences. In the normal course, creditor and debtors, buyers and sellers, both gained from routine transactions, at least in the sixty years spanned by the mutiny and the First World War that saw land

---

[62] Umar-ud-Din vs Janto, P.H.C., 1906.

[63] Vesey-FitzGerald, 'Projected Codification'.

extension and growing peasant exports. But disputes did break out when market fluctuations caused unexpected shocks to income.

In theory, were such shocks in some way anticipated and insured against, and were there laws to protect the party worst-off by an unanticipated shock from fulfilment of contract, disputes might not occur. In practice, no such laws or insurance existed, and the trades were conducted in an institutional vacuum. The disputants themselves thought that the state would protect them from unfair enforcement or unfair breach of contracts. And curiously enough, the state thought that customs and conventions would provide adequate means of settling disputes, without new laws being necessary. Two well-known episodes from the late nineteenth century—the indigo mutiny and the Deccan riots—show well how the vacuum that was sustained because of these premises worsened situations of conflict.

In the first half of the nineteenth century, indigo was a major exportable from India, the demand for which was sustained by rapid growth in usage of blue dye in textile printing.[64] With the end of the Company's monopoly trading rights, it emerged as a lucrative but risky commodity for private trade. Indigo was procured mainly from northern India and Bengal. In Bengal, indigo was produced in factories owned by European capitalists. The factories directly entered agreements with the peasants to buy leaves. Land ownership in this time vested with the zamindars. In this scenario, there were two methods commonly used by the manufacturers to procure indigo. The manufacturers could grow indigo themselves on estates that they purchased or leased in from a zamindar (called *nij* or own farming) or contract with peasants for growing the crop in lands on which the latter had tenant rights (called raiyati or peasant farming). Although own farming limited the scope of breach of contract, it was not a popular mode of farming, presumably because the European indigo capitalists' interest in land was limited to one crop, and they were not ordinarily willing to assume all the risks and obligations connected with ownership of the zamindari estates.

---

[64] A fuller account of the dispute, complete citation of the relevant scholarship, and a longer statement of my interpretation of the blue mutiny can be found in 'Indigo and Law in Colonial India', forthcoming.

Contract farming, while more popular, involved serious disputes almost throughout the lifetime of the trade in Bengal. The standard method of ensuring contract enforcement was an old one, already popular in textiles, silk, or opium. The contractor advanced a sum of money, and did not fully clear the credit account when the crops came in. The threat of losing the unpaid balance on a previous transaction was expected to induce the supplier to fulfil the terms of the current transaction. Indigo followed this precedence. Additionally, planters hired as officers those members of the rural society 'better able to secure ... cultivation, from their intimate connexion with the cultivators'.[65] This hybrid between dubious customary authority and a dubious agreement functioned with minor frictions for almost sixty years. In 1860, it collapsed completely as peasants in lower Bengal refused to sow the crop after taking advances. The planters-manufacturers filed a large number of suits in the magistrates' courts alleging that the action was in breach of written agreements. The episode has become known as the blue mutiny.

Throughout the official and unofficial documentation on indigo, references to caste and community remain conspicuously obscure. The social identity of the intermediaries and factory officers using which, the planters thought, they would be 'better able to secure cultivation', failed to make any impact. Peasants themselves appear to have acted on the basis of class rather than caste and community in resisting the planter. In lower Bengal, where some planters-turned-zamindars tried to put pressure upon the holders of privileged tenants, the key figures among the opposition were identifiable as superior tenants. They received moral support from church organizations and representatives thereof, who again tried to mobilize a large section of the peasantry. Community was invisible in this dispute.

Why did the conflict occur? The mainstream view in Indian historiography holds that the planters ordinarily enforced indigo contracts by coercive means, in connivance with the courts and the police, and the 1860 episode saw an outburst of pent-up resentment against a colonial-capitalist form of exploitation.[66] Planters were not

---

[65]   John O'Brien Saunders, editor of *Englishman* and former planter, British Parliamentary Papers, *East India (Indigo Commission), Minutes of Evidence*, London, 1861, p. 139.

[66]   S. Bhattacharya, 'The Indigo Revolt of Bengal', *Social Scientist*, 5 (1978),

always gentlemanly, and yet, available data do not suggest that coercion was successful, or that the business had always been unprofitable for the peasants. Far from using the courts to their advantage, the planters bitterly complained about the ineffectiveness of legal redress almost throughout the career of the trade. Direct coercion was a symptom of the failure of formal law to solve these disputes

In essence, the blue mutiny was a trade dispute rather than a political conflict. The disputes arose from the design of the contract. The typical indigo contract did not specify the quantity of leaves to be delivered, but the extent of land to be sown with indigo. As long as the price of the competing crop rice did not increase relative to that of indigo in a sustained way, this form of the agreement made sense. Indigo cultivation was profitable for peasants, and the contract set by land area saved on information cost. But an agreement that made no provision for contingencies such as relative price shifts made peasants worse-off if the price of rice increased relative to indigo. Between 1855 and 1860, that is exactly what happened. The planters could either offer a higher price for indigo or threaten the peasants of legal action for breach of contract. With a few days left of the sowing season, desperate planters took the latter road.

When the dust settled, planters and officers concluded that the performance of contracts by means of obsolete loyalty and weak contracts was not feasible any more, and sales required a contract law. The demand for such a law had been a long-standing one. Only a few years before the blue mutiny, the planters had stated before a Parliamentary Committee that 'a good law of contract is, and much required for all classes, ... The present law of complaining before the civil courts is so expensive and tedious, it is in fact an encouragement to ill-disposed people to break their contracts.'[67] 'Indigo being the most valuable product of Bengal', another planter stated before the

---

pp. 13–23; Sugata Bose, *Peasant Labour and Colonial Capital, Rural Bengal since 1770*, Cambridge: Cambridge University Press, 1993; Blair B. Kling, *The Blue Mutiny. The Indigo Disturbances in Bengal, 1859–1862*, Philadelphia: University of Pennsylvania Press, 1966; B. Chowdhury, *Growth of Commercial Agriculture in Bengal, 1757–1900*, Calcutta: Calcutta University Press, 1964; B. Hartmann and J. Boyce, *A Quiet Violence: View from a Bangladesh Village*, London: Zed Press, 1984; Indrajit Ray, 'The Indigo Dye Industry in Colonial Bengal. A Re-examination', *Indian Economic and Social History Review*, 41(2), 2004, pp. 199–225.

[67] G. MacNair, indigo planter, British Parliamentary Papers, *Select committee*

Indigo Commission, 'I consider the contract law peculiarly adapted to that product'.[68] The question of a contract law had been debated time and again by the Law Commissions of India. On each occasion the discussion had been inconclusive.[69] The executive branch of the administration saw the indigo situation as 'errors of law'.[70] A commission of enquiry agreed with that view. The decisive step came in 1862, when an administrative note prepared by the Secretary of State initiated the proceedings for the creation of a contract law in India.[71] The note mentioned that indigo was the proximate motivation behind the move.[72] In 1866, when the draft of a new law was proposed, it marked a break with legal tradition. Perhaps for the first time in Indian history, the state that framed the Contract Act 'freely availed itself of its supreme power to define what shall henceforth be the law of the land'.[73] The claim of the community was formally overturned. Other spheres where this radical principle was extended in the next decade were trusts, negotiated instruments, transfer of property, promissory notes, evidence, wills and probates, and specific relief.

If the blue mutiny was a dispute over sale, the Deccan riots were a dispute over loans. The land mortgage market was largely a British Indian creation. In a world where money was scarce (the best loans in India carried 12 per cent interest rate per year, about double that in Western Europe, 5–6, in the nineteenth century), land mortgage became quickly popular with both lenders and debtors. As cotton prices soared in the Bombay–Deccan when the American civil war

---

to inquire into progress and prospects for promotion of European colonization and settlement in India second report, minutes of evidence, London, 1857–8, p. 4.

[68] Planter Thomas Larmour, British Parliamentary Papers, *East India (Indigo Commission), Minutes of Evidence*, p. 133.

[69] In 1835, a proposal that indigo contracts be registered before a magistrate was rejected by Thomas Macaulay as being impracticable. In 1839, a draft act that could enforce the contracted use of land was reviewed by the Governor General and returned to the Commission with the message that the matter needed further consultation.

[70] Minute by the Lieutenant Governor of Bengal, 5 June 1854, B.P.P., *Selections from the records*, p. 6.

[71] British India was administered by the Governor General in India, advised by a Council, and the Secretary of State in London. The Lieutenant Governor was in charge of provincial administration.

[72] B.P.P., *East India (Contract Law): A copy of the legislative despatch*, p. 1.

[73] Rattigan, 'Influence of English Law', p. 52.

disrupted cotton supplies to England, peasants took loans against land mortgage. Communities of small-scale bankers migrated from Marwar and Gujarat into the cotton growing villages to meet this need. When the boom ended in a disastrous price crash, peasants were confronted, possibly for the first time in generations, with the prospect of losing their ownership titles because of an adverse balance sheet. Neither that reason for losing land nor the outsider status of those who looked set to possess land made sense. Anti-moneylender riots broke out in Poona and Ahmednagar districts in the summer of 1875. As in the indigo episode, there was almost no loss of life. In a few dozen houses belonging to Gujarati and Marwari moneylenders, property and account books were burnt. The event unnerved officers, and some of them feared that similar outbursts might recur in other regions where peasants were falling prey to a cycle of debt.[74]

The dispute was a commercial one. There was no element of insurgency. Far from entertaining a grudge against the state, the peasants looked up to the state as a protector of customary rights to land. Curiously, official post-mortems tried, and failed, to read the riots in terms of loyalties of a customary kind, as an expression of antagonism between peasant caste and moneylender caste, and as the organization of protest along caste lines. It was soon evident that this episode did not fit the caste story well at all. Diverse groups of peasants came together in orchestrating arson. If there was any leadership, it came not from caste elders, but from village headmen, a relic of the old regime and a part of the administrative system rather than that of the village community.[75] Class, rather than caste, was the platform for mobilization.

The reason why the episode generated so much official worry and documentation was the legal implications of the situation. The riots were not a case for political intervention. History is replete with examples showing that a mortgage taken at high prices can lead to a transfer of assets unless price risks are insured against. A debtor does not have to be a poor peasant to be subjected to such risks. But insurances are rarely available or demanded when they are available.

[74] Neil Charlesworth, 'Myth of the Deccan Riots of 1875', *Modern Asian Studies*, 6(4), 1972, pp. 401–21.

[75] I.J. Catanach, 'Agrarian Disturbances in Nineteenth Century India', *Indian Economic and Social History Review*, 3(1), 1966, pp. 65–84.

How should then peasant property be protected? Administration intervened in the only way it could—by instituting laws that restrained the moneylender's powers to repossess mortgaged land. A big disincentive to land mortgage dealings by professional bankers, the move drove the credit market transactions to greater insularity. It privileged credit and exchange relationships between peasants and peasants over similar relationships between peasants and outsiders, thereby deepening differentiation.

CONCLUSION

The paradox of institutional change in rural India, it was mentioned in the beginning of this chapter, was that the power of the collective persisted despite definition of clear private titles in land. In this chapter, I outline three reasons for this persistence. First, local power structures had a great deal of influence on who was to receive these titles. In the end, dominant peasant lineages did retain much of their power, even though non-cultivating elites with indirect interest in land lost out politically or lost interest in agriculture. Second, the evolution of law followed an erratic course. Although private land titles were favoured by administrators in agriculture, succession laws remained rooted in tradition. Traditionalism in the realm of landed property meant that the law courts often upheld the claims of the joint family over the claims of individuals within it. This aspect of land laws suppressed transactions in the land market, possibly contributing to the rapid rise in rents in the twentieth century. Third, inside the production process, the need for optimal use of assets meant that some assets were continued to be used jointly, such as water, animals, and common lands. Wealth inequality and caste power went hand in hand.

Market exchange had planted the seeds of an endogenous collapse of the peasant community, however. The collectives we do encounter in the nineteenth century were a far cry from the groups that formed around military chiefs, who broke in land, cleared forests and pastures, negotiated taxes and rents, and revolted when the terms of agreement were broken. Increasingly, the collectives consisted of the male kin of a cluster of families in control of resources, including a legal title to land. They had been demilitarized and decollectivized, and recast as the joint family or lineage instead. In part, the change came about because trade and credit divided up peasants into debtors and creditors, trade disputes led to laws that privileged peasant-capitalists, property law recognized the rights of the joint family where it could be found, even though these concepts were beginning to be challenged in the court room.

Through case laws, the legal fiction of the joint family suffered faster attrition after the end of colonial rule in 1947.

Epilogue

The book relates how rules of cooperation formed in South Asia, were held together, and how they changed in more modern times. Guilds composed of kinsmen coordinated the actions of merchants, artisans, peasants, and workers in the pre-colonial business world. Rulers respected these institutions. Communities of this kind, endogamous guilds aided by regional states, regulated the accumulation and use of land, labour, capital, and knowledge. By the benchmarks of the early modern world, they performed these tasks efficiently, to which the highly refined craftsmanship and flourishing long-distance trade bear witness. These institutions could adapt, and new groups stake claims to customary rights, but such moves needed political support to be successful.

From the late-eighteenth century, an emerging new economy shaped by foreign trade, industrialization, and colonial rule weakened personal ties. The moral order that once governed relationships inside merchant and banking communities proved inadequate in addressing disputes between members and struggles for control of collective resources. Increasing scope of contract created a space for disputes over breach of contract. Laws and associations that could bridge communal borders became necessary and, in the new regime, possible. In agriculture, peasant collectives were threatened when private ownership rights were given precedence over user rights. With the growth of technical education, one of the functions the artisan collectives had performed before—impart training and preserve useful knowledge—became less relevant. Employers in modern factories initially relied on work-teams that shared some social ties and worked under a headman. These teams made recruitment and supervision easier. But the employers increasingly saw such teams as a burden, because they feared loss of control over the labour of the individual worker by inserting the headman in collective bargaining processes. Overall, informal and personal ways of doing business was in decline.

But they did not decline quickly. New types of risks facing the migrant worker or the merchant were met by reviving bonds of kinship. Furthermore, both during and after colonial rule, potential decline of the old rules of cooperation was slowed by state policy deliberately seeking to preserve a formal role for caste, clan, and community in economic organization. Being subject to these diverse pulls, institutional change in the region happened in a discordant way, at a slow pace while unleashing huge conflicts.

The book follows the transition up to the end of colonial rule in the region, and suggests that the story has relevance for historians of the world and students of contemporary India. I suggest that the actions of economic actors were simultaneously market-driven and 'embedded', or anchored in honour-based relationships. Both dimensions are important for a balanced history of institutional change. I propose further that these relationships derived legitimacy and enforcement, not from religion, but from a contract between the state and society. That implicit contract was withdrawn in the eighteenth century, and was, in any case, incompatible in the new global-industrial economy. The collectives became unstable as a result.

What forms came in its place? Among merchants and bankers, there was an imperceptible creative destruction of the community as individuals, families, and other associational rules became prominent. Successful entrepreneurs succeeded by skilfully using old ties and formal institutions. Peasants, artisans, and workers in the twentieth century also display evidence of compromise and dualism.

Hybrids carried costs. With workers, the cost appeared in the shape of headmen in the work-place filtering the authority of the employers on the workers. In modern industry and banking, managing agents and Indian private banks joined together the formality of law and the informality of the community, at times using such flexibility positively and at times using it for private gains at the expense of their principles, for such a world had weakened both formal and informal checks upon predatory and irresponsible behaviour. In the sphere of property and contract law, the simultaneous emergence of common law courts and a code-based law-book overwhelmed the judicial process.

It is on this point of a discordant and costly persistence of collectives that the narrative carries a contemporary relevance. Some of the discord referred earlier continue to the present day. The community principle was not allowed to dissipate on its own in independent India, though it was placed on a different foundation. The legal right of communities to demand protection was framed in the nineteenth century in religionist terms and encompassed property rights. In post-colonial India, the scope of protection offered was narrowed, being made available to a constrained set of castes in the affirmative action regime, but they were more effectively enforced.

Much else besides has changed in the last 50 years. The sphere of global transactions expanded. Colonial and communal property, marriage, inheritance, and succession laws suffered huge wear and tear. The legal regime moved steadily away from scriptures and codes. Chapter 3 discussed how industrial houses tended to part company with the community as a system of value and move towards unorthodox partnerships, assertive individuals, and accumulation of personal wealth and consumption. In the course of this change, business brand shifted from caste and community to fix upon families. Dhirubhai Ambani in the 1980s became a phenomenon by symbolizing a further evolution in this pattern—shift of brand of managerial acumen from the family to the individual. Like Napoleon, he decided to found a dynastic empire in turn. After the liberalization of 1985–95, flood of foreign capital, rise of the engineer–entrepreneur, services firms, globalization of Indian firms, old families dividing, state–business partnership on technology, perhaps even a new pattern of business participation in politics, have all reconfigured the world of industry and commerce beyond recognition.

And yet, to the extent the state protects any or some communities, the use of the community as a platform for building cooperation continues. The community is almost irrelevant today as a device to instil a moral code or a device to impart training. Yet, in the clamour for state jobs, and in the supply of labour and capital in small town industry and trade, community still serves as a platform for bargaining and mutual help. Among family-run businesses, the elders display a yearning for the old times and the younger generation frustrates them. The persistence of collectivist practices in these fields continues to produce competitive pressures and political conflicts, as the recent and ongoing struggle over job and education quotas, communal riots in industrial towns, and the still ongoing fragmentation of the idea of the business family would suggest.

In the winter of 2008, Indian business witnessed the unravelling of a corporate fraud, described by the *Economist* magazine as India's Enron. The surprising aspect of the fraud was that it could be kept hidden from public view in a highly visible company, a 'blue-chip', for years. Although its services were visible, its management was not, apparently because the owner had recruited board members mainly from his own community, and the members' sectarian loyalty proved stronger than their responsibility to the shareholders. A report published in the *Economist* on this episode observed, 'about half of the 30 companies in the Sensex, India's benchmark stock market index, are run by business families'. 'They don't always understand the new rules', an Indian businessperson informed the magazine. This sentence could have come from a nineteenth century newspaper report on failed banks of Calcutta. The discordant transition described in the book is far from over.

Bibliography

A District Officer (1869). *Notes on North-western Provinces of India*, London: W.H. Allen.

Abraham, Meera (1988). *Two Medieval Merchant Guilds of South India*, New Delhi: Manohar Publications.

Acemoglu, Daron, Simon Johnson, and James A. Robinson (2001). 'The Colonial Origins of Comparative Development: An Empirical Investigation', *American Economic Review*, 91(5), pp. 1369–401.

Adas, Michael (1974). 'Immigrant Asians and the Economic Impact of European Imperialism: The Role of the South Indian Chettiars in British Burma', *Journal of Asian Studies*, 33, pp. 385–401.

Ahmad, Muhammad Basheer (1941). *The Administration of Justice in Medieval India*, Aligarh: The Aligarh Historical Research Institute.

Ahuja, Ravi (1999). 'The Origins of Colonial Labour Policy in Late Eighteenth-Century Madras', *International Review of Social History*, 44, pp. 159–95.

Akerlof, George A. (1997). 'Social Distance and Social Decisions', *Econometrica*, 65(5), pp. 1005–27.

——— (1980). 'A Theory of Social Custom, of which Unemployment may be One Consequence', *The Quarterly Journal of Economics*, 94(4), pp. 749–75.

——— (1976). 'The Economics of Caste and of the Rat Race and Other Woeful Tales', *The Quarterly Journal of Economics*, 90(4), pp. 599–617.

Akbar, Muhammad (1948). *The Administration of Justice by the Mughals*, Lahore: Muhammad Ashraf.

Alam, Muzaffar and Sanjay Subrahmanyam (ed) (1998). *The Mughal State 1526–1750*, New Delhi: Oxford University Press.

All India Handicrafts Board (1964). *Report on Hand Printed Textile Industry in Madurai (Madras)*, New Delhi: Government Press.

Allen, Calvin H. Jr. (1981). 'The Indian Merchant Community of Masqat', *Bulletin of the School of Oriental and African Studies, University of London*, 44(1), pp. 39–53.

Amin, Shahid (1994). 'Small Peasant Commodity Production and Rural Indebtedness: The Culture of Sugarcane in Eastern U.P., c. 1880–1920', in Sugata Bose (ed.), *Credit, Markets and the Agrarian Economy of Colonial India*, New Delhi: Oxford University Press, pp. 80–135.

Anderson, M.R. (2003). 'Work Construed: Ideological Origins of Labour Law in British India to 1918', in Peter Robb (ed.), *Dalit Movements and the Meanings of Labour in India*, New Delhi: Oxford University Press.

——— (1993). 'Islamic Law and the Colonial Encounter in British India', in David Arnold and Peter Robb (eds), (1996), *Institutions and Ideologies: A SOAS South Asia Reader*, London: Curzon Press, pp. 165–185.

Anonymous (1930). *Famous Parsis: Biographies and Critical Sketches of Patriots, Philanthropists, Politicians, Scholars and Captains of Industry*, Madras: G. A. Natesan.

——— (1844). 'Report on the State of the Police in the Lower provinces for the First Six Months of 1842', *Calcutta Review*, 1, pp. 189–217.

——— (1719). *Thirty Four Conferences between the Danish Missionaries and the Malabarian Bramans or Heathen Priests in the East Indies* (tr. from High Dutch by J. Thomas Philipps), London: St. Paul's.

Arasaratnam, S. (1979). 'Trade and Political Dominion in South India, 1750-1790: Changing British–Indian relationships', *Modern Asian Studies*, 13(1), pp. 19–40.

Asher, Catherine B. and Cynthia Talbot (2006). *India before Europe*, Cambridge: Cambridge University Press.

Athar Ali, M. (1993). 'The Mughal Polity — A Critique of Revisionist Approaches', *Modern Asian Studies*, 27(4), pp. 699–710.

Bagchi, A.K. (1997). *The Evolution of the State Bank of India, Volume 2: The Era of the Presidency Banks, 1876-1920*, London and New Delhi: Sage Publications.

——— (1994). 'European and Indian Entrepreneurship in India 1900–30', in R.K. Ray (ed.), *Entrepreneurship and Industry in India 1800–1947*, New Delhi: Oxford University Press.

——— (1982). *The Political Economy of Underdevelopment*, Cambridge: Cambridge University Press.

——— (1976). 'Deindustrialization in India in the Nineteenth Century: Some Theoretical Implications', *Journal of Development Studies*, 12(2), pp. 135–64.

Baillie, N.B.E. (1869). *A Digest of Moohummudan Law on the Subjects to which it is Usually Applied by British Courts of Justice in India*, Part Second (Doctrines of the Imamea Code of Jurisprudence), London: Smith Elder & Co.

——— (1865). *A Digest of Moohummudan Law on the Subjects to which it is Usually Applied by British Courts of Justice in India*, London: Smith Elder & Co.

Bailey, F.G. (1957). *Caste and the Economic Frontier: A Village in Highland Orissa*, Manchester: Manchester University Press.

Baker, C.J. (1981). 'Colonial Rule and the Internal Economy in Twentieth Century Madras', *Modern Asian Studies*, 15(3), pp. 565–602.

Balfour, Edward (1844). 'Migratory Tribes of Natives in Central India', *Journal of the Asiatic Society of Bengal*, 13, pp. 1–15.

Bandopadhyay, Arun (1992). *The Agrarian Economy of Tamil Nadu, 1820-1855*, Calcutta: K.P. Bagchi.

Bandopadhyay, Brajendranath and Sajanikanta Das (eds) (1997). *Bharat-chandra Granthabali*, Calcutta: Bangiya Sahitya Parishat.

Banerjee, Kum Kum (1986), 'Grain Traders and the East India Company: Patna and its Hinterland in the Late Eighteenth and Early Nineteenth Centuries', *Indian Economic and Social History Review*, 23(4), pp. 403–29.

Banerjee, S.N. and J. S. Hoyland (1922). *The Commentary on Father Monserrat on His Journey to the Court of Akbar 1580-1582*, London: Humphrey Milford.

Barbosa, Duarte (1866). *A Description of the Coasts of East Africa and Malabar: In the Beginning of the Sixteenth Century*, London: Hakluyt Society.

Bardhan, P. K. (2005). 'Institutions Matter, but which Ones?', *Economics of Transition*, 13(3), pp. 499–532.

——— (1980). 'Interlocking Factor Markets and Agrarian Development: A Review of Issues', *Oxford Economic Papers*, 32(1), pp. 82–98.

Bates, Crispin (1994). 'Regional Dependence and Rural Development in Central India: The Pivotal Role of Migrant Labour', in David Ludden (ed.), *Agricultural Production in Indian History*, New Delhi: Oxford University Press.

Bayly, C. A. (2002). 'Epilogue to the Indian Edition', in Seema Alavi (ed.), *The Eighteenth Century in India*, New Delhi: Oxford University Press.

——— (1983). *Rulers, Townsmen and Bazaars: North Indian Society in the Age of British Expansion 1770-1870*, New Delhi: Oxford University Press.

——— (1973). 'Patrons and Politics in Northern India', *Modern Asian Studies*, 7(3), pp. 349–88.

Bayly, Susan (1999). *Caste, Society and Politics in India from the Eighteenth Century to the Modem Age*, Cambridge: Cambridge University Press.

Bell, D.S. (2006). 'Historiographical Reviews: Empire and International Relations in Victorian Political Thought', *The Historical Journal*, 49(1), pp. 281–98.

Bengal (1940). *Report of the Land Revenue Commission Bengal*, vol. I, Calcutta: Government Press.

Benton, Lauren (1999). 'Colonial Law and Cultural Difference: Jurisdictional Politics and the Formation of the Colonial State', *Comparative Studies in Society and History*, 41(3), pp. 563–88.

Berman, H.J. (1983). *Law and Revolution: The Formation of the Western Legal Tradition*, Cambridge Mass.: Harvard University Press.

Bernier, François (1916). *Travels in the Mogul Empire A.D. 1656–1668*, London: Humphrey Milford.

Bernstein, Henry (1994). 'Agrarian Classes in Capitalist Development', in Leslie Sklair (ed.), *Capitalism and Development*, London: Routledge, pp. 40–71.

Beveridge, Henry, ed. (2006). *The Tuzuk-i-Jahangiri*, New Delhi: Low Price Publications.

Bhadra, Gautam (1980). 'Mogaljuge Bharatiya Banik' [The Merchant in Mughal India], *Ekshan*, 4(3–5), pp. 56–91.

Bhargava, Meena (1993). 'Perception and Classification of the Rights of the Social Classes: Gorakhpur and the East India Company in the Late Eighteenth and Early Nineteenth Centuries', *Indian Economic and Social History Review*, 30(3), pp. 215–37.

Bhattacharya, Ardhendu (1930). 'Extracts from a Survey of the Small Urban Industries of Lucknow in United Provinces', *United Provinces Provincial Banking Enquiry Committee 1929-30*, 4 vols, Allahabad.

Bhattacharya, Bijanbihari (ed.) (1961). *Ketakadas Kshemananda: Manasa-mangal*, Calcutta: Sahitya Akademi, reprinted 2005.

Bhattacharya, Neeladri (1994). 'Lenders and Debtors: Punjab Countryside, 1880-1940', in Sugata Bose (ed.), *Credit, Markets and the Agrarian Economy of Colonial India*, New Delhi: Oxford University Press.

Bhattacharya, S. (1978). 'The Indigo Revolt of Bengal', *Social Scientist*, 5, pp. 13–23.

Bhattacharya, Sabyasachi (1966). 'Cultural and Social Constraints on Technological Innovation and Economic Development: Some Case Studies', *Indian Economic and Social History Review*, 3(3), pp. 240–67.

Bin Wong, Roy (1997). *China Transformed: Historical Change and the Limits of European Experience*, Ithaca, NY: Cornell University Press.

Blake, S.P. (1991). *Shahjahanabad: The Sovereign City in Mughal India, 1639–1739*, Cambridge: Cambridge University Press.

——— (1979). 'The Patrimonial-Bureaucratic Empire of the Mughals', *Journal of Asian Studies*, 39(1), pp. 77–94.

Bombay (1940). *Report of the Textile Labour Inquiry Committee*, vol. II (Final Report), Bombay: Government Press.

Bombay Mill Owners' Association (1927). *Proceedings of the Bombay Strike Enquiry Committee*, vol. III, Bombay: Bombay Millowners Association.

Bose, S. (1993). *Peasant Labour and Colonial Capital. Rural Bengal since 1770*, Cambridge: Cambridge University Press.

Bourguignon, F. and C. Morrisson (2002). 'Inequality among World Citizens: 1820-1992', *American Economic Review*, 92(4), pp. 727–44.

Bowrey, Thomas (1895). *A Geographical Account of Countries round the Bay of Bengal, 1669 to 1679*, Cambridge: Haklyut Society, reprinted Delhi: Asian Educational Services.

Breman, Jan (1989). *Taming the Coolie Beast: Plantation Society and the Colonial Order in Southeast Asia*, New Delhi: Oxford University Press.

Brennig, Joseph A. (1986). 'Textile Producers and Production in Late Seventeenth Century Coromandel', *Indian Economic and Social History Review*, 23(4), pp. 333–56.

—— (1977). 'Chief Merchants and the European Enclaves of Seventeenth Century Coromandel', *Modern Asian Studies*, 11(3), pp. 321–40.

Brimmer, A.F. (1955). 'The Setting of Entrepreneurship in India', *Quarterly Journal of Economics*, 69, pp. 553–76.

British Parliamentary Papers, House of Commons (1957–58). *Select Committee to Inquire into Progress and Prospects for Promotion of European Colonization and Settlement in India Second Report, Minutes of Evidence*, London.

—— (1888–9). *Copies of Government of India Despatch, dated the 22nd day of June 1889, with its Enclosures, including reports by Mr. Tucker and, of Memorial of the Indian Association of Calcutta, dated the 12th day of April 1888 (in continuation of House of Lords' Return (No. 14), 5th March 1889*, London.

—— (1861). *East India (Indigo Commission), Minutes of Evidence*, London.

—— (1861). *East India (Indigo Commission), Report of the Indigo Commission*, London.

—— (1773). *Seventh Report from the Committee of Secrecy appointed to enquire into the State of the East India Company together with an Appendix referred to in the said Report*.

Bronson, Bennet (1996). 'Metals, Specialisation, and Development in Early Eastern and Southern Asia', in Bernard Wailes (ed.), *Craft Specialization and Social Evolution: In Memory of V. Gordon Childe*, Philadelphia: University of Pennsylvania Press.

—— (1986). 'The Making and Selling of Wootz: A Crucible Steel of India', *Archeomaterials*, 1(1), pp. 13–51.

Buchanan, Francis (1807). *A Journey from Madras, through the Countries of Mysore, Canara, and Malabar, etc.*, London: E. Caddell for the East India Company.

Burden, E. (1909). *Monograph on the Wire and Tinsel Industry in the Punjab*, Lahore: Government Press.

Calkins, P.B. (1968–9). 'A Note on Lawyers in Muslim India', *Law & Society Review*, 3(2/3), pp. 403–6.

Carter, Marina (1995). *Servants, Sirdars and Settlers: Indians in Mauritius, 1834-1874*, New Delhi: Oxford University Press.

Catanach, I.J. (1966). 'Agrarian Disturbances in Nineteenth Century India', *Indian Economic and Social History Review*, 3(1), pp. 65–84.

Chakrabarty, Dipesh (1989). *Rethinking Working-Class History: Bengal, 1890-1940*, Princeton: Princeton University Press.

Chakravarty, Lalita (1978). 'Emergence of an Industrial Labour Force in a

Dual Economy—British India, 1880–1920', *Indian Economic and Social History Review*, 15(3), pp. 249–327.

Chakravarty-Kaul, M. (1996). *Common Lands and Customary Law. Institutional Change in North India over the Past Two Centuries*, New Delhi: Oxford University Press.

Champakalakshmi, R. (1987). 'Urbanisation in South India: The Role of Ideology and Polity', *Social Scientist*, 15(8/9), pp. 67–117.

Chandavarkar, Rajnarayan (1994). *The Origins of Industrial Capitalism in India: Business Strategies and Working Classes in Bombay, 1900-1940*, Cambridge: Cambridge University Press.

Charlesworth, Neil (1972). 'Myth of the Deccan Riots of 1875', *Modern Asian Studies*, 6(4), pp. 401–21.

Chatterjee, Kumkum (1992). 'Trade and Darbar Politics in the Bengal Subah, 1733-1757', *Modern Asian Studies*, 26(2), pp. 233–73.

Chaudhuri, B. B. (2008). *Peasant History of Late Pre-colonial and Colonial India*, New Delhi: Pearson Longman.

—— (1983). 'Agrarian Relations: Eastern India', in Dharma Kumar (ed.), *The Cambridge Economic History of India*, vol. 2, Cambridge: Cambridge University Press.

—— (1975). 'The Process of Depeasantization in Bengal and Bihar, 1885-1947', *Indian Historical Review*, 2(1), pp. 105–65.

—— (1964). *The Growth of Commercial Agriculture in Bengal, 1757-1900*, Calcutta: Quality Printers.

Chaudhuri, K. N. (1978). 'Some Reflections on the Town and Country in Mughal India', *Modern Asian Studies*, 12, pp. 77–96.

Chaudhury, Sushil (1995). *From Prosperity to Decline: Eighteenth Century Bengal*, New Delhi: Manohar Publications.

Cipolla, C.M. (1972). 'The Diffusion of Innovations in Early Modern Europe', *Comparative Studies in Society and History*, 14(1), pp. 46–52.

Clark, Gregory (2004). 'Explaining Employment Institutions—A Historical Perspective', University of California, Davis, mimeo.

—— (1991). 'Yields per Acre in English Agriculture, 1250–1860: Evidence from Labour Inputs', *Economic History Review*, 44(3), pp. 445–60.

Cohn, B.S. (1999). *Colonialism and its Forms of Knowledge*, New Delhi: Oxford University Press.

—— (1961). 'From Indian Status to British Contract', *The Journal of Economic History*, 21(4), pp. 613–28.

—— (1960). 'The Initial British Impact on India: A Case Study of the Benares Region', *The Journal of Asian Studies*, 19(4), pp. 418–31.

—— (1959). 'Some Notes on Law and Change in North India', *Economic Development and Cultural Change*, 8(1), pp. 79–93.

Commander, Simon (1983). 'The Jajmani System in North India: An Examination of Its Logic and Status across Two Centuries', *Modern Asian Studies*, 17(2), pp. 283–311.

Dalton, E.T. (1868). 'The "Kols" of Chota-Nagpore', *Transactions of the Ethnological Society of London*, 6, pp. 1–41.

Das, R.K. (1931). *Plantation Labour in India*, Calcutta: R. Chatterjee.

Das Gupta, Ashin (2001). *The World of the Indian Ocean Merchant, 1500–1800: Collected Essays of Ashin Das Gupta*, New Delhi: Oxford University Press.

——— (1970). 'The Merchants of Surat, c. 1700–1750', in E. Leach and S. N. Mukherjee (eds), *Elites in South Asia*, Cambridge: Cambridge University Press.

Dave, I.R. (1976). *The Saurashtrians of South India*, Rajkot: Saurashtra University.

Davis, Donald R. (2005). 'Intermediate Realms of Law: Corporate Groups and Rulers in Medieval India', *Journal of the Economic and Social History of the Orient*, 48(1), pp. 92–117.

De Haan, Arjan (1997). 'Unsettled Settlers: Migrant Workers and Industrial Capitalism in Calcutta', *Modern Asian Studies*, 31(4), pp. 919–49.

Della Valle, Pietro (1892). *The Travels of Pietro Della Valle in India*, London: Hakluyt Society.

Derrett, J.D.M. (1976). 'Rajadharma', *Journal of Asian Studies*, 35(4), pp. 597–609.

Desai, R.C. (1948). 'Consumer Expenditure in India, 1931–2 to 1940–1', *Journal of the Royal Statistical Society. Series A (General)*, 111(4), pp. 261–308.

Dharma Kumar (1965). *Land and Caste in South India: Agricultural Labour in Madras Presidency in the Nineteenth Century*, Cambridge: Cambridge University Press.

Dirks, N.B. (1992). 'Castes of Mind', *Representations*, 37, pp. 56–78.

——— (1986). 'From Little King to Landlord: Property, Law and the Gift under the Madras Permanent Settlement', *Comparative Studies in Society and History*, 28(2), pp. 303–33.

——— (1982). 'The Pasts of a *Palaiyakarar*: The Ethnohistory of a South Indian Little King', *Journal of Asian Studies*, 41(4), pp. 655–83.

Dobbin, Christine (1970). 'The Parsi Panchayat in Bombay City in the Nineteenth Century', *Modern Asian Studies*, 4(2), pp. 149–64.

Eisenstadt, S.N. (1964). 'Modernization and Conditions of Sustained Growth', *World Politics*, 16(4), pp. 576–94.

Elvin, Mark (1984). 'Why China Failed to Create an Endogenous Industrial Capitalism: A Critique of Max Weber's Explanation', *Theory and Society*, 13(3), pp. 379–91.

Engerman, Stanley L. (1997). 'Cultural Values, Ideological Beliefs, and Changing Labor Institutions: Notes on their Interactions', in John N. Drobak and J.V.C. Nye (eds), The Frontiers of the New Institutional Economics, San Diego: Academic Press.

Engerman, Stanley L. and Kenneth L. Sokoloff (1997). 'Factor Endowments, Institutions, and Differential Paths of Growth among New World Economies', in Stephen Haber (ed.), *How Latin America Fell Behind*, Stanford, CA: Stanford University Press, pp. 260–304.

Fewsmith, Joseph (1983). 'From Guild to Interest Group: The Transformation of Public and Private in Late Qing China', *Comparative Studies in Society and History*, 25(4), pp. 617–40.

Foltz, Richard C. (1998). *Mughal India and Central Asia*, Oxford and Karachi: Oxford University Press.

Forster, George (1808). *A Journey from Bengal to England*, vol. II, London: A. Faulder.

Fox, Richard G. (1967). 'Family, Caste, and Commerce in a North Indian Market Town', *Economic Development and Cultural Change*, 15(3), pp. 297–314.

Frank, André Gunder (1967). *Capitalism and Underdevelopment in Latin America: Historical Studies of Chile and Brazil*, New York: Monthly Review Press.

Frank, André Gunder, and Barry K. Gills (eds) (1996). *The World System: Five Hundred Years or Five Thousand?*, London and New York: Routledge.

Franks, H. George (undated). *Panchayats of the Peshwas*, Poona.

Freitas, Kripa (2006). 'The Indian Caste System as a Means of Contract Enforcement' (unpublished), Illinois: Northwestern University.

Fryer, Geoffrey (1979). 'John Fryer, F.R.S. and His Scientific Observations, Made Chiefly in India and Persia between 1672 and 1682', *Notes and Records of the Royal Society of London*, 33(2), pp. 175–206.

Fryer, John (1993). *Travels in India in the Seventeenth Century—Thomas Roe and John Fryer*, New Delhi: Asian Educational Services.

Fukazawa, H. (1991). *The Medieval Deccan: Peasants, Social Systems and States—Sixteenth to Eighteenth Centuries*, New Delhi: Oxford University Press.

———(1983). 'Non-Agricultural Production: Maharashtra and Deccan', in T. Raychaudhuri and Irfan Habib (eds), *The Cambridge Economic History of India*, vol. 1, Cambridge: Cambridge University Press.

Gadgil, D. R. (1959). *Origins of the Modern Indian Business Class*, New York: Institute of Pacific Relations.

Galenson, David (1982). *White Servitude in Colonial America: An Economic Analysis*, New York: Cambridge University Press.

Gellner, David (1995). 'Religion and the Transformation of Capitalism', in Richard H. Roberts (ed.), *Religion and the Transformations of Capitalism: Comparative Approaches*, London: Routledge.

Gilmartin, D. (2003). 'Cattle, Crime and Colonialism: Property as Negotiation in North India', *Indian Economic and Social History Review*, 40(1), pp. 33–56.

Goody, J. (1996). *The East in the West*, Cambridge: Cambridge University Press.

Gordon, Stewart and John F. Richards (1985). 'Kinship and Pargana in Eighteenth Century Khandesh', *Indian Economic and Social History Review*, 22(4), pp. 371–97.

Gordon, Stuart (1977). 'The Slow Conquest: Administrative Integration of Malwa into the Maratha Empire, 1720–1760', *Modern Asian Studies*, 11(1), pp. 1–40.

Goswami, Omkar (1985). 'Then Came the Marwaris: Some Aspects of the Changes in the Pattern of Industrial Control in Eastern India', *Indian Economic and Social History Review*, 22(3), pp. 225–49.

Gough, Kathleen (1981). *Rural Society in Southeast India*, Cambridge: Cambridge University Press.

——— (1979). 'Dravidian Kinship and Modes of Production', *Contributions to Indian Sociology*, 13(2), pp. 264–92.

Granovetter, Mark (1985). 'Economic Action and Social Structure: The Problem of Embeddedness', *American Journal of Sociology*, 91(3), pp. 481–510.

——— (1983). 'The Strength of Weak Ties: A Network Theory Revisited', *Sociological Theory*, 1, pp. 201–33.

Greif, Avner (2001). 'Impersonal Exchange and the Origin of Markets: From the Community Responsibility System to Individual Legal Responsibility in Premodern Europe', in Masahiko Aoki and Yūjirō Hayami (eds), *Communities and Markets in Economic Development*, Oxford: Oxford University Press.

——— (1994). 'Cultural Beliefs and the Organization of Society: A Historical and Theoretical Reflection on Collectivist and Individualist Societies', *Journal of Political Economy*, 102(5), pp. 912–50.

Greif, Avner, Paul Milgrom, and Barry R. Weingast (1994). 'Coordination, Commitment, and Enforcement: The Case of the Merchant Guild', *The Journal of Political Economy*, 102, pp. 745–76.

Griffiths, Percival (1967). *The History of the Indian Tea Industry*, London: Weidenfield and Nicholson.

Grose, John Henry (1772). *A Voyage to the East Indies*, London.

Growse, F. S. (1883). *Mathura: A District Memoir* (third edition), Allahabad: Government Press.

Guha, Ranajit (1963). *A Rule of Property for Bengal: An Essay on the Idea of Permanent Settlement*, Paris: Mouton Publishers.

Guha, Sumit (1989). 'The Handloom Industry of Central India: 1825–1950', *Indian Economic and Social History Review*, 26(3), pp. 297–318.

——— (1987). 'The Land Market in Upland Maharashtra', *Indian Economic and Social History Review*, 24(2), pp. 117–44.

Gune, V. T. (1953). *The Judicial System of the Marathas*, Poona: Sangam.

Gupta, Dipankar (ed.) (1991). *Social Stratification*, New Delhi: Oxford University Press.

Habib, Irfan (1982). 'Agrarian Economy', in T. Raychaudhuri and Irfan Habib (eds), *The Cambridge Economic History of India*, vol. I, Cambridge: Cambridge University Press, pp. 62–89.

———— (1980). 'Aspects of Agrarian Relations and Economy in a Region of Uttar Pradesh during the 16th Century', *Indian Economic and Social History Review*, 17(1), pp. 205–32.

———— (1975). 'Colonialization of the Indian Economy, 1757–1900', *Social Scientist*, 3(8), pp. 23–53.

———— (1969). 'Potentialities of Capitalistic Development in the Economy of Mughal India', *The Journal of Economic History*, 29(1), pp. 32–78.

Habib, Irfan and Dhruv Raina (eds), *Social history of science in colonial India*, New Delhi: Oxford University Press.

Hall, K. R. (1981). 'Peasant State and Society in Chola Times: A View from the Tiruvidaimarudur Urban Complex', *Indian Economic and Social History Review*, 18(3-4), pp. 393–95.

Hallward, N. L. (1920). *William Bolts. A Dutch Adventurer under John Company*, Cambridge: Cambridge University Press.

Hamilton, Alexander (1995). *A New Account of the East Indies being the Observations and Remarks of Capt. Alexander Hamilton*, vol. 1, London, 1739, reprinted New Delhi: Asian Educational Services.

Hamilton, Gary (1996). 'The Organizational Foundations of Western and Chinese Commerce: A Historical and Comparative Analysis', in G. Hamilton (ed.), *Asian Business Networks*, Berlin: Walter de Gruyter, pp. 43–58.

Hamilton, Walter (1815). *The East India Gazetteer; containing particular Descriptions of the Empires, Kingdoms, Principalities, Provinces, Cities, Towns, Districts, Fortresses, Harbours, Rivers, Lakes, &c. of Hindostan and the Adjacent Countries beyond the Ganges and the Eastern Archipelago*, London: John Murray.

Hardgrove, Anne (2004). *Community and Public Culture: The Marwaris in Calcutta, c. 1897–1997*, New York: Columbia University Press.

Harnetty, Peter (1991). 'Deindustrialization Revisited: The Handloom Weavers of the Central Provinces of India', *Modern Asian Studies*, 25(3), pp. 455–510.

Hartmann, B. and J. Boyce (1984). *A Quiet Violence: View from a Bangladesh Village*, London: Zed Books.

Hasan, Farhat (2004). *State and Locality in Mughal India: Power Relations in Western India, c. 1572–1730*, Cambridge: Cambridge University Press.

Hatekar, Neeraj (1996). 'Information and Incentives: Pringle's Ricardian Experiment in the Nineteenth Century Deccan Countryside', *Indian Economic and Social History Review*, 33(4), pp. 437–57.

Haynes, Douglas (2001). 'Artisan Cloth-Producers and the Emergence of Powerloom Manufacture in Western India 1920–1950', *Past and Present*, 172, pp. 170–98.

—— (1996). 'The Logic of the Artisan Firm in a Capitalist Economy: Handloom Weavers and Technological Change in Western India, 1880–1947', in Burton Stein and Sanjay Subrahmanyam (eds), *Institutions and Economic Change in South Asia*, New Delhi: Oxford University Press.

—— (1991). *Rhetoric and Ritual in Colonial India: The Shaping of a Public Culture in Surat City, 1852–1928*, Berkeley: University of California Press.

—— (1987). 'From Tribute to Philanthropy: The Politics of Gift Giving in a Western Indian City', *The Journal of Asian Studies*, 46(2), pp. 339–60.

Haynes, D.E. and T. Roy (1999). 'Conceiving Mobility: Weavers' Migrations in Pre-colonial and Colonial India', *Indian Economic and Social History Review*, 36(1), pp. 35–67.

Heber, Bishop Reginald (1828). *Narrative of a Journey through the Upper Provinces of India, Calcutta to Bombay, 1824–1825*, vol. 1, London: John Murray.

Heesterman, J.C. (1985). *The Inner Conflict of Tradition: Essays in Indian Ritual, Kingship and Society*, Chicago: University of Chicago Press.

Hegde, K.T.M. (1973). 'A Model for Understanding Ancient Indian Iron Metallurgy', *Man* (new series), 8(3), pp. 416–21.

Hicks, J.R. (1969). *A Theory of Economic History*, Oxford: Clarendon Press.

Hoffmann, J. (1915), 'Principles of Succession and Inheritance among the Mundas', *The Journal of the Bihar and Orissa Research Society*, pp. 5–19.

Hossain, Hameeda (1989). *The Company Weavers of Bengal: The East India Company and the Organisation of Textile Production in Bengal 1750–1813*, New Delhi: Oxford University Press.

Houbert, J. (1981). 'Mauritius: Independence and Dependence', *Journal of Modern African Studies*, 19, pp. 75–105.

Humphreys, S.C. (1969). 'History, Economics, and Anthropology: The Work of Karl Polanyi', *History and Theory*, 8(2), pp. 165–212.

Hunter, W.W. (1885). *The Imperial Gazetteer of India*, vol. I, London: Trubner & Co.

Iliopoulou, Despina (2001). 'The Uncertainty of Private Property: Indigenous versus Colonial Law in the Restructuring of Social Relations in British India', *Dialectical Anthropology*, 26(1), pp. 65–88.

Inden, Ronald (1998). 'Orientalist Construction of India', in Peter J. Cain and Mark Harrison (eds), *Imperialism: Critical Concepts in Historical Studies*, London: Routledge.

—— (1986). 'Tradition against Itself', *American Ethnologist*, 13(4), pp. 762–75.

India, Government of (1931). *Report of the Royal Commission on Labour in India*, Calcutta: Government Press.

——— (1931). *Royal Commission on Labour in India, Vol. VI, Part II, Evidence Recorded in Assam*, Calcutta: Government Press.

——— (1931). *Royal Commission on Labour in India, Vol. I, Part II, Oral Evidence Recorded in Bombay Presidency*, Calcutta: Government Press.

——— (1931). *Royal Commission on Labour in India, Vol. I, Part I, Written Evidence Recorded in Bombay Presidency*, Calcutta: Government Press.

——— (1910). *Report of the Committee on Emigration from India to the Crown Colonies and Protectorates*, London: HMSO.

——— (1906). *Proceedings of the Assam Labour Enquiry Committee in the Recruiting and Labour Districts*, vol. I (evidence), Calcutta: Government Press.

——— (1903). *Report of the Indian Irrigation Commission 1901–1903*, Part-II – Provincial, London: HMSO.

——— (1842). *Correspondence Relative to the Introduction of Indian Labourers into the Mauritius*, London: HMSO.

——— (1841). *Correspondence between the Government of India and the Court of Directors relating to the Hill Coolies*, Calcutta: Government Press.

——— (1841). *Exportation of Hill Coolies*, Calcutta: Government Press.

India (1927). *Report of the Indian Tariff Board (Cotton Textile Industry Enquiry) 1927*, vol. III (evidence of the Bombay, Ahmadabad, and Baroda Millowners' Associations), Calcutta: Government Press.

——— (1927). *Report of the Indian Tariff Board (Cotton Textile Industry Enquiry) 1927*, vol. III (evidence of local governments, and so on), Calcutta: Government Press.

——— (1908). *Indian Factory Labour Commission, vol. II, Evidence*, Simla: Government Press.

Irschick, Eugene R. (1989). 'Order and Disorder in Colonial South India', *Modern Asian Studies*, 23(3), pp. 459–92.

Irwin, John (1954). *Shawls*, London: HMSO.

Islam, M.M. (1995). 'The Punjab Land Alienation Act and the Professional Moneylenders', *Modern Asian Studies*, 29(2), pp. 271–91.

Ito, Shoji (1966). 'A Note on the 'Business Combine' in India', *The Developing Economies*, 4, pp. 367–80.

Jain, B. S. (1970). *Administration of Justice in Seventeenth Century India*, New Delhi: Metropolitan Book.

Jain, R.K. (1984). 'South Indian Labour in Malaya 1840–1920: Asylum Stability and Involution', in Kay Saunders, ed., *Indentured Labour in the British Empire 1834–1920*, London and Canberra: Australian National University Press.

Jha, J.C. (1996). *Aspects of Indentured Inland Emigration to North-East India 1859-1918*, New Delhi: Indus Publications.

Jones, E.L. (1988). *Growth Recurring: Economic Change in World History*, New York: Oxford University Press.

Jung, Al-Haj Mahomed Ullah Ibn S. (1926). *A Dissertation on the Administration of Justice of Muslim Law preceded by an Introduction to the Muslim Conception of the State*, Allahabad: Allahabad Law Journal Press.

Kaiwar, Vasant (1994). 'Property Structures, Demography and the Crisis of the Agrarian Economy of Colonial Bombay Presidency', in David Ludden (ed.), *Agricultural Production in Indian History*, New Delhi: Oxford University Press.

Kale, Madhavi (1998). *Fragments of Empire: Capital, Slavery, and Indian Indentured Labor in the British Caribbean*, Philadelphia: University of Pennsylvania.

Kane, P.V. (1946). *History of Dharmasastra (Ancient and Medieval Religious and Civil Law in India)*, Poona: Bhandarkar Oriental Research Institute, vol. 3; vol. 5, part I.

Kannappan, Subbiah (1985). 'Urban Employment and the Labor Market in Developing Nations', *Economic Development and Cultural Change*, 33(4), pp. 699–730.

Kapp, K. William (1963). *Hindu Culture, Economic Development, and Economic Planning in India*, Bombay: Asia Publishing House.

Kerr, Ian J. (2006). 'On the Move: Circulating Labor in Pre-Colonial, Colonial, and Post-Colonial India', *International Review of Social History*, supplement, 51, pp. 85–109.

Kling, Blair B. (1966). *The Blue Mutiny. The Indigo Disturbances in Bengal, 1859–1862*, Philadelphia: University of Pennsylvania Press.

Kooiman, D. (1989). *Bombay Textile Labour: Managers, Trade Unionists and Officials*, New Delhi: Manohar Publications.

Kranton, R.E. and A.V. Swamy (2008). 'Contracts, Hold-up, and Exports: Textiles and Opium in Colonial India', *American Economic Review*, 98(3), pp. 967–89.

——— (1998). 'The Hazards of Piecemeal Reform: British Civil Courts and the Credit Market in Colonial India', *Journal of Development Economics*, 58(1), pp. 1–24.

Krishnamurty, J. (1972). 'The Growth of Agricultural Labour in India', *Indian Economic and Social History Review*, 9(4), pp. 327–32.

Krishnan, V. (1959). *Indigenous Banking in South India*, Bombay: Bombay State Cooperative Union.

Kosambi, Meera and John E. Brush (1988). 'Three Colonial Port Cities in India', *Geographical Review*, 78(1), pp. 32–47.

Kugle, S. A. (2001). 'Framed, Blamed and Renamed: The Recasting of Islamic Jurisprudence in Colonial South Asia', *Modern Asian Studies*, 35(2), pp. 257–313.

Kumar, Dharma (1989). 'A Note on Land Control', in Peter Robb (ed.), *Rural India: Land, Power and Society under British Rule*, New Delhi: Oxford University Press.

—— (1975). 'Land Ownership and Inequality in the Madras Presidency: 1853-54-1946-47', *Indian Economic and Social History Review*, 12(3), pp. 229–61.

Kumar, Ravinder (1965). 'Rural Life in Western India on the Eve of the Brtish Conquest', *Indian Economic and Social History Review*, 2(3), pp. 201–20.

Lai, Walton Look (1993). *Indentured Labor, Caribbean Sugar: Chinese and Indian Migrants to the British West Indies 1838-1918*, Baltimore: Johns Hopkins University Press.

Laidlaw, James (1995). *Riches and Renunciation: Religion, Economy and Society among the Jains*, Oxford: Clarendon Press.

Lakha, Salim (1985). 'Character of Wage Labour in Early Industrial Ahmedabad', *Journal of Contemporary Asia*, 15(4), pp. 421–41.

Lal, B.V. (1984). 'Labouring Men and Nothing More: Some Problems of Indian Indenture in Fiji', in Kay Saunders (ed.), *Indentured Labour in the British Empire 1834-1920*, London and Canberra: Australian National University Press, pp. 126–57.

—— (1983). *Girmitiyas: The Origins of the Fiji Indians*, Canberra: Australian National University.

Lal, Deepak (2007). *The Hindu Equilibrium: India c. 1500 B.C.-2000 A.D.*, New Delhi: Oxford University Press.

Lamb, Helen (1955). 'The Indian Business Communities and the Evolution of an Industrialist Class', *Pacific Affairs*, 28, pp. 101–16.

—— (1953). 'The Emergence of an Indian Business Class', mimeo.

Leff, N.H. (1978). 'Industrial Organization and Entrepreneurship in the Developing Countries: The Economic Groups', *Economic Development and Cultural Change*, 26, pp. 661–75.

Liège, J. L. (1986). 'Indentured Labour in the Indian Ocean and the Particular Case of Mauritius', *Intercontinenta*, 5, pp.

Ludden, David (1999). *The New Cambridge History of India IV.4: An Agrarian History of South Asia*, Cambridge: Cambridge University Press.

—— (1988). 'Agrarian Commercialism in Eighteenth Century South India: Evidence from the 1823 Tirunelveli Census', *Indian Economic and Social History Review*, 25(4), pp. 493–519.

—— Ludden, ed. (1994). *Agricultural Production*, Delhi: Oxford University Press.

Lynch, O.M. (1969). *The Politics of Untouchability*, New York.

Macnaghten, Francis W. (1824). *Considerations on Hindoo Law as it is current in Bengal*, Serampore: Mission Press.

Mahadevan, Raman (1978). 'Immigrant Entrepreneurs in Colonial Burma—An Exploratory Study of the Role of Nattukottai Chettiars of Tamil Nadu 1880-1930', *Indian Economic and Social History Review*, 15(3), pp. 329–58.

Maine, Henry S. (1876). *Village-Communities in the East and West*, New York: Henry Holt & Co.

Majumdar Choudhury, S.N. (1930). 'Extracts from a Survey of the Small Urban Industries of Benares' United Provinces', in *United Provinces, United Provinces Provincial Banking Enquiry Committee 1929-30*, vol. 2, Allahabad: Government Press, pp. 371–91.

Malcolm, John (1832). *A Memoir of Central India*, vol. 2, London: Parbury Allan and Co.

Manucci, Niccolao (1907). *Storia do Mogor*, vol. 3, London: John Murray.

Markovits, Claude (1999). 'Indian Merchant Networks Outside India in the Nineteenth and Twentieth Centuries: A Preliminary Survey', *Modern Asian Studies*, 33(4), pp. 883–911.

Martin, Montgomery (1838). *The History, Antiquities, Topography, and Statistics of Eastern India ... Collated from the Original Documents of the E.I. House*, vol. 1, London: W.H. Allen.

Marx, Karl (1958). *Capital*, vol. 1, edited by F. Engels (the English tr. of the third edition by Samuel Moore and Edward Aveling), Moscow: Progress Publishers.

Mayer, Peter (1993). 'Inventing Village Tradition: The Late 19th Century Origins of the North Indian "Jajmani System" ', *Modern Asian Studies*, 27(2), pp. 357–95.

Mazumdar, D. (1973). 'Labour Supply in Early Industrialization: The Case of the Bombay Textile Industry', *Economic History Review*, 26(3), pp. 477–96.

Meillassoux, Claude (1972). 'From Reproduction to Production', *Economy and Society*, 1(1), pp. 93–105.

Menski, W. (2003). *Hindu Law*, New Delhi: Oxford University Press.

Mentz, S. (2005). *The English Gentleman Merchant at Work: Madras and the City of London 1660-1740*, Copenhagen.

Milgrom, Paul R., Douglass C. North, and Barry R. Weingast (1990). 'The Role of Institutions in the Revival of Trade', *Economics and Politics*, 2(1), pp. 1–23.

Mill, James (1975). *The History of British India*, first published 1817, Chicago: University of Chicago Press.

——— (1858). *The History of British India from 1805 to 1835*, edited by Horace Wilson, London: James Madden.

Mines, Mattison (1984). *The Warrior Merchants: Textiles, Trade, and Territory in South India*, Cambridge: Cambridge University Press.

——— (1972). *Muslim Merchants*, New Delhi: Shri Ram Centre for Industrial Relations and Human Resources.

Misra, A.M. (2000). 'Business Culture and Entrepreneurship in British India, 1860-1950', *Modern Asian Studies,* 34(2), pp. 333–48.

Mizushima, Tsukasa, 'Mirasi System as Social Grammar: State, Local Society, and Raiyat in the 18th-19th South India'. Available at *http://www.l.u-tokyo.ac.jp/~zushima9/pdf(for%20hp)/1-28.doc.*

Mokyr, J. (2002). *Gifts of Athena: Historical Origins of the Knowledge Economy,* Princeton: Princeton University Press.

Mohapatra, Prabhu (2007). 'Eurocentrism, Forced Labour, and Global Migration: A Critical Assessment', *International Review of Social History,* 52, pp. 110–115.

—— (2006). '"Following Custom"? Representations of Community among Indian Immigrant Labour in the West Indies, 1880–1920', *International Review of Social History,* supplement, 51, pp. 173–202.

Moll-Murata, Christine (2008). 'Chinese Guilds from the Seventeenth to the Twentieth Centuries: An Overview', *International Review of Social History,* 53, supplement, pp. 213–47.

Moore, J. Barrington (1967). *Social Origins of Dictatorship and Democracy,* Boston.

Moosvi, Shireen (2008). *People, Taxation, and Trade in Mughal India,* New Delhi: Oxford University Press.

—— (1987). *The Economy of the Mughal Empire c.1595,* New Delhi: Oxford University Press.

Moreland, W.H. (1920). *India at the Death of Akbar: An Economic Study,* London: Macmillan Publishers.

Morris, Morris D. (1979). 'South Asian Entrepreneurship and the Rashomon Effect, 1800–1947', *Explorations in Economic History,* 16(4), pp. 341–61.

—— (1979). 'Modern Business Organisation in India, 1850–1947', *Economic and Political Weekly,* 14.

—— (1967). 'Values as an Obstacle to Economic Growth in South Asia: An Historical Survey', *Journal of Economic History,* 27(4), pp. 588–607.

—— (1965). *Emergence of an Industrial Labour Force in India,* Berkeley and Los Angeles: University of California Press.

—— (1963). 'Towards a Reinterpretation of Nineteenth Century Indian Economic History', *Journal of Economic History,* 23(4), pp. 606–18.

—— (1960). 'The Recruitment of an Industrial Labour Force in India, with British and American Comparisons', *Comparative Studies in Society and History,* 2(3), pp. 305–28.

Morris, Morris D., Tapan Raychaudhuri, Bipan Chandra, and Toru Matsui (1969). *Indian Economy in the Nineteenth Century: A Symposium,* New Delhi: Indian Economic and Social History Association.

Mukherjee, B. N. (1936-7). 'Dari Industry of Patna', *Annual Report,* Patna: College Chanakya Society.

Mukund, K. (2005). *The View from Below: Indigenous Society, Temples and the Early Colonial State in Tamilnadu 1700-1835*, Hyderabad: Orient Longman.

Myers, Charles A. (1958). *Labor Problems in the Industrialization of India*, Cambridge MA: Harvard University Press.

Nakazato, Nariaki (1997). 'Regional Patterns of Land Transfer in Late Colonial Bengal', in Peter Robb, Kaoru Sugihara, Haruka Yanagisawa (eds), *Local Agrarian Societies in Colonial India: Japanese Perspectives*, Delhi: Manohar Publications.

Naqvi, S. (1972). 'Marx on Pre-British Indian Society', *Indian Economic and Social History Review*, 9(1), pp. 380–412.

Nandy, Ashis (1973). 'Entrepreneurial Cultures and Entrepreneurial Man', *Economic and Political Weekly*, 8, pp. M98–M106.

Neild, Susan (1979). 'Colonial Urbanism: The Development of Madras City in the Eighteenth and Nineteenth Centuries', *Modern Asian Studies*, 13(2), pp. 217–46.

Neild-Basu, Susan (1984). 'The Dubashes of Madras', *Modern Asian Studies*, 18(1), pp. 1–31.

Newman, R. K. (1981). *Workers and Unions in Bombay, 1918-1929*, Canberra: Australian National University Press.

Nigata, Marie Louise (2008). 'Brotherhoods and Stock Societies: Guilds in Pre-modern Japan', *International Review of Social History*, supplement, 53, pp. 121–42.

North, D.C. (2005). *Understanding the Process of Economic Change*, New York: Academic Press.

——— (1981). *Structure and Change in Economic History*, New York: Norton Publishers.

North, Douglass C. and Robert Paul Thomas (1973). *The Rise of the Western World: A New Economic History*, New York: Cambridge University Press.

North, D.C. and B.R. Weingast (1989). 'Constitutions and Commitment: The Evolution of Institutions Governing Public Choice in Seventeenth-Century England', *Journal of Economic History*, 49(4), pp. 803–32.

Northrup, David (1995). *Indentured Labor in the Age of Imperialism 1834-1922*, Cambridge: Cambridge University Press.

Olson, Mancur (2000). *Power and Prosperity*, New York: Basic Books.

——— (1982). *The Rise and Decline of Nations*, New Haven: Yale University Press.

——— (1971). *The Logic of Collective Action: Public Goods and the Theory of Groups*, New Haven: Yale University Press.

Orme, Robert (1805). *Historical Fragments of the Mogul Empire, of the Morattoes, and of the English concerns in Indostan from the Year MDCLIX*, London: F. Wingrave.

Otter, S.D. (2001). 'Rewriting the Utilitarian Market: Colonial Law and Custom in mid-Nineteenth-Century British India', *The European Legacy*, 6(2), pp. 177–88.

Ovington, J. (1929). *A Voyage to Surat in the year 1689*, London: Humphrey Milford.

Palsetia, Jesse S. (2001). *The Parsis of India: Preservation of Identity in Bombay City*, Leiden: Brill.

——— (2005). 'Merchant Charity and Public Identity Formation in Colonial India: The Case of Jamsetjee Jejeebhoy', *Journal of Asian and African Studies*, 40(3), pp. 197-217.

Panda, Chitta (1996). *The Decline of the Bengal Zamindars: Midnapore, 1870-1920*, New Delhi: Oxford University Press.

Panikkar, K.N. (2007). 'Cultural Trends in Precolonial India: an Overview', reprinted in S. Irfan Habib and Dhruv Raina (eds), *Social History of Medicine ain Colonial India*, New Delhi: Oxford University Press.

Papanek, H. (1973). 'Pakistan's New Industrialists and Businessmen: Focus on the Memons', in Milton Singer (ed.), *Entrepreneurship and Modernization of Occupational Cultures in South Asia*, Durham: Duke University Press.

Parry, Jonathan (1998). 'Mauss, Dumont, and the Distinction between Status and Power', in Wendy James and N.J. Allen (eds), *Marcel Mauss: A Centenary Tribute*, New York and Oxford: Berghahn Books.

——— (1986). 'The Gift, the Indian Gift and the "Indian Gift"', *Man*, 21(3), pp. 453-73.

Parthasarathi, Prasannan (2001). *The Transition to a Colonial Economy, Weavers, Merchants and Kings in South India, 1720-1800*, Cambridge: Cambridge University Press.

Patel, S.J. (1952). *Agricultural Labourers in Modern India and Pakistan*, Bombay: Asia Publishing.

Patnaik, Utsa (1990). *Agrarian Relations and Accumulation: The 'Mode of Production' Debate in India*, Bombay. Published for SAMEEKSHA Trust by Oxford University Press.

Peabody, Norbert (2003). *Hindu Kingship and Polity in Precolonial India*, Cambridge: Cambridge University Press.

Pearson, M.N. (1990). 'Merchants and States', in J. Tracy (ed.), *The Political Economy of Merchant Empires. State and World Trade 1350-1750*, Cambridge: Cambridge University Press.

——— (1990). 'Review of *Two Medieval Merchant Guilds of South India* by Meera Abraham', *The Journal of Asian Studies*, 49, pp. 953-4.

Perlin, Frank (1985). 'State Formation Reconsidered: Part Two', *Modern Asian Studies*, 19(3), pp. 415–80.

——— (1983). 'Proto-industrialisation in Precolonial South Asia', *Past and Present*, 98, pp. 30–95.

Polanyi, Karl (1957). *The Great Transformation*, Boston: The Beacon Press.

Pomeranz, K. (2000). *The Great Divergence: China, Europe, and the Making of the Modern World Economy*, Princeton: The Princeton University Press.

Pouchepadass, Jacques (2000). *Land, Power and Market: A Bihar District under Colonial Rule, 1860-1947*, New Delhi: Sage Publications.

––––– (1992). 'Land, Power and Market: The Rise of the Land Market in Gangetic India', in Peter Robb (ed.), Rural India, New Delhi: Oxford University Press.

Prakash, B.A. (1988). 'Agricultural Backwardness of Malabar during the Colonial Period: An Analysis of Economic Causes', *Social Scientist*, 16(6/7), pp. 51–67.

Prakash, Om (2007). 'From Negotiation to Coercion: Textile Manufacturing in India in the Eighteenth Century', *Modern Asian Studies*, 41(6), pp. 1331–68.

––––– (1998). *European Commercial Enterprise in Pre-Colonial India*, Cambridge: Cambridge University Press.

Punjab (1941). *Artisans of Lahore*, Lahore: Government Press.

Raheja, Gloria Goodwin (1988). 'India: Caste, Kingship, and Dominance Reconsidered', *Annual Review of Anthropology*, 17, pp. 497–522.

Rajasekhar, D. (1991). 'Commercialization of Agriculture and Changes in Distribution of Land Ownership in Kurnool District of Andhra (c. 1900–50)', in S. Bhattacharya, Sumit Guha, Raman Mahadevan, Sakti Padhi, and G.N. Rao (eds), *The South Indian Economy*, New Delhi: Oxford University Press.

Ramaswamy, Vijaya (2004). 'Vishwakarma Craftsmen in Early Medieval Peninsular India', *Journal of the Economic and Social History of the Orient*, 47, pp. 548–82.

––––– (1985). 'Artisans in Vijayanagar Society', *Indian Economic and Social History Review*, 22(4), pp. 417–44.

––––– (1985). 'The Genesis and Historical Role of the Master Weavers in South Indian Textile Production', *Journal of the Economic and Social History of the Orient*, 28, pp. 294–325.

Rana, R.P. (1981). 'Agrarian Revolts in Northern India during the Late 17th and Early 18th Century', *Indian Economic and Social History Review*, 18(3-4), pp. 287–325.

Ranga, N.G. (1930). *Economics of Handlooms*, Bombay: Taraporevala.

Rankin, George (1946). *Background to Indian Law*, Cambridge: Cambridge University Press.

––––– (1945). 'Hindu Law To-Day', *Journal of Comparative Legislation and International Law*, 3rd Ser., 27(3/4), pp. 1–17.

Rattigan, W.H. (1901). 'The Influence of English Law and Legislation upon the Native Laws of India', *Journal of the Society of Comparative Legislation*, New Ser., 3(1), pp. 46–65.

Ray, Indrajit (2004). 'The Indigo Dye Industry in Colonial Bengal. A Re-examination', *Indian Economic and Social History Review*, 41(2), pp. 199–225.

Ray, Indrani (1971). 'The French Company and the Merchants of Bengal (1680-1730)', *Indian Economic and Social History Review*, 8(1), pp. 41–55.

Ray, Ratnalekha (1979). *Change in Bengal Agrarian Society, c. 1760–1860*, New Delhi: Manohar Publications.

Ray, Ratna and Rajat Ray (1975). 'Zamindars and Jotedars: A Study of Rural Politics in Bengal', *Modern Asian Studies*, 9(1), pp. 81–102.

Ray, Rajat Kanta (1995). 'Asian Capital in the Age of European Domination: The Rise of the Bazaar, 1800-1914', *Modern Asian Studies*, 29(3), pp. 449–554.

Raychaudhuri, Tapan (1983). 'The Mid-Eighteenth Century Background', in Dharma Kumar (ed.), *The Cambridge Economic History of India, c. 1757–1970*, Cambridge: Cambridge University Press.

——— (1983). 'Non-agricultural Production' and 'The State and the Economy: The Mughal Empire', in T. Raychaudhuri and Irfan Habib (eds), *The Cambridge Economic History of India*, vol. 1, Cambridge: Cambridge University Press.

——— (1969). *Bengal under Akbar and Jahangir*, Delhi: Munshiram Manoharlal.

Read, Thomas T. (1934). 'The Early Casting of Iron: A Stage in Iron Age Civilization', *Geographical Review*, 24(4), pp. 544–54.

Reich, David, Kumarasamy Thangaraj, Nick Patterosn, Alkes L. Price and Lalji Singh (2009). 'Reconstructing Indian Population History', *Nature*, 461, pp. 489–95.

'Retired Mill Manager' (1903). 'Hints on the Management of Cotton Mills', *Indian Textile Journal*, 14, p. 81.

Richards, John F. (1995). *The Mughal Empire*, Cambridge: Cambridge University Press.

——— (1990). 'The Seventeenth Century Crisis in South Asia', *Modern Asian Studies*, 24(4), pp. 625–38.

Robb, Peter (1997). *Ancient Rights and Future Comforts: Bihar, the Bengal Tenancy Act of 1885 and British Rule in India*, Richmond: Curzon Press.

——— (1992). 'Peasants' Choices? Indian Agriculture and the Limits of Commercialization in Nineteenth Century Bihar', *Economic History Review*, 45(1), pp. 97–119.

——— (1988). 'Law and Agrarian Society in India: The Case of Bihar and the Nineteenth Century Tenancy Debate', *Modern Asian Studies*, 22(2), pp. 319–54.

——— (1979). 'Hierarchy and Resources: Peasant Stratification in Late Nineteenth Century Bihar', *Modern Asian Studies*, 13(1), pp. 97–126.

Robert, Bruce L. (1985). 'Structural Change in Indian Agriculture: Land and Labour in Bellary District, 1890–1980', *Indian Economic & Social History Review*, 22(4), pp. 281–306.

Rostow, W. W. (1959). 'The Stages of Economic Growth', *Economic History Review*, 12(1), pp. 1–16.

Roy, Tirthankar (2011). 'Indigo and Law in Colonial India', *Economic History Review*, 64(S1), pp. 60–75.

—— (2008). 'Knowledge and Divergence from the Perspective of Early Modern India', *Journal of Global History*, 3, pp. 361–87.

—— (2008). 'Sardars, Jobbers, *Kanganies*: The Labour Contractor and Indian Economic History', *Modern Asian Studies*, 42(4), pp. 971–98.

—— (2007). 'A Delayed Revolution: Environment and Agrarian Change in India', *Oxford Review of Economic Policy*, 23(2), pp. 239–50.

—— (2007). 'Out of Tradition: Master Artisans and Economic Change in Colonial India', *Journal of Asian Studies*, 66, pp. 963–91.

—— (2006). 'Roots of Agrarian Crisis in Interwar India: Retrieving a Narrative', *Economic and Political Weekly*, 41(54), pp. 5389–5400.

—— (2006). *The Economic History of India 1857–1947*, New Delhi: Oxford University Press.

—— (2005). *Rethinking Economic Change in India: Labor and Livelihood*, London: Routledge.

—— (2002). 'Acceptance of Innovations in Early Twentieth-century Indian Weaving', *Economic History Review*, 55(3), pp. 507–32.

—— (1999). *Traditional Industry in the Economy of Colonial India*, Cambridge: Cambridge University Press.

—— (1997). 'Capitalism and Community: A Case-study of the Madurai Sourashtras', *Indian Economic and Social History Review*, 34(4), pp. 437–63.

—— (1993). *Artisans and Industrialization: Indian Weaving in the Twentieth Century*, New Delhi: Oxford University Press.

Rudner, D.W. (1994). *Caste and Capitalism in Colonial India: The Nattukottai Chettiars*, Berkeley and Los Angeles: University of California Press.

—— (1987). 'Religious Gifting and Inland Commerce in Seventeenth-Century South India', *Journal of Asian Studies*, 46(2), pp. 361–79.

Saberwal, S. (1976). *Mobile Men: Limits to Social Change in Urban Punjab*, New Delhi.

Sahai, N. (2005). 'Crafts in Eighteenth Century Jodhpur: Questions of Class, Caste and Community Identities', *Journal of the Economic and Social History of the Orient*, 48, pp. 524–51.

San Bartolomeo, Paolino da (1800). *A Voyage to the East Indies, Containing an Account of the Manners, Customs, & c. of the Natives with a Geographical Description of the Country. Collected from Observations made during a Residence of Thirteen Years, between 1776 and 1789*, London: J. Davis.

Sanjiva Row, T. *The All India Digest, Section II (Civil) 1811-1911*, vols. I-, Madras: The Law Printing House.

Sarkar, Jadunath (1952). *Mughal Administration* (fourth edition), Calcutta: M.C. Sircar.

Sastry, K.R.R. (1925). *South Indian Gilds*, Madras: Indian Publishing House.

Saumerez Smith, R. (1996). *Rule by Records: Land Registration and Village Custom in Early British Punjab*, New Delhi: Oxford University Press.

Saunders, A.J. (1920–22). 'The Sourashtra Community in Madura. South India', mimeo, Madura.

Scoville, James (2003). 'Discarding Facts: The Economics of Caste', *Review of Development Economics*, 7(3), pp. 378–91.

Scrafton, Luke (1770). *Reflections on the Government of Indostan. With a Short Sketch of the3 History of Bengal, From MDCCXXXVIIII to MDCCLVI; and an Account of the English Affairs to MDCCLVIII*, London: W. Strahan.

Sen, Dinesh Chandra (1914). *Banga Sahitya Parichay*, vol. 1, Calcutta: Calcutta University.

Sen, Samita (2004). '"Without His Consent?": Marriage and Women's Migration in Colonial India', *International Labor and Working-Class History*, 65, pp. 77–104.

Sen, S.R. (1997). *Restrictionism during the Great Depression in Indian Tea Jute and Sugar Industries*, Calcutta: Firma KLM.

Sen, Sukumar (1959), *Bangala Sahityer Itihas* [A History of Bengali Literature], vol. 1 of 4, Calcutta: Eastern Publishers.

Setalvad, M.C. (1960). *The Common Law in India*, London: Steven and Sons.

Sethi, Rajiv and E. Somanathan (2003). 'Understanding Reciprocity', *Journal of Economic Behavior and Organization*, 50(1), pp. 1–27.

Sharma, R.C. (19), *Ardhakathanak*, Bombay: Indico.

Singer, Milton (1966). 'Religion and Social Change in India: The Max Weber Thesis Phase Three', *Economic Development and Cultural Change*, 14, pp. 497–505.

Singh, J.D.K.S. (1981). *The Handloom Industry in Madurai City*, Madurai.

Sinopoli, Carla M. (2003). *The Political Economy of Craft Production: Crafting Empire in South India, c. 1350–1650*, Cambridge: Cambridge University Press.

Sivasubramonian, S. (2000). *National Income of India in the Twentieth Century*, New Delhi: Oxford University Press.

Smith, Sheila (1993). 'Fortune and Failure: The Survival of Family Firms in Eighteenth Century India', in Geoffrey Jones and Mary B. Rose (eds), *Family Capitalism*, London: Routledge.

Sokoloff, Kenneth L. and Stanley L. Engerman (2000). 'Institutions, Factor Endowments, and Paths of Development in the New World', *Journal of Economic Perspectives*, 14(3), pp. 217–32.

Southall, Aidan (1988). 'The Segmentary State in Africa and Asia', *Comparative Studies in Society and History*, 30(1), pp. 52–82.

―――― (1987). 'On Mode of Production Theory: The Foraging Mode of Production and the Kinship Mode of Production', *Dialectical Anthropology*, 12(2), pp. 165–92.

Specker, Konrad (1989). 'Madras Handlooms in the Nineteenth Century', *Indian Economic and Social History Review*, 26(2), pp. 131–66.

Stein, Burton (2003). 'Eighteenth Century India: Another View', in P.J. Marshall (ed.), *The Eighteenth Century in Indian History. Evolution or Revolution*, Delhi: Oxford University Press.

―――― (1985). 'State Formation and Economy Reconsidered: Part I', *Modern Asian Studies*, 19(3), pp. 387–413.

―――― (1980). *Peasant, State and Society in Medieval South India*, New Delhi: Oxford University Press.

Stein, Burton and Sanjay Subrahmanyam (eds) (1996). *Institutions and Economic Change in South Asia*, New Delhi: Oxford University Press.

Stokes, Eric (1973). 'The First Century of British Colonial Rule in India: Social Revolution or Social Stagnation?', *Past and Present*, 58, pp. 136–60.

Strange, Thomas (1875). *Hindu Law with Reference to Such Portions of it as Concern the Administration of Justice in the King's Courts in India* (fifth edition), Madras: Higginbothams.

Subrahmanian, Lakshmi (2007). 'Merchants in Transit: Risk-sharing Strategies in the Indian Ocean', in H. P. Ray and E. A. Alpers (eds), *Cross Currents and Community Networks: The History of the Indian Ocean World*, New Delhi: Oxford University Press.

Subrahmanyam, Sanjay (1998). 'Hearing Voices: Vignettes of Early Modernity in South Asia, 1400–1750', *Daedalus*, 127(3), pp. 75–103.

―――― (1992). 'The Mughal State—Structure or Process? Reflections on Recent Western Historiography', *Indian Economic and Social History Review*, 29(3), pp. 307–9.

―――― (1990). *The Political Economy of Commerce: Southern India 1500-1650*, Cambridge: Cambridge University Press.

―――― (1988). 'A Note on Narsapur Peta: A 'Syncretic' Shipbuilding Centre in South India, 1570–1700', *Journal of the Economic and Social History of the Orient*, 31(3), pp. 305–11.

Sudhir, P. and P. Swarnalatha (1992). 'Textile Traders and Territorial Imperatives: Masulipatnam, 1750-1850', *Indian Economic and Social History Review*, 29(2), pp. 145–69.

Sugarman, David (1993). 'Simple Images and Complex Realities: English Lawyers and Their Relationship to Business and Politics, 1750-1950', *Law and History Review*, 11(2), pp. 257–301.

Swai, Bonaventure (1979). 'East India Company and Moplah Merchants of Tellicherry: 1694–1800', *Social Scientist*, 8(1), pp. 58–70.

Swarnalatha, P. (2001). 'Revolt, Testimony, Petition: Artisanal Protests in Colonial Andhra', *International Review of Social History*, pp. 107–29.

Taira, Koji (1997). 'Factory Labour and the Industrial Revolution in Japan', in K. Yamamura (ed.), *The Economic Emergence of Modern Japan*, Cambridge: Cambridge University Press, pp. 239–93.

Talbot, Cynthia (2001). *Precolonial India in Practice: Society, Region, and Identity in Medieval Andhra*, New York: Oxford University Press.

Thomas, E. (1871). *The Chronicles of Pathan Kings of Delhi*, London: Thornton.

Thompson, William (1782). *Travels in Europe, Asia, and Africa; describing characters, customs, manners, laws, and productions of nature and art containing various remarks on the political and commercial interests of Great Britain and delineating in particular a new system for the government and improvement of the British settlements in the East Indies: Begun in the year 1777 and finished in 1781*, vol. 2, London: J. Murray.

Thorner, Alice (1962). 'The Secular Trend in the Indian Economy, 1881–1951', *Economic Weekly*, 14, pp. 1156–65.

Thorner, Daniel (1966). 'Marx on India and the Asiatic Mode of Production', *Contributions to Indian Sociology*, 9, pp. 33–66.

——— (1962). '"Deindustrialization" in India, 1881–1931', in D. and A. Thorner (eds), *Land and Labour in India*, New York: Asia, pp. 70–81.

Thornton, Douglas M. (1898). *Parsi, Janina, and Sikh, or, Some Minor Religious Sects in India: The Maitland Prize Essay for 1897*, London: The Religious Tract Society.

Thurston, Edgar (1909). *Castes and Tribes of Southern India*, vols. I–VII, Madras: Government Press.

Timberg, T.A. (1994). 'Three Types of the Marwari Firm', in R.K. Ray (ed.), *Entrepreneurship and Industry in India 1800–1947*, New Delhi: Oxford University Press.

——— (1978). *The Marwaris, from Traders to Industrialists*, New Delhi: Vikas Publishing House.

Tomlinson, B.R. (1993). *The Economy of Modern India*, Cambridge: Cambridge University Press.

——— (1981). 'Colonial Firms and the Decline of Colonialism in Eastern India 1914–47', *Modern Asian Studies*, 15(3), pp. 455–86.

Toreen, Olof (1771). *A Voyage to China and the East Indies by Peter Osbeck ... Together with A Voyage to Suratte by Olof Toreen Chaplain of the Gothic Lion East Indiaman ...*, vol. 2, London: Benjamin White.

Torri, Michelguglielmo (1998). 'Mughal Nobles, Indian Merchants and the Beginning of British Conquest in Western India: The Case of Surat 1756–1759', *Modern Asian Studies*, 32(2), pp. 257–315.

——— (1991). 'Trapped inside the Colonial Order: The Hindu Bankers of Surat and Their Business World during the Second Half of the Eighteenth Century', *Modern Asian Studies*, 25(2), pp. 367–401.

Tripathi, Dwijendra (2004). *The Oxford History of Indian Business*, New Delhi: Oxford University Press.

────── (1981). 'Occupational Mobility and Industrial Entrepreneurship in India: A Historical Analysis', *The Developing Economies*, 19(1), pp. 52–68.

United Provinces (1930). *United Provinces Provincial Banking Enquiry Committee 1929-30*, 4 vols., Allahabad: Government Press.

Verhoeven, J.D., A.H. Pendray, and W.E. Dauksch (1998). 'The Key Role of Impurities in Ancient Damascus Steel Blades', 50 (9), pp. 58–64. Also available at http://www.tms.org/pubs/journals/JOM/9809/Verhoeven-9809.html

Verma, Tripta (1994). *Karkhanas under the Mughals*, New Delhi: Pragati Publications.

Vesey-FitzGerald, S. (1947). 'The Projected Codification of Hindu Law', *Journal of Comparative Legislation and International Law*, 3rd Ser., 29(3/4), pp. 19–32.

Vicziany, M. (1986). 'Imperialism, Botany and Statistics in Early Nineteenth-Century India: The Surveys of Francis Buchanan (1762-1829)', *Modern Asian Studies*, 20(4), pp. 625–60.

Wacha, D.E. (1914). *The Life and Life Work of J.N. Tata*, Madras: Ganesh and Publishers.

Wallerstein, Immanuel (1974). *The Modern World System: Five Hundred Years or Five Thousand?*, London and New York: Routledge.

Washbrook, D.A. (2004). 'South India 1770–1840: The Colonial Transition', *Modern Asian Studies*, 38(3), pp. 479–516.

────── (1997). 'From Comparative Sociology to Global History: Britain and India in the Pre-History of Modernity', *Journal of the Economic and Social History of the Orient*, 40(4), pp. 410–43.

────── (1994). 'The Commercialization of Agriculture in Colonial India: Production, Subsistence and Reproduction in the 'Dry South', c. 1870-1930', *Modern Asian Studies*, 28(1), pp. 129–64.

────── (1990). 'South Asia, the World System, and World Capitalism', *Journal of Asian Studies*, 49(3), pp. 479–508.

────── (1981). 'Law, State and Agrarian Society in Colonial India', *Modern Asian Studies*, 15(3), pp. 649–721.

Weber, Max (1978). *Economy and Society*, ed. by G. Roth and C. Wittich, Berkeley: University of California Press.

────── (1958). *The Religion of India: The Sociology of Hinduism and Buddhism*. Translated and edited by Hans H. Gerth and Don Martindale, Glencoe: The Free Press.

White, David L. (1991). 'From Crisis to Community Definition: The Dynamics of Eighteenth-Century Parsi Philanthropy', *Modern Asian Studies*, 25(2), pp. 303–20.

—— (1987). 'Parsis in the Commercial World of Western India, 1700–1750', *Indian Economic and Social History Review*, 24(2), pp. 183–203.

Wilson, Jon E. (2007). 'Anxieties of Distance: Codification in Early Colonial Bengal', *Modern Intellectual History*, 4(1), pp. 7–23.

Wink, André (1986). *Land and Sovereignty in India. Agrarian Society and Politics under the Eighteenth Century Maratha Svarajya*, Cambridge: Cambridge University Press.

Wiser, William (1936). *The Hindu Yajmani System*, Lucknow: The Lucknow Publishing House.

Wittfogel, K. (1957). *Oriental Despotism*, New Haven: Yale University Press.

Wolf, Eric (1982). *Europe and the People without History*, Berkeley and Los Angeles: University of California Press.

Wrightson, Keith (2006), *English Society 1580–1680*, London: Routledge.

Yanagisawa, Haruka (1993). 'The Handloom Industry and its Market Structure: The Case of the Madras Presidency in the First Half of the Twentieth Century', *Indian Economic and Social History Review*, 30(1), pp. 1–27.

Yusuf Ali, Abdullah Ibn (1900). *A Monograph on Silk Fabrics Produced in the North-Western Provinces and Oudh*, Allahabad: Government Press.

Index

Aligarh school 46, 58, 60, 61
apprenticeship 130, 132, 135, 144–7, 151, 152
Ardhakathanak 14
Arthasastra 50
artisan caste, community 26, 91, 104, 116, 129, 26, 130, 131, 135–8, 142, 144, 145, 149–152
Assam 86, 154, 162, 165, 173–180
association, assembly 17–19, 92, 130, 134, 140, 142, 148, 149, 152
Aurangzeb 12, 70

Banjara 14
Banking (see also credit, rural) 122–4
Barbosa, Duarte 97
Bartolomeo, Paolino da San 9–11, 93
Benares 14, 143–5, 148, 195
Bengal 6, 12, 13, 22, 66, 76–8, 104, 106, 107, 136139, 141, 160–2, 164, 165, 173, 175, 199, 201–3, 206–9, 213–16
Bengali firms, merchants 113, 123
Bernier, François 7, 10, 11, 15, 131
Bohra 94, 120
Bombay 27, 92, 93, 99, 108, 109, 111–14, 118, 199, 121, 123, 126, 154, 172, 181–3, 185–8
Bombay-Deccan 144, 195, 216
Bowrey, Thomas 7, 8, 10–12
Brahmin, Brahman 13, 15, 48, 50–3, 56, 57, 59, 60, 68

Calcutta 26, 78, 107, 111–14, 118, 119, 123–28, 154, 159, 162, 165, 168, 169, 174, 181
caste (see also, community, guild, purity, pollution, panchayat)
    precolonial India 12–15, 22, 91

and jati 17–18, 20
    concept 21–2, 30, 32, 35, 39, 42, 110, 128
Chambers of commerce 117
Chandimangal 13
Chettiar 117–18, 210
China 2–4, 17, 47
class, class consciousness 159, 180, 184, 187, 191, 212, 214, 217
colonialism, colonization 5, 38, 39, 43, 78
colonial law (see also land law, property right, women, company law, contract law, common law) 78–88
commercial disputes (see also commercial law) 100–5
commercial institutions 95–98
commercial law (see also contract) 1, 6, 23, 25, 84–6, 94–5, 98, 102, 105
common law 62, 65, 67–9, 78, 84, 85, 87
common property resources 194
community (see also caste, endogamous guild, law and justice, merchant, labourer, artisan)
    defined 16–24
    and state 25, 60
company law 114, 115, 120
contract, contract enforcement 4, 5, 22–5, 204, 213, 214–16
contract law 216
Coromandel 136–8
cotton famine 114, 216, 217
credit, rural 115, 117, 191, 201, 203–6, 210, 214, 218, 219

de-industrialization 139
Della Valle, Pietro 9
distributional coalitions 35
divergence (see Europe–Asia comparison)

East India Company, Dutch 107
East India Company, English 25, 90, 108, 109
Europe, guild 3–4, 34, 42, 86
Europe, states 39
Europe–Asia comparison 31, 33, 37, 38–41, 46–7, 49, 86, 89
European firms, colonial India 124–8

family, joint (see joint family)
Fazl, Abul 131
Fryer, John 8–9

Ghoshal, Joynarayan 14
Great Depression 125
Grose, John Henry 97, 98
guild, artisan 130, 131, 133, 134, 140–3, 146, 148–151
guild, endogamous (see also community, caste) 2, 4, 5, 12, 16, 18, 20, 26, 27, 37, 42, 43, 89, 111, 115, 119, 129, 130, 133, 148, 151, 220
guild, European (see Europe, guild)
Gujarat 90, 94, 107, 111, 113, 120, 121, 136, 206, 217
Gujarati, firms, merchants 64, 107, 111, 113, 120, 121

Hamilton, Alexander 9
Headman (see also sardar, jobber, kangany) 154, 155, 161, 166–8, 173, 180, 182, 188, 189
Hindu law 56, 71, 81–5, 209

indenture 159, 160, 166, 171, 173, 174
Indian Ocean 23, 105, 106
indigo trade 101, 113, 118, 204
Indigo mutiny 77, 86, 214–16
industrialization 26, 114, 115, 119, 120, 123, 125, 128, 180, 188, 220
Institutional economic history 36, 39, 46
Islamic law 62, 81

Jain, Banarasidas (see Ardhakathanak)
Japan 4
jobber (see also headman) 176, 181–7
joint family 16, 82, 84, 88, 91, 113, 120

kangany (see also headman) 160, 166, 167, 178

karkhana 131, 132, 143–5, 148, 151
kingship, precolonial 48–58

labour law 155, 164, 172, 178, 180, 183
labourer, caste and community 26–7, 153, 154, 155, 157–9, 162, 166, 173, 180, 187, 188
land law 193, 204, 208–12
land market 192, 203, 204, 207, 208, 211
land tenure (see zamindari, ryotwari)
law and justice
    precolonial (see kingship, Hindu law)
    labour (see labour law)
    Maratha (see Maratha state, law and justice)
    Mughal (see Mughal, Mughal India)
    Bengal (see Bengal)
    Colonial (see colonial law)
Lucknow 142, 144–6, 151

Madras 11, 107, 108, 154
Madras Presidency 75, 149, 173, 174, 203, 206
Madras–Deccan (see Madras Presidency)
Madurai 149–151
Maine, Henry 30, 31, 33, 60, 64
Malabar 11, 13, 195, 199, 203
Managing agency 120–3
Manasamangal 12–13, 22, 66
Manucci, Niccolao 10, 11, 15, 22, 97
Maratha state, law and justice 49, 59, 71, 73
marriage (see also endogamous guild, caste) 37, 52–6, 65, 84, 85, 89, 98, 113, 116, 118, 128, 133, 136, 147
Marwaris 26, 91, 112, 118–20, 124
Marx, Karl 33, 39, 46, 60
Mauritius 154, 156, 159, 164, 165, 169, 171, 172, 174,
Megasthenes 54
merchant castes, communities 26, 69, 95, 98–100, 106–8
migration
    merchants 26, 119
    labourers 28, 153, 156, 161, 162, 164, 165, 170, 174–6, 179, 180, 183, 221
Mill, James 14, 46, 61
Mughal, Mughal India
    state 12, 58–60, 191
    law and justice 60–71

trade, finance, industry 23, 89–90,
131–3
army 63, 64
Mutiny 86
Mysore 74, 75

Orme, Robert 11
Ovington, J. 8

panchayat 68, 72–4
Parsi 91, 93, 94, 99, 107–14, 119–121
Parsi panchayat 93, 109, 110
peasants, caste and community 26–27,
190, 192, 193, 195, 197–9, 201, 202–4,
208–12, 214, 216–18
Pelsaert, Francisco 131
Permanent Settlement (see zamindari)
pollution 21, 22
property right 4, 20, 27, 28, 30, 39–41, 190–2,
196–8, 201, 204, 206, 207, 209, 210
Punjab 63, 146–8, 204–6, 208–12
Purity (see also marriage) 52–4, 56, 57, 63,
65, 74, 83

Ray, Bharatchandra 13–14

ryotwari tenure 199, 201, 202

sardar (see also headman) 160, 167–80, 182
Scrafton, Luke 10, 15
Sind 90, 206
slavery 158–60
substantivism 32, 33
Surat 90, 97, 98, 106–8, 112

temples 130, 133, 134, 136
tenancy 206–8
trade 149, 204, 205, 208, 212, 214
Toreen, Olof 15

village community 17–18, 31, 60
Vijayanagar 10, 23, 57, 58, 133

Weber, Max 14, 17, 22, 30–3
women
artisans 145, 146, 151
property rights 82–4, 210
relationship with community 70, 74
wage-workers 158, 159, 169, 176, 177

zamindari tenure 199–201, 207, 213